THE AGASHAN

DISCOURSES

THE AGASHAN DISCOURSES

The Agashan Teachers Speak on the
Who, What, Where, When, and *Why*
of Life on the Earth Plane

Compiled and Edited
By
WILLIAM EISEN

Teachings Received through the Instrumentality of
Reverend Richard Zenor, Trance Intermediary

DeVORSS & COMPANY
P.O. Box 550, Marina Del Rey, CA 90291

The Agashan Discourses: An Agashan Book by William Eisen
Copyright © 1978 by William Eisen

First Edition

ISBN 0-87516-242-8
Library of Congress Catalog Card Number: 77-85424

Manufactured in the United States of America
by DeVorss & Company, Publishers

This book is dedicated to Richard Zenor Slocum, without whose devotion to duty and dedicated service as the trance intermediary for Agasha and the other Teachers of Light, not a word of this volume could have been written.

Appreciation is also extended to Walter Vincent Anderson, whose original compilation of material proved to be the inspiration behind this present work, and to the many Agashans who have contributed to its editing. I am especially grateful, among others, to Catherine Roller, Henrietta Bernstein, and James Crenshaw for their invaluable assistance.

TABLE OF CONTENTS

8

INTRODUCTION

By William Eisen

During the past 35 years or so (since the early 1940's), a group of Egyptian and Atlantean Ascended Masters of great antiquity has been quietly and unpretentiously lecturing and conducting classes in Los Angeles through the deep trance mediumship of an extremely sensitive and well-known psychic instrument, the Reverend Richard Zenor of the Agasha Temple of Wisdom. This manifestation is made possible through Richard Zenor's amazing ability to self induce, at will, the unconscious trance state while simply relaxing in a chair in front of a large audience. In this state his body can then be animated by a new and completely different entity, and these Master Teachers then take over and use his vocal cords to communicate with those of us in the 20th century in much the same way that you would use your telephone.

All of the trance lectures since 1949 have been tape recorded, and they constitute a veritable encyclopedia of information relative to the laws governing mankind, and man's relationship with God. In other words, the philosophy so taught attempts to answer practically all of the questions one is liable to ask relative to *who, what, where, when,* and *why*

15

of life on the earth plane today. The Master Teacher Agasha, the principal speaker for this organization of Ascended Masters, states that at the end of every age must come the clarification of all that had been misinterpreted before, and that now, in the "Grand Finale" of the present cycle or age, is the time for these things to be understood by the world at large.

In our first volume, *Agasha: Master of Wisdom*,[1] the reader was told of the *saga* or narrative aspect of Agasha's manifestation because it was basically a history or a biography of this great sage. In it, the reader was taken on a spiritual journey into the past, way back to the inception of this saga 7,000 years ago in Egypt, or Austa as it was known then. He was given detailed information on an advanced pre-dynastic Egyptian civilization, the purpose of the Great Pyramid and how it was constructed, the essence and basic teachings of the Agashan philosophy, some new concepts relating to the laws governing time and space, and some predictions relative to the return of the Atlanteans and the coming new Golden Age of Peace. He was also taken into some of the great Spiritual Centers that now exist on the earth, and he met a few of these great Ascended Adepts who are still living in the flesh today.

In this present volume, *The Agashan Discourses*, the reader will be introduced to the *sage* or teaching aspect of Agasha's manifestation. It is therefore a compilation of a total of 16 different talks on a variety of subjects. Here, the reader will be given specific information as to how reincarnation works, the nature and evolution of the universe and of man, your life in the ethereal world after so-called physical death, the etheric planes, the anim or "ghost" of the atom, and the mechanics of soul projection with some practical information on how to achieve out-of-the-body experiences. You will also be told the reported true story of the birth, life, and death of Jesus of Nazareth and the reason for his manifestation. This 11th discourse, incidentally, will be given by that masterful storyteller, Kraio himself. And then lastly, you will be taken back to your original birth in the great Core of Life, told the story of your journey through the Cosmos up to where you are today, and given a preview of your final manifestation as a veritable god in the 16th and concluding discourse titled "Pillars of Light."

This is your future; this is your heritage as you embark with us on the second phase of this new and exciting journey into consciousness. Here, you may imagine that you are yourself attending the classes and listening as the Teachers speak directly to you, the reader, no matter where you be at the moment. Here, you may actively participate in discussions relative to the mysteries of your own Being, because the discourses are given by the Teachers themselves, in their own words, and in their own style and manner. You may participate in this way because the classes are eternal, and the universal truths expressed on any one evening are equally as valid on any other evening.

Perhaps at this time, however, we should point out that if any of the readers of this work wish to listen to a transcription of the actual tape of any one of the discourses or lectures presented here, we unfortunately cannot comply with this request because the lectures per se do not exist precisely in the way that they are given. One must understand that in a typical Agashan class, which covers a period of time of approximately two hours, Agasha as well as the other Teachers who manifest will speak on a multitude of different topics and subjects. Agasha says that he tries to cover as many subjects as he can in the course of an evening, and so therefore he weaves back and forth from one subject to another, emphasizing points which he feels are appropriate for that particular class.

Now this is not to deny the sheer elegance of any one class as an entity in itself; indeed not, for they are most beautifully presented. And even magically so, I might add, because Agasha states that he is directing his words to the soul and not to the outer consciousness. He speaks in this manner to try to awaken the inner man; therefore the listener will usually find himself in a state of meditation.

The editors, therefore, in compiling the material for this present work, were faced with this problem at the outset. We could have transcribed a few classes intact exactly as they were given and presented them as the second volume in this series. But if we had followed this course of action, the tremendous philosophical concepts as given by Agasha over a period of some 35 years could hardly have been touched. And then too, much of the material is repetitious with many of the classes overlapping each other in subject content. Besides, we were not attempting to speak to the soul, as Agasha does, but we were attempting to present to the world at large the essence of the entire philosophy as given by Agasha over these many years. This then involved a good deal of editing of the tapes so that the subject matter could be broken out into its various divisions and topics.

Therefore, when Agasha gives us a lecture on the Soul Pattern, let us say, which is the 9th discourse of this present work, we are in reality giving the reader excerpts from his teachings on several different classes on this same general topic of the soul. We have also taken considerable poetic license in editing, etc., so as to tie together these various excerpts into one complete whole and present them as one lecture. This may seem a bit odd perhaps, but it was the only way to solve the problem under the circumstances. But the editors feel that the end justifies the means because in this way you, the reader, will be in a position to understand just what Agasha has been saying on this subject over a period of many years. However, the words are still his, the phraseologies are his, and the discourses are given in his own inimitable style and presentation.

We should also say a few words at this time about the general format of the Agashan classes. It is 8:30 P.M. on a Monday evening. The lights are dimmed and Richard Zenor goes into trance. Soon his body becomes limp, apparently in a very deep state of sleep. Then with the suddenness of an electric shock it jerks back to life, and the first voice we hear is that of Dr. Navajo, the medium's doorkeeper, the one who guards the entrance to the Temple known as Richard Zenor. Perhaps a better terminology would be to refer to it as the Temple of Richard Zenor's Being, but in any event it is Dr. Navajo who alternately opens the door and then closes the door as the various Teachers from the Higher Orders enter the Temple and take control of the Zenor instrument or telephone.

Dr. Navajo will then begin the class by asking those assembled to recite the affirmation. This affirmation, incidentally, was given by Agasha many years ago and it is always used to open every class. Then Dr. Navajo will usually give a discourse on various aspects of the Agashan philosophy, and this may last for anywhere from five minutes to almost an hour at times. In his last life he was a medicine man of the Navajo Indian tribe, in the area now known as New Mexico, but you would never know it to hear him speak because he has an excellent command of the English language. In fact, he is a very knowledgeable teacher in his own right, even though he tells us he is only elaborating and clarifying information originally given by Agasha. Yet he fulfills a very definite function insofar as his words are directed to the outer, conscious mind, whereas Agasha speaks to the inner man or the soul. Many students will remain alert during Dr. Navajo's talk, but they will fall into a state of meditation as soon as Agasha takes over. And Agasha will do this quite abruptly, sometimes even in the middle of a sentence. When Agasha's light takes over the body, Navajo is gone.

Agasha's manifestation in every class always occurs in two separate and distinct phases. The forepart of his talk is always given from the floor of the platform where he has placed the medium's body in the yoga lotus position, swaying back and forth as he conducts the class. It is in this portion of the class that Agasha gives his major lesson for the evening. Then he will end his talk by slipping back into a sitting position up on the chair while he counts to three and asks the class to sound the A-U-M.

The second or last part of the class has no particular format per se. Sometimes Agasha will himself conduct the remainder of the class, but on the whole, perhaps two or three or even a half-dozen or so other Master Teachers will come and speak at some length from the various orders and degrees which make up a consciousness known as the Consciousness of Immensity. Their voices and personalities are all distinctly different. Then at the conclusion of the class, Agasha will return and close it with the usual, "Manzaholla." However, it is Dr. Navajo himself who always utters the final words before Richard Zenor returns to the body and awakens from the trance state.

The Master Teacher Kraio's voice is particularly moving. It is soft, and low, and filled with great love and compassion as he tells us many stories about his life, his birth, and the mission he had to perform during his last physical incarnation as Jesus of Nazareth in Palestine. Today he is known as Kraio. We have selected nine of these little talks for inclusion in the 11th discourse of this work; but this is only a sampling. If we were to include them in their entirety, it would become a complete book in itself. Do we have any proof that this is indeed actually the voice of the great Master? No, we do not. But if you will allow yourself the luxury, just for the moment, of trying to believe and accept the philosophy expressed in the other chapters of these volumes, why then should this particular discourse be the exception?

Let us remember that these classes have been going on now for over 35 years. (The Agasha Temple of Wisdom was formally incorporated on May 5, 1943, but the actual classes began a few years prior to this date.) This is a long period of time for any class to be in manifestation. Of course, the format has not always been the same and in the beginning, before Agasha began conducting his classes on a regular basis, Dr. Navajo could speak English only very limitedly. In those early days it was Dr. Adams who was the principal speaker, and Margie, who is now a mature feminine teacher and helper, was but a child guide.

Moreover, since that time a tremendous amount of material has been received and recorded. Many teachers have manifested, and Agasha himself has talked and lectured on practically every subject imaginable. If one were to play the more than 2,200 classes that have been tape recorded just since the year 1949, you would have to listen for eight hours a day, seven days a week, and for more than eighteen months to hear them all. And this does not include the material given by Agasha for the years prior to the availability of the tape recorder in 1949. For these classes, one would have to depend upon shorthand notes and a few disk and wire recordings. Thus the potential research that can be done in the future is almost inexhaustible.

How much of this material has been published down through the years? Unfortunately, not a great deal. James Crenshaw first brought Agasha's philosophy to the attention of the reading public in 1950 with the publication of his classic work, *Telephone Between Worlds*.[2] It is now in its tenth printing. He also wrote a series of articles for *Psychic Observer*[3] which became a yearly feature for this psychic journal; but these articles dealt mainly with the prophecies given each year through the Zenor instrument, and not so much with the philosophy itself.

Then in 1953 Gordon Collier included a bit more of the Agashan material in a book called *Will You Be Alive in 1965?*[4] The title was updated in a subsequent edition to read 1975, and then changed once again to 1985 as the years went by; but it has remained in print and the material is basically the same as it was originally given. Among other things, it relates to predictions from several different sources for these "latter days," which according to Agasha will last until the year 2020.

About the only other books about Agasha to be published

up until the present year were two that were compiled and edited by Philip Hastings, a friend of mine and a fellow disciple for many years. One of these is a booklet titled *Wisdom of Agasha*,[5] but its small size bears little relationship with the impact of its words. It was first printed in 1962. The other is a delightful little volume where Margie, one of the guides who communicates regularly through the Zenor telephone, answers some questions about life in the astral world as well as on the application of the philosophy on the earth plane. It was published in 1965 and is titled *Margie Answers You*.[6] Some of the material also appeared for a while as a regular monthly feature in *Chimes*,[7] a psychic magazine of considerable repute.

Therefore, aside from the above, we find that very little has actually been published on the Agashan philosophy itself since James Crenshaw first gave us *Telephone Between Worlds* back in 1950. But a lot can happen in the interim, and a great amount of additional material has been given by Agasha since this book was originally written. This then is the reason for these two new volumes that are being published at this time: *Agasha: Master of Wisdom* and the present work, *The Agashan Discourses*.

To understand how they came to be written, we have to return to the year 1969. The writer had just moved back into Los Angeles, and was once again attending the Agashan classes. He had originally discovered them in 1952 and had become an avid student, having attended practically every class over an eight-year period up until the year 1960. Then circumstances forced him away for a while, but it seemed good to be back. He had never really been away in mind or spirit, only in body. The classes have a way of growing on one, becoming a part of your very life; and once you have attended the classes for any length of time, you never really break away from the philosophy completely.

I could see that Agasha's great program, which had not been clearly understood earlier, now fairly cried out for an in-depth study of the entire philosophy. What had been published at that time had only scratched the surface of the tremendous depth of Agasha's philosophical thought. And what was more, there was available to anyone who would need them literally hundreds of hours of lectures, all recorded on tape, to draw from in the preparation of such a study.

Several of the students had already started transcribing the material. Of course, the prophecies were being transcribed and had been all along, but occasionally someone would also transcribe and type up a portion of one of Agasha's talks that was especially moving. This was most important, I remember thinking at the time, for it seemed to me that the philosophy itself was the very heart of his entire message. The excerpt from Agasha's talk would then be put up on the bulletin board or passed out to some of the disciples if copies were available.

One of those who had started transcribing and then editing the philosophical portion of these discourses was Walter Anderson, a very dedicated student and a fellow disciple of Agasha from the time he first entered the class in 1953 up until the time of his passing into the spirit world in 1968. His teacher was Manzaholla, and we spoke about him in the Manzaholla chapter of *Agasha: Master of Wisdom.*

I believe that it was sometime in the year 1963 that Walter became inspired. He started by borrowing some tapes, taking them home, and then painstakingly transcribing and editing them, in longhand, and from a playback machine without even a foot control. He worked on this project diligently, whenever he could find the time, for over five years, until he eventually ended up with a manuscript of 120 typewritten pages just a few weeks before his death. It was still unfinished and it did not have a title, but the material that he had selected was edited so beautifully and expressed Agasha's philosophy so profoundly that when it was first shown to me after I returned to the Temple in 1969, I found it impossible to put aside until I had finished reading it.

This then was the answer, I remember thinking at the time, only the manuscript that I had in my hand was far too short. It was simply humanly impossible to adequately express the entire philosophy of the Agashan teachers in just 120 pages. Even though the material was very beautifully written and edited, there were many subjects not covered, and it fairly demanded further expansion and elucidation. Therefore this writer, after having realized what could be accomplished with just a little more effort, then set out to complete and finish a task which a very dedicated fellow disciple, Walter Anderson, had begun some six years earlier.

Starting then in early 1970, I embarked upon that very same path. But I knew that in order to present the philosophy in depth, a great number of lectures would first have to be transcribed and then cataloged and indexed as to subject matter. Walter had attempted to do this, but he was hindered by his inadequate and laborious method of transcribing the tapes. Consequently, he simply did not have enough material to fall back upon in order to cover a particular subject thoroughly. The solution then was obviously an electric typewriter, an adequate playback machine with a foot pedal, and a great amount of patience and perseverance. Obtaining the first two items was easy; the last proved more difficult.

But on the whole it proved to be a labor of love as I listened, typed, and watched in a sort of hypnotic state as the words of Agasha almost magically appeared on page after page after page. Eventually I found that I had accumulated a total of 2,687 pages of typewritten material, all dutifully transcribed, word for word, from a total of 117 different classes.

Looking back on it, I remember this experience as being absolutely fascinating; indeed, it was almost a mystical experience. I didn't have to think; I just typed and absorbed every word as I typed. Some of the tapes that I had borrowed were recorded from earlier classes before I had entered the movement, and so being new for me they were doubly interesting. It was just as if I were there, attending that very same class. I paid no particular attention to punctuation, as I concentrated basically on typing out each word as it was uttered. The punctuating and editing could come later.

But all of these pages would be of no value to the forthcoming books without an adequate index. Therefore the next step was an index, but even indexing the material proved to be no small effort. However, the problem was soon solved by allocating two lines of my index to express the essence of each page of material, and eventually I had a credible index/summary of each of the classes that had been transcribed. This index/summary is now a small volume in itself of some 150 single-spaced pages (300 pages if they were double-spaced), and even it is fascinating reading in that it graphically emphasizes the vast amount of diversified material, on literally hundreds of subjects, that has been given even in just a few of the Agashan classes.

With the index complete, I was now ready to start work on the final manuscript; and needless to say, this too proved to be a more formidable task than I had originally anticipated. Originally I had planned on just adding some additional material to the Anderson manuscript, fill in the gaps so to speak, and thus end up with a single credible volume which would fully express that which has now come to be known as the Agashan philosophy. But unfortunately, this was not to be the case. If it had been this way, my job would have been far easier, believe me. Writers have often said that sometimes the characters that they have created seem to take over the book and then dictate to the author what he is to write. And this seems to be precisely what happened in this particular case.

The book—or rather I should now say books because it later became apparent that the material was not easily adaptable to only one volume—just seemed to write itself. Now I do not mean to imply any form of physical phenomena; no,

I don't mean that at all. But I feel that somehow I was directed from within myself to produce the chapters and compile the material exactly in the way that it is presented in these two volumes: *Agasha: Master of Wisdom* and its companion volume, *The Agashan Discourses*.

And it was really almost effortless! But by that, I certainly don't mean to say that I didn't have to spend literally hundreds of hours writing, composing, and then rewriting again. And even though the discourses in this present volume were taken directly from the tapes, there was still a tremendous amount of editing involved. But be that as it may, I still wish to make the point that after experiencing a certain amount of duress, everything just seemed to fall into place in its rightful category.

Sometimes I would find that I had transcribed just exactly the right material to complement the material that Walter had transcribed, or that someone else had transcribed. It must be remembered that other students had also transcribed a rather substantial amount of material that was made available for my use. Therefore it was through the efforts of several individuals that these books were finally brought into manifestation.

"The Grand Finale" (the final chapter of *Agasha: Master of Wisdom*) was perhaps one of the most difficult chapters in that it involved a good deal of research. But nevertheless I still seemed to know just how to compose its contents and prepare its general theme even before it was written. I could very definitely feel another presence seemingly directing my every effort. Now this is not only applicable to this one particular chapter, but the same thing could be said for the entire contents of both books as well. Perhaps this is not an unusual phenomenon; but it certainly seemed unusual to me.

I also found that in compiling the various topics, chapters, and discourses that go on to make up both volumes, I really could not use as much of the Anderson material as I had originally intended. I tried wherever possible to do so, but sometimes I would find other material that seemed to fit better into the subject matter of the particular chapter or discourse I was working on. With the vast amount of material that I eventually had to choose from, I actually ended up with far more material than I could ever possibly use in these two volumes. However, I am forever grateful for Walter's original manuscript, for without its inspiration, I might never have had the courage to even attempt these two works.

One other point. The very beautiful painting that appears on the frontispiece of this book is also located above the stairway that leads to the contact room at the Agasha Temple of Wisdom. It was painted in the 1950's by a very gifted artist and a fellow disciple of the Agashan organization for many years. His name is Robert Zimmerman. It was so chosen because it is a symbolic representation of you, the reader, ascending the great stairway of life, listening to the discourses and passing your initiations, and by so doing, gaining entrance to the Spiritual Temples in the Higher Orders of Consciousness.

So come with us, then, into these Halls of Higher Learning and actively participate in the discourses. Picture yourself upon that stairway, and listen to Agasha as he walks with you through the pages of this book. May the light of his wisdom illuminate your path.

Los Angeles, California, October, 1977
William Eisen

NOTES

1. William Eisen, *Agasha: Master of Wisdom* (Los Angeles, DeVorss & Co., 1977)

2. James Crenshaw, *Telephone Between Worlds* (Los Angeles, De-Vorss & Co., 1950, 1977)

3. *Psychic Observer* (Ralph G. Pressing, publisher, Jamestown, N.Y.)

4. Gordon Collier, *Will You Be Alive in 1985?* (Ossining, N.Y., The Book of Destiny, 1953, 1971)

5. Philip Hastings, *Wisdom of Agasha* (Los Angeles, DeVorss & Co., 1962, 1977)

6. Philip Hastings, *Margie Answers You* (Los Angeles, The Agasha Temple of Wisdom, 1965)

7. *Chimes* (Leigh and June Denton, publishers, Encinitas, Calif.)

FIRST DISCOURSE

REINCARNATION

By Agasha

MY BLESSED DISCIPLES—greetings and bless each and every one tonight, and may I express my gratitude for your wonderful cooperation. I know that it shall continue throughout the years that we plan to carry out our wonderful program for our message to be perpetuated down through the ages. I also know that as you work with me, as you bear with me, being ever so patient while you are being trained, you will be in a more receptive mood to accept the things that I am desirous of putting across unto you blessed disciples.

We realize that in the scientific world today, and particularly in medical science, mankind is continually learning much pertaining to human expression. The psychologists and the psychiatrists are busy in their departments, and they have learned considerably, I will grant you that. It is all well and good and in due order; yet I realize that in those departments they have lacked the real education relative to human expression and human behavior.

Therefore, be it known unto all of you disciples tonight that in medical science—even though they are proving a great deal subject to the human anatomy—the researchers still realize that birth is the most mysterious factor to be reckoned with. It seems that in medical science birth is considered to be only that which can be observed with the physical eye. Yet you in occult science understand rebirth. You understand it to be the return of the souls unto the physical plane. You understand how this law of reincarnation that brings you back into the physical operates, and you realize that much is retained in the soul of which the mortal self is oblivious. But many of you disciples would like to know a little more about this subject; so therefore in the forepart of the class tonight, I will bring unto your attention the importance of birth and bringing children into this life, or rather bringing souls into this life, and thus enabling them to express themselves and to have their karmic relations whatever they may be.

The Reincarnational Plane

But first let us have a better understanding of the reincarnational plane, and let us try to realize just where this plane of consciousness exists. If I were to project myself to the reincarnational plane from the Consciousness of Immensity, I would have to descend first through the great Cosmic Consciousness, then come down through the Celestial Planes, and from the Celestial project myself down through the astral divisions. It is from the astral divisions that the reincarnating soul would embark. But then I would continue on through these divisions to the mental plane; and then just below the mental plane, in between the mental and the physical, I would come in contact with that plane of consciousness which is called the reincarnational plane.

There in the reincarnational plane—which normally we pierce and pass through without stopping, as it has no significance to anyone unless he is specifically looking for the reincarnational plane—we find these minute souls. When I say "minute souls," I mean these Sparks of Divinity. They are the atom souls who are waiting for their time to be reborn upon the earth plane.

These are the ones who at one time had roamed the astral world. There, they had had their experiences and they had prepared themselves by learning various things such as art, literature, or this or that. Then after a period of time, and while they were in a state of meditation, they suddenly lost their outer body and passed out of the astral world. The millions of them probably had not even embraced the subject of reincarnation. But nevertheless, after passing out of the astral body, they reverted back to their original state which we will call the Spark of Divinity. The law of divinity then brought these souls unto the reincarnational plane, there to remain until the right magnetic or spiritual attraction will bring a particular soul into the immediate atmosphere of the parent who is to bring it into manifestation.

The Return of the Soul unto the Earth

Now there are millions of women in this life who are destined to bring souls into manifestation; likewise there are millions of women who are not to bring children into the world. They are denied the privilege, and rightfully so, because of what they had done in their previous lives in reference to bringing children into this existence. Therefore, inasmuch as they had perhaps served magnificently in past generations, there need not be the necessity of bringing through their own channelship souls into this present generation, and we accept that as truth. Yet we realize that birth is one of the most interesting studies, and also one of the most mysterious, to the scientific mind.

We must come to understand that as the soul is lingering in the auric vibration or the immediate atmosphere of the parent, as I have so informed you in the past, it takes on the anims (spiritual atoms) and rebuilds a kingdom of its own. It takes on the vibrations and various other thoughts that will be inherent, we might say, in that soul when that soul actually comes into manifestation.

Now there is no group of people in the spiritual consciousness that directs the souls, necessarily, unto the earth plane.

This happens to be an automatic process, working through a divine law that was very well established long before, we will say, you had ever come into the flesh. The law was there. We realize then that, it being a God law, it must be an automatic process. Yet we, as individuals on the path, can observe such manifestations and can hover very close to the reincarnational plane. There, we can then observe the soul as it is being attracted unto the parent. Do you find this interesting, children?

Multiple Births

Now as we are observing the souls in the auric force, let us suppose that there are two, three, or four souls who are to be brought into life simultaneously. We realize that this happens occasionally upon the earth plane; we also realize that it happens within the animal kingdom more frequently. However, we are in reference to human expression now. So let us suppose that we are observing one, two, three, or four souls endeavoring to come into life.

Now then, if we were to observe such as I refer to, am I as a teacher, or are you as a disciple, in a position to make mighty sure that these souls actually are brought into manifestation? Do we need to nurture, as it were, these souls to insure that nothing goes wrong with the parent and thus help her to bring them into manifestation? It would be my privilege to assist, and your privilege too, the same as it be my privilege to assist you disciples at this time. Yet we must try to recognize and bear in mind that as the souls are lingering in the auric force, there may be one, two, or even three (if there were to be quadruplets as it were) denied the privilege of coming into manifestation.

In other words, while four went through the procedure of birth, in this instance three were stillborn. Only one remains to live upon the physical plane. The souls who were stillborn must then go into the astral kingdom and grow, mature, and go to school the same as if they had lived here upon the earth plane. It is interesting, isn't it?

Now then, let us strive to understand in our disciple consciousness tonight that it would be my privilege, if I were
doing that particular type of work, to do whatever I could
(we will say even helping them karmically) to work with the
parent and with the souls in order to enable them to come
into manifestation. There is a need for that soul expression;
there is a need for that parent to have that experience. As
you know, on very, very rare occasions there will be four
brought into manifestation. This being so rare, why of
course it is treated in the same light.

Twins, as you can well recognize, are quite often brought
into manifestation, and when this occurs they usually have
a certain destiny to fulfill. There is a karmic relation between
the twins that must be reckoned with, although on the
surface the twins would not be in a position to know what
their mission is. However, their souls are very much aware
of this mission, but as to whether the twins fulfill it is another question. They may take different paths, and as they
take different paths we find then that there may be a mistake
made by the twins, and thus they will not bring about that
which was preordained or destined before they were brought
into manifestation.

So therefore, we realize that although you are destined to
do a thing, or at least we will say that you are supposed (that
is a better word) to do a certain thing in this embodiment,
you can miss the cue. You can miss this or that vibration and
make the mistake of your life; in other words, you can miss
the opportunity. There is no guarantee that you will fulfill
that which you were sent back to do. You understand and
accept this to be true, don't you? You were sent back to do
a certain thing, but you do an entirely different thing, thus
in turn not learning your lesson, piling up more karma for
yourself, and not fulfilling your mission.

Now let us revert back to the parent who brings more than
one into this life. Let us refer to a mother who brings in, we
will say as a supposition, twelve children. Now some of you
think that having such a large family at the present time is

sinning; but there are those who bring into this life many souls, particularly in the foreign lands. In some countries there is that which causes them to bring in many souls, as many as they can bring in.

You would say, "Well, where in the world does the poor mother have any rest, or any happiness, in bringing in all of those children?" She works, she slaves, yet all she does is to enable souls to come into this life. What is wrong? The thing is, blessed ones, that in her own consciousness she is fulfilling that which she desires to fulfill. She is paying karma, number one; and number two, in her own right she is happy in bringing forth the life into manifestation, in all probability.

You have all gone through that stage at some time or another in your evolution. As to when, it doesn't matter, but you have my word for it. At some time or another it had taken place in your life because, as I have so informed you in this organization, you have been male and you have been female. The only way that you can work harmoniously in a lifetime is by having had the experiences of being both male and female.

Karmic Relationships

Sometimes a would-be parent will deny a particular soul from coming into manifestation, and as far as that is concerned it may indeed be a proper denial. Why is this so? The answer is that the mother may be blocking the way, unconsciously to her outer self, because of an inharmonious karmic relationship.

You see, there are souls who know about reincarnation and who are desirous of returning to the earth plane. For it is that they had been taught by certain organizations upon the earth that when a person reaches the stage whereby he desires to return back to the earth to have a reembodiment and to be a certain individual—or we will say to be rich or whatever it might be—then that person may linger toward a parent and even try to choose his parent. Yet it often does not work that way.

There is a karmic vibration working unbeknownst to him that will bring him back into the physical body and unto a parent who is not necessarily the parent that the outer consciousness had chosen, but an entirely different parent with whom he had had relationships, we will say, dating back many generations or even thousands of years earlier. It might have been a brother, a sister, a mother, a father, or whatever it might be; but there is some relationship there that will attract his soul and bring it back into manifestation.

You have karmic debts to pay on the earth plane. Of course, this is not applicable to everyone you meet on the earth plane, but the principal things that manifest or come into your lives are the things that you must work out with the particular individual or individuals involved. Yet we must strive to understand that as the soul is returning unto the earth plane, it is oblivious in its outer consciousness, we will say, as to its previous lives; but there within the Spark of Divinity, it knew it all the time. That is the God Consciousness. That is the part of the great force of divinity which enables us to be given another opportunity to repay our karmic debts.

We recognize that this Spark of Divinity is the same spark that has always returned to the earth plane. But first it must return to the reincarnational plane, only to be reborn after living for a time in the mother's aura. It will live there until such time that it is able to take over the newly created body from the germinal kingdom and thus be reborn unto the earth plane. We also recognize the fact that there is no direction, necessarily, by souls on this side of life to send other souls back unto the earth plane. Then why has the soul returned? The answer is, blessed disciples, that it has returned to make amends.

Therefore, we find then that we are serving upon the earth plane. We are serving by bringing life into manifestation, life which is so mysterious to the material scientist. We accept it by saying, "Only God knows," and this is true. Yet we are the gods who can know, we are the gods who can understand, and infinitely so, and we are also the gods who can recognize how that same life is brought into manifestation. This, of course, applies to all species on the earth as well as in the various divisions of the earth consciousness.

A Story of Two Souls

Let us suppose now that we have—well we don't have to suppose it because it is true—but let us just say that we have millions in spirit, in the astral world, who do not embrace reembodiment. Therefore they don't want to study it; they don't want to accept it. They just simply accept what they see and know that they were John Jones, so to speak, upon the physical plane. And they still are John Jones in the astral world. Very well.

But here is a little example of one, we might say, who is advanced. Here comes a soul who has lived in the astral world for perhaps 40 or 50 years. He was not inspired on the earth plane at all; he did not embrace reincarnation. Nor did he embrace reincarnation in the astral world; he simply embraced that which was taught in the realm that he had found himself in. But then after 40 or 50 years of learning and growing after his earthly departure, he is inspired. All of a sudden he has the awakening!

And the moment that he has the awakening in the astral world, he is going to open the door—automatically. It will be an automatic process, indeed. Then immediately thereafter, he will have a sincere desire to more or less isolate himself from his associates in the astral world, and they will then step aside leaving him to himself. He is now by himself, and while he is in that isolated state, so to speak, he is listening to the soul. He is being inspired by the soul and the soul is bringing forth information that he could not receive before. Yes indeed, he has had the awakening.

So therefore, here comes the teacher. The teacher will then appear before him as a spirit from the higher planes of life, very much the same as I appear here through this channel unto you. He will come to him in a vague sort of way, at first, until he can become so attuned to the astral beings. Then the teacher will gradually teach him, inform him, and tell him of the things in the higher orders. It will be strange to the disciple at first because prior to now he has been oblivious to the higher and finer things of the Consciousness of Immensity. But henceforth, he will be visited by the teacher at various times, and the teacher will then most assuredly explain the process of life—the apparent mysteries of life.

Now that the disciple is ready, he can be told about reembodiment. But even though he had been oblivious prior to this time, mind you, basically he knew. He understood within the soul even though outwardly he had been oblivious. But now he is becoming conscious of this fact; he has accepted it from the teacher who has descended from the Consciousness of Immensity at the right and proper time. The teacher will undoubtedly now give him information about reembodiment and prepare him for his return onto the earth.

Of course, this is only one process of the teacher's many functions, but the disciple has asked for it, and so he shall be given the truth. The teacher will prepare him by telling him of the approximate time that he will give up his astral body and return onto the earth plane. But it may not be for a generation or two hence, and so the disciple accepts all of this in much the same manner as a child upon the earth plane accepts physical death in the apparent far distant future. Yes, he will have many years to become prepared.

Now that the disciple is informed that he is to return to the earth plane, what does the teacher do then? The teacher can, mind you, being a teacher from the higher Consciousness of Immensity, actually look up the record and find not only the date, but also who the actual soul is who is destined to become the future parent of the disciple! This may not be for a generation or so hence, and more than likely the future parent is still in the astral world. So the teacher, knowing the records, may then say unto the disciple, "Over here, in this division of the astral world, is a certain individual. I can take you there and you can meet this individual, this lady. Then as you go there and meet her, please understand that 200 years from now this lady will be living on the earth plane and she will become your mother."

Now this is given 200 years in advance by this teacher! You understand how advanced the teacher would have to be in order to be in a position to carry on such a program, don't you? Yes indeed, he was able to read the Akashic Record, interpret it, and then reveal unto the outer consciousness of the disciple what was so written therein. But let us not confuse this with "directing" a soul back onto the earth plane. This is an interesting feature tonight, isn't it?

So then let us go on quietly and try to accept this in the light in which I give it. Please understand that this is a disciple on the path who is informed that he is going to return onto the earth plane, we will say as a supposition, in 200 years. All right. In the meantime he is in the astral world for 200 years. What is he doing all this time in the astral world? He is growing, he is progressing, he is visiting the Consciousness of Immensity. He visits the Consciousness of Immensity precisely the same as some of you children, unbeknownst to your outer consciousness, go there and then return while your physical body is in the state called sleep.

We will assume then that he was well on the path when he was finally met by his teacher. Very well. If this were not so, then for the 200 years that he might be with this particular lady, he would not necessarily know that she is going to be the channel through which he is destined to return to the earth plane. But then they may become the very best of friends. They may learn together, progress together, have their experiences together, or whatever it might be. They may even, through the aid and direction of the teacher, visit various planets and have many, many experiences. Perhaps the woman will know about reincarnation, and let us assume that she does. Perhaps she has also seen in her own soul that she will be the parent of this particular friend of hers (or whoever it might be in the astral world). She has seen that in 200 years she is actually committed, and if she has been able to do this, she may even discuss it many times with her future "son."

All right. Let us say now that 200 years have passed. The teacher had visited them on a number of occasions during these 200 years, and they had both become advanced individuals. It is time now for the woman, or the future mother, to reincarnate. Thus, during a state of meditation and in accordance with a sincere soul desire, her outer consciousness suddenly becomes oblivious, and the soul then descends unto the reincarnational plane and eventually goes through the process called birth.

Now the interesting feature that I want to bring out tonight is that the future son, the one who through the law of destiny is to become this woman's son, is sometimes permitted at the discretion of the teacher to witness the process of this child, or this soul, being brought into manifestation. But this certainly does not apply to all individuals, mind you. It only applies when one is advanced and knows the whole picture before it is to take place; then he might be permitted to have the experience and observe the process. Remember, it is all automatic. This is only a case where these two souls wanted the experience of knowing in advance. It is a good example to give you tonight because your teachers would like for you to have this information.

The process goes on. The child, or we should now say the young lady or the young woman, reaches the age of 18. But all the time that this child has been growing up in life, having her experiences or whatever it be, the soul who is to be brought onto the earth plane as her son has been observing her actions. This also was permitted because the experience was needed and it was not, we will say, for self-satisfaction. Very well. The young woman becomes 18, a young age in the physical body upon the earth plane indeed, but that is the way it is supposed to be. It is now about time for this other soul to come into manifestation.

Now over here on this side the teacher had actually, in this case mind you, prepared the soul to return, and the astral body is then left to disintegrate. The disintegration of the astral body is a natural process, incidentally, for when the spirit steps out and there is no life force remaining in the astral body, then that astral body becomes only a shell in the astral world and it begins to fade away. This occurs only after the silver cord of life (as you call it on the earth plane) is severed from the astral body in a similar manner as when it is severed from the physical body at physical death.

Then the soul must go back into that Spark of Divinity, where it will then either ascend into a higher state of consciousness and bring into manifestation a new spiritual body, or descend into the reincarnational plane and await rebirth once more in the physical level of expression.

Well, let us go back to where we were. In this case the soul is returning onto the physical plane, and now all of a sudden the time has come. The first preparatory step towards its eventual rebirth is to leave the astral body, which it does. But the soul then goes back into its Spark of Divinity where it will pierce through the various planes separating its present location in the astral world from the reincarnational plane.

First it pierces through all the astral planes, unbeknownst mind you, to the astral beings in the astral world. Then it pierces through the mental plane, a plane that is created not only by the consciousness of men upon the earth, but also through the actions of men upon the earth. Finally it comes to rest in the reincarnational plane, and therein it awaits the exact moment when the atmosphere or, in other words, the auric vibration of the parent is brought into play. When this occurs, the action will be directed by the teacher in the example that I am giving you tonight—not in all cases, but in this particular case it will be under the direction of the teacher.

At this point in time the soul, or rather the Spark of Divinity that represents the soul, now comes into manifestation within the auric force of the parent, and there it will linger for several months. All the while it will be taking on vibrations, absorbing vibrations, until such time as the soul comes back into manifestation.

Now what is the result of all of this? Here we have a child who has had all of these previous experiences, mind you, resulting from knowing this woman in the other world for a period of 200 years. And here we have this young lady. There she is. She is now the proud mother of this boy, and he has finally come into manifestation. What is the result from all this? The result, blessed disciples, is this: as the child grows, as the child reaches the age of three, as the child reaches the age of five, there is a nearness, a very closeness that is far beyond normal mother love when we say that the mother loves the child or loves the boy. There is something even stronger than what the mother can explain herself, you understand. Perhaps you might even call it possessive love, or whatever else it might be termed. But in the case that we bring to your attention, it is an example of a very, very strong connection.

Very well then. We find that the boy now reaches the age of 21, and there is still that strong tie. Perhaps that boy is to become a great artist, or a great musician, or a great what-ever it might be. If this occurs, it is because that mother and that boy, or we will say the two souls, had become accom-plished artists or musicians or whatever in the astral world prior to their earthly incarnation. We are assuming that both the mother and the son are talented in their respective fields. This prior learning then, being retained by the soul, is ex-pressed in another generation or two generations later upon the physical plane. There is that karmic tie. Do you follow me on that point, disciples? Does this give you a better explanation, children of the earth?

Of course, what I have given is just an example. But you can apply this same life principle to millions of souls when you give recognition to the subject, when you get to the depth of all of these things that bring everything into manifestation. In the particular case that I have just brought to your attention, please understand that this is a case where the ones involved had actually worked out the plan without interfering with the divine plan—without violating the law. Of course you really couldn't interfere with the divine plan because it only works one way, but you can actually become so infinitely attuned whereby these things are given to you in advance. I might add that this is so only if you have reached the divine state where you are ready for such information to be given unto you.

Now do you see how we are hemmed in on the earth plane by false ideas and the things that we conjure up? When we start digging into the occult, and into the science of the occult world, then we realize that we can fathom everything that is apparently mysterious to the average lay mind. Isn't that true? So therefore, that is what we are going to do in the future in our occult science. But first we must strive to realize and understand our position on the earth plane. It makes no difference whether this be menial activity or then again whether it be something great that we are supposed to accomplish; for once we understand our position, we can then know back of that why we are the individuals that we are.

Your Relations with Your Family

Let us turn now to your relations with your family. If you say that your brother was your brother in a previous life, or that your sister was your sister many lives ago, it is in all probability true. It is true because you have these relations. The same thing can be said about your relationship with your parents.

Let us suppose that you were born into a family where the parent was extremely mean to you. Your father was abusive, or your mother was abusive, and you wanted to run away and you did—as soon as you could, that is. You were not a wanted child and they said that you were this and that; you heard negative things and you lived in an inharmonious atmosphere. What lesson were you supposed to learn? Your parents were supposed to learn a lesson, but they failed. You also were born into that family to learn a lesson, but how are you going to learn that lesson? You ran away.

The fact remains, disciples, that running away or not, you are to reach the consciousness of the Divine State and recognize the lack of understanding within your parents. Now I certainly do not mean the lack of understanding within the soul itself, for within the soul lies the God Consciousness. I merely mean that your parents had not come unto the divine realization of the God Consciousness within, and therefore they are what we term "young souls." They have not learned, they have not unfolded, and they are merely mortals motivating upon the physical plane.

However, you as an individual may have a very wonderful consciousness, you may be ever so divine, and you may be ever so spiritual in the midst of hell and confusion and so on. Yet there you are, brought into that family that is very opposite from your own consciousness. Do you understand? Have you not observed these things upon the earth plane? I know you have, and no doubt you yourself may have been born into a family like that at one time or another in your earthly career.

This also explains relations between brothers and sisters. You have brothers, you have sisters, yet you are not at all like your brothers or your sisters. You are just as far from them as you can possibly be; in fact, you even get along better with strangers or with other people. But as far as getting along with your own brothers or sisters—you just don't. You find that the so-called stranger is the one you invariably turn your affections to, or the one whom you may want to discuss matters with. You never do this with your own family because there isn't that nearness; there is always that bickering and fighting among your brothers and sisters. Indeed, here also is a lesson to be learned.

You must always remember and bear this in mind: as much love as you might have for your parents, you were only to come through them as a channel on the earth plane. They merely acted as a channel so that you could be born into this world. Of course, as a child you are to honor and obey your mother and father as it is said; there is respect that you must pay, indeed so. And this respect should last throughout your life. But try to realize that you are not to be a slave to it. They were only channels that enabled you to come into this manifestation.

Perhaps you may not feel very close to your father or your mother; in fact, you may feel very far apart. Yet circumstances might force you to be with them. You might be forced to do what they want you to do because of a karmic condition. If this be so, then there is a lesson for you to learn and there is a lesson for them to learn. Yet they may not learn it and you may not learn it. Do you follow me on that point? Do you see what I mean by that statement?

In summary then, it seems that every case is different upon the earth plane. Yet we have similar cases. Your case may be this one or it may be that one, but nevertheless you must strive to learn the lesson that is there for you to learn. You are not placed there to be among certain other individuals by happenstance. There is a definite reason that you were born into the family that you find yourself in. Yet you must remember that your mother and father were only channels through which you were to come into manifestation. And this is precisely the same as when you enabled many other souls to come into manifestation in other generations down through the many millions of years in which you have re-embodied yourself upon the earth plane.

All these things are vital to your education in the occult field of expression. Rub your hands together, sound the A-U-M, and call out your disciple number. One . . . two . . . three . . . AUM.

SECOND DISCOURSE

THE REBIRTH PROCESS

By Dr. Navajo

Good evening, friends. Let us say the affirmation, please.

I am master of myself.
I am all powerful,
And nothing can come to me
Of an inferior nature.
I am peace.
I am power.
I am all there is.

WELL FRIENDS, here we are again to continue our activity with our blessed Agasha when he descends to control the channel. In the past Agasha has given us much information on the subject of reincarnation and rebirth, and especially during a class a short time ago. However, since that time many of the disciples have requested me to cover the subject a little more thoroughly and fill in the gaps, so to speak, that were not covered during that particular class. Therefore, in the time allotted me before he takes over, I am

45

going to endeavor to restate and summarize the basic principles of this fascinating subject as given by Agasha.

Reincarnation: What It Is All About

Reincarnation is the basic principle of life itself in the
evolution of mankind: that which has enabled man to evolve
and become the human that we are in evidence of to date or,
if need be, which enables man to become a higher being than
what we are today. This can be accredited to the action and
the unfolding of the soul. No one determines rebirth for
you—only the soul determines. It is the God within who
indicates the moment of your return unto the flesh and the
intermingling or relationship, the working out of karma,
with human beings on the earth plane.

Reincarnation is the only logical explanation of the mystery of life. You become that which you are through your
learning, your behavior, your working in harmony with and
not violating God's laws. You are the result of your actions
of the past in this life that you are in evidence of at this
moment. When you first came into this incarnation you were
the result of the actions of a previous life and the many lives
you had lived. You were the result of what you had accomplished and what you had failed to conquer.

Regardless of one's believing or not believing, rebirth is
automatic and compulsory until a soul has the Grand Awakening and ascends unto the Consciousness of Immensity. If
you have not accepted this principle as the means of evolving
to become a greater entity than what you represent yourself
to be today, then you must awaken the God Kingdom. Let
it prove to you that rebirth is the only way in which you can
improve and be challenged. Let it enable you to understand
everything that has transpired in this individual life. Listen
to the voice within as it indicates the way that makes it possible for you to conquer that which is to be conquered in this
given life.

Once this principle of reincarnation is accepted, all things are seen in a different perspective. You will not be antagonistic to problems, for you will know that you are being made aware of mistakes made in a past life, or else you are learning needed lessons in this incarnation. Trials are not given as punishment but are presented as a means of helping you to learn lessons and make amends. Then through these actions you evolve and progress toward the ultimate state, whatever that may be.

The Length of the Cycle Between Lives

The question often arises, "After passing from the earth plane, how long does one live in the astral world before again incarnating?" Agasha tells us that the period varies, and this is one of the statements regarding rebirth that should be clarified in the occult world. Some groups appear to be far removed in their opinion from the statements given by Agasha or what the teachers bring forth. These groups arbitrarily indicate that there is a positive and definite set time for each spirit to return to the earth plane. This, according to the Agashan teachers, is not true. It varies, and down through the years we have evidence of that.

It is quite rare in this period of our evolution for an entity to come back to the earth plane after only a very short sojourn in the astral consciousness. We do, however, have a record of such an action. The entity, returning rather quickly, at an early age began recalling that she had a short time before lived in an adjacent city. She indicated her parents, gave their names, and added a great deal of substantiating evidence. All of this was later proved and authenticated.

Another situation of record concerns a young man who awakened around three or four o'clock in the morning. He was startled for a moment at the very real experience he had just gone through—an incident so definite and so complete that he was convinced that he had long ago lived in a small community in the state of Massachusetts. He had seen himself standing in a country cemetery reading a name on a memorial stone. As he studied it, he was suddenly impressed that this was his name in a previous life. He immediately made a note of everything connected with the incident, and the following summer he made a point to vacation in that vicinity. Finding it no problem to locate the small village and the cemetery, he shortly was standing at the exact spot as he had seen it in those early morning hours. Everything was the same: the grave, the name, and the date given on the tombstone—1776.

These are two incidents of reincarnation which indicate a different span of time in rebirth. You usually live in the astral world for a longer time than you live in the physical body. The average life in this consciousness covers a span of about 200 years, and one could well question, "If you are wide awake for 200 years, what are you doing all this time?" Agasha answers this by saying, "It is a consciousness of action and variety; you are busy earning, working, and learning."

Rebirth: A Controversial Subject

The fact that one has lived for sometimes hundreds of years in the astral consciousness does not necessarily mean that he should believe in reincarnation. His belief will depend entirely upon the awakening of the God-Self within. When one leaves the earth plane, he gravitates to the level of his own understanding; this is a consciousness where he will encounter similar ideas and vibrations. If he knew nothing of reincarnation or refused to study it in the physical plane, it is not likely that he would meet those who understand it over here in the astral plane. They would naturally be of the same opinion and report adversely when communicating.

You see folks, there is here in the astral world as much disagreement regarding reincarnation as there is on your earth plane. You on the earth plane, communicating with Spirit by the hundreds and thousands through mediums all over the world, are continually faced with the pros and cons of reembodiment—some say one thing, some another.

Therefore, the one question that plagues seekers of truth in the occult field in reference to rebirth is this vast difference of opinion expressed by many entities of the astral world regarding it.

When Does the Soul Take Over the Body?

Another controversial point that invariably is brought up in any discussion regarding rebirth is that pertaining to the precise moment that the soul takes over the newly formed body. To answer this question intelligently, we must move back to the moment of conception when the most minute force of the germinal kingdom is brought forth. We realize that it will take a certain period of time, according to what we have learned through experience and observation, for the body to grow and expand. During this time it is being fed by the parent and being prepared to be brought into manifestation in the manner in which it should be.

During this period of waiting, the soul is hovering in the immediate aura of the mother. It is being nurtured by her and it is taking on the vibrations of the parents. It is well if there is an attunement, a good relationship, between the parents during this time.

Now when does the soul take over the body? The teachers say that the exact moment when this occurs varies with the individual. This is determined by the soul. But when life is felt by the mother, you are most certainly in evidence of the soul having taken over and entered the newly formed body. This is usually around the fourth month of pregnancy.

What Happens When There Is a Miscarriage?

The mother, in carrying the fetus, might have an early miscarriage; then, of course, the child could not take over and enter. When I speak of "child," I mean the entity to be reborn. It is not aware that it is to reembody. It is only through the attraction, the inner relations, that it is to become the child of the parents. But if there were this type of miscarriage, a mother, after a reasonable period of time, might again become pregnant, and the soul that was to come forth as a result of the previous conception would take over at the proper time and be reborn through this new pregnancy.

If no vehicle for rebirth is available, the soul, needing the earthly experiences and having failed to come into life, will return to the reincarnational plane. There it will await a new opportunity to come unto another parent.

The same situation would exist in the case of an abortion in the early stages of pregnancy. If this is performed prior to the time life would be felt by the mother, then life is not taken; the soul is merely prevented from taking over the body and coming into manifestation. This action is legitimate when the mother's health could be adversely affected or when hardship would be involved.

But in the case of a miscarriage in the latter stages of pregnancy or in the case of the stillborn, the soul of the child had for the moment taken over, and so it would return to the astral plane where the child would grow to maturity in that consciousness. Thus many a "would-be mother" has a son or a daughter, unbeknownst to her, living and growing and expanding here in the astral world.

On the Immaculate Conception

The attitude of parents in attracting souls to be brought into this life is important. Therefore if a highly evolved soul is to be attracted unto the parents, it would appear that the parents themselves should likewise be in a high, harmonious spiritual state.

The thing for us to keep in mind is that a conception may be called "immaculate" when there is a true mating, a true relationship, a harmonious vibration emanating from the one to the other—the male and the female—a most beautiful relationship! This condition is most difficult for us to describe using the words available to us in the language of today. Rebirth under such conditions as I speak of could very well be called an immaculate conception.

This then leads us up to the many misstatements made

regarding this doctrine of the Immaculate Conception and the ultimate consequences which led to the concept of virgin birth. There are many on the earth plane who believe that such a birth actually happened in the birth of Jesus; they also believe that it never happened before. Knowing that this is a universe governed by God's laws, which are immutable, it seems logical to believe that if such a thing happened once it could happen many times, or it never happened at all. Agasha tells us that this very subtle doctrine, insofar as it relates to the birth of Jesus, is to be taken more symbolically than literally. Here again is another one of the misconceptions that needs to be clarified.

We must always remember that when we speak of birth, we are referring to one of God's immutable laws which are never subject to change. Therefore, the items we have to consider when we refer to the basic principle that produces life are the action, the component parts, and that which is relevant to produce whatever it may be—fruit, animal, this or that. Then through their interaction, germination, and fermentation, life is brought forth.

Your Astral Death Just Before You Were Born

Life in the astral world is not static. We are as free here as you are on the earth plane. We may, after having resided in some particular consciousness for a period of time, then desire to go into another kingdom, not necessarily a higher kingdom, but a new kingdom because we had become interested in other things. This is normal, and if we were to do this it would raise no particular questions. Remember, you will live in the astral world for a period ranging from 100 to 300 years on the average, and this is a considerable length of time. You will exist in a consciousness that will enable you to see yourself in the light; yet you might have no idea of ever going back to the earth plane. You may not believe in reincarnation, and you may not have advanced yourself to a place where you might at least investigate it.

Then suddenly you disappear from society. This departure

is different in that it is not of your own volition, and those in your category who, like you, do not believe in reembodiment will for a time think it strange. In wonderment they will question, "Where did he go? What happened? Did he fade away into the nothingness?" And with no understanding the question will never be answered to their satisfaction.

Regardless of one's belief in reference to rebirth, the action at the proper time is automatic. In this disappearing act, the soul passes out of the astral body, the outer casing, and goes back into its original state, the Spark of Divinity. It is the sublimated astral body that is left to disintegrate. However, this is not within the sight of those we call the onlookers. The soul then is in a form that we would refer to as being egg-shaped, and it leaves the astral world and moves into the reincarnational plane.

The Soul Seeks Its Parents

One could now question, "How does the soul know when to make the decision to be drawn or to go into the immediate atmosphere of the parent to be?" The answer is that since God is all knowing, it does not have to consult the mortal mind, the outer mind, if you want to put it in that light. The God Kingdom, being infinite, brings the action about through an affinity or a relationship with the past. The incarnating soul could in another life have been the parent, but now it returns to be the child. The matter of location as to where the parent is now living is of no importance. It could be the same country, it could be 10,000 miles away, or it could be most anywhere; but the soul would find the spirit of the parent and thus be brought out of the darkness and into the light to be reborn.

All is brought about through the inner workings of the mind. The outer mind does not know and is not in a position to know. It is utterly oblivious to all of this and this is in order. It is God's way, and it is concealed from the mortal mind so that the outer mind cannot question or interfere with God's law.

Thus we find the soul appearing in the immediate atmosphere of the mother to be. It hovers there and bides its time. It has now become very minute, and it represents the very essence of life because it is encased within the Spark of Divinity which is an integral part of God. As I have just pointed out, if you were to gaze upon that soul with microscopic vision, you would find it to be an extremely minute, egg-shaped form hovering in the mother's aura.

But just think of the lives that had been lived by that soul! Who can say how many? Think of the millions of years involved in that soul's unfoldment, and then think of the numberless events connected with each incarnation. And the absolutely, positively incredible thing is that the record of all of this—including every solitary word uttered either sincerely, facetiously, or even in anger—is all contained therein. Within that hovering soul is the record of every incarnation ever lived. Just think of it! It is as Agasha has so often said, "Within the soul is stored the record of all."

A Look at Reincarnation in General

Let us now take a look at the overall picture of souls returning back unto the physical plane. Often the devotees of reincarnation bring a great deal of ridicule unto themselves by making unsubstantiated claims regarding certain individuals. If a particular bright light comes forth in the field of invention, many will immediately tag him as being the reincarnation of Thomas A. Edison. This is a bit beyond normal reasoning.

Thomas Edison was a wonderful channel and has, no doubt, busied himself with the things that previously concerned him and with the advancement of such activities in the present period. He and the other great men advanced in science, the political field, medicine, art, music, and the like are constantly assisting and helping to improve the work of their colleagues in their own particular field on the earth plane. Like always attracts like, and it will always be so. But this certainly does not mean that the person being helped is necessarily the reincarnation of the one famous in history.

We are also aware of the reincarnationist who claims that he had been in a previous life some great king or queen. Now this might be true. But on the other hand it might simply be an ember to keep his or her very substantial ego aglow. This does not deny the fact that sometimes you do come back to humble yourself when you were not humble before. As a person, perhaps in a previous life you had others at your beck and call, and then you abused the privilege. So then now you are back in this life all the more to be tested. You have to learn to be humble and not to be aggressive.

Another very important point to be brought out is that if a person becomes very powerful, or if he amasses a great fortune, or if he finds himself in a position where in any way he controls the lives of others, he must be absolutely sure not to use this power in the wrong direction. There is a law to balance this: the law of retribution, the law that governs all things. We must all balance the scale in each of our lives. That means my life, your life, the other person's life. I am what I am through the actions of the past, and who can find fault with that?

On Recalling Your Previous Lives

There are many in the occult field who state that they are in a position to tell you how many lives you had lived in a certain cycle, and then they might perhaps give you a complete description of many of these lives. Agasha tells us that this is not always true, since many people who try to give readings are digging deep into the field of imagination. Even though the information is given in all sincerity, he brings out that the number of psychics in the outer world today who have the ability to pry into the soul and find out what one has experienced are few.

Even to one who has studied and unfolded, the soul is often reluctant to give out much information relative to previous lives. The reason for this—aside from the confusion it would bring—lies in the fact that the soul must reach a certain pinnacle of unfoldment before it will reveal certain factors that need to be brought out to prove things unto the disciple. When these pinnacles are reached, the soul reveals much information to the outer consciousness.

Why should you be recalling all of the things that you had done in a previous life? It is even difficult enough to recall many things that happened in this life, and there are many other things that you do not care to recall at all. Surely in other lives you had such experiences, and if you should be in this life so unfortunate that you are able to recall all events, you would then indeed be wallowing in a sea of turmoil and bewilderment.

Agasha states that while the Divine Higher Self knows all of your incarnations, it is well to remember that you, the mortal self, are now under and always have been under the dictates of this Higher Self. Your soul was reborn into the particular cycle of life where you now find yourself. You are in this situation to learn, to make amends, and to strive ever to cleanse and purify yourself of the desires and passions of the mortal. This does not mean to not use them and enjoy them; it simply means to learn not to be controlled by them. By accomplishing that which your soul had set out for you to accomplish, and by not failing in this life as you had in others, this might very well make it possible for you to advance into a consciousness whereby it would not be necessary for you to ever again return onto the earth plane.

This then is a summary of the general philosophy of reincarnation and rebirth as given by Agasha during these many years. As a simple Navajo Indian, I hope that I have been able to shed a little more light on this subject by simply restating tonight that which he had given in previous classes.

Well folks, Agasha's light is building up in the center of the room now, and it looks like I am going to have to step aside. Oh, oh, here he comes now . . . . . .

THIRD DISCOURSE

THE LAW OF EVOLUTION

By Agasha

My blessed children—Manzaholla and bless each and every disciple who, fully realizing that we are well on the path, endeavors to understand the intricacies of life. And one of the most intricate subjects of all of them is the study of the evolution of mankind. This principle of evolution, along with its related laws, is in my opinion one of the most interesting subjects that can ever be brought unto the higher disciple.

We can speak scientifically and understand many things which are given to you by the scientific minds on earth. Yet when these minds endeavor to prove unto the lay mind that they are absolutely correct in their deductions, we must realize that in reality they are only speculating. On the other hand, I am not speculating when I return unto the earth because it is my desire to give you the pure and unadulterated information in a simplified form, so simple that even a child may very readily understand it.

Yet there are times when I seem to go off on a tangent, as you would call it upon earth. I speak at random because I am endeavoring to cover as much as I possibly can in the course of an evening. Consequently, it does tend to confuse some of you disciples as you endeavor to follow me when often I speak rather hurriedly and may change my thought rather abruptly as some other thought may cross my consciousness. I have reduced my vibration to a very great extent when I manifest through this channel and sometimes, as I had explained many months ago, I am thinking much faster than I can speak. Thus you might say that I am trying to catch up with myself, if you know what I mean.

The True Meaning of Evolution

In any discussion of the evolution of mankind, we must try to realize and try to acquaint ourselves with the fact or idea that in reality it is Consciousness itself evolving through bodies and form that is the basis for the true evolution of Man, and not strictly the evolution of the body. We must also realize that we were before this world was born. This is of prime importance for any true understanding. We have been in physical forms on other planets, but we have evolved through these forms, through these respective bodies, up to where we are today. We were mammoth people at one time, we were midgets at one time, and we were odd-looking, perhaps, in comparison with our appearance today. But it is our consciousness evolving through form that is so all important.

So therefore we can say that before this small earth of yours was brought into manifestation, we were on other planets. We have gone through the same process on other planets that we are going through now, but each time that we came onto a new planet we were just a little bit higher than what we had been on the previous planet. Now we may have appeared upon other planets in a different body; we may have lived more of an animalistic life, that may be true. But on the other hand, it may not have been any more of an animalistic life than what we went through in our earlier evolution upon this present planet.

We Were Always a Divine Entity

Now blessed disciples of the earth, we must strive to understand another important factor which becomes more or less the key to any correct understanding of the evolution of mankind. This important proposition—or knowledge, rather, as it is no longer a supposition—is that before we came to this earth, we were a divine entity. And before we had come onto other planets, we were a divine entity. But if we had lived on other planets in the various bodies that we inhabited in the dense plane, then this means that we were evolving there on those planets the same as we have evolved here on this earth.

At this point one might ask, "If it is true that when we first came upon this planet we were a little bit higher than what we were on a previous planet, then did we arrive here in that higher state, or did we have to revert back to our original condition in the beginning? In other words, did we continue to grow, expand, and evolve from where we had left off at the previous planet, or did we have to start all over again, as it were, from a lower form of life?"

Before I answer this question, I would like to have you understand that there is a gap whereby the spirit does not return unto the earth plane or any other physical plane. There was a lapse of time whereby the spirit remained in the ethereal world until conditions were proper on the forthcoming planet for the mortal mind and mortal body to formulate and begin to evolve.

This then explains the belief of many down through the ages that they had come to the earth in a primitive form from other planets, and that they would have to spend some time here on the earth plane before they could return to the beauty which they were supposed to inherit on some other planet or star. Rather primitively they were embracing the higher teachings of occultism which state that in reality we are all divine entities. However, both the vision as well as the learning of these evolving souls were limited, thus pro-hibiting them from understanding the things that are given us today and the wonderful things that were given during the great period of Atlantis.

Therefore, in answer to the question just posed, we must strive to understand that when human expression incarnates for the first time on a particular planet, it cannot do so until a suitable physical vehicle is there to receive it. And since all life came from the sea, through the process of evolution new life forms are constantly being evolved. Thus we find that out of necessity, we had to begin our evolution on this planet Earth in a lower life form as it evolved out of the sea.

Now if you were to ask if we had also gone through all of the life processes of the earth plane, I would most certainly have to answer that indeed we did, although not necessarily on this particular planet. We very definitely first went through water, fire, and all the elemental forms. Then our bodies evolved with the aid of the germinal kingdom through all the lower forms of life to become the human expression that we are today. This is a fundamental law. There is no other way.

You realize, of course, that the physical body that you inhabit today went through numerous lower forms of life while evolving and growing within your mother's womb after the union of two very minute and tiny life cells. This same cycle is repeated innumerable times, not only with the rebirth of each new physical vehicle or body, but also with the rebirth of an entire new species on a particular earth plane. "Is this retrogression?" you ask. Of course not. It is only seemingly so.

The soul took over your physical body after it had evolved to a certain point within your mother's womb. Yet your outer consciousness can only remember, we will say, back to perhaps the third year of this present physical life. There-fore, in a like manner we can say that the higher conscious-ness of the human expression which had evolved to a high degree on a previous planet will not fully awaken within the new physical vehicle until it, too, has evolved to a certain degree of consciousness. Thus we have a gap, or a lapse in time. The higher outer consciousness of the soul sleeps until a suitable time for its reawakening within the new life form. Yet the inner consciousness of the soul is always awake and conscious of the God Kingdom within. I hope this brings a little more light and understanding to this fundamental but somehow difficult concept for the average disciple to fully understand.

How Human Life Came to this Planet

Now prior to the time of the mammoth animals and early plant life, millions and millions of years were required for the earth to go through its cooling process. And, of course, your material science is in agreement with occult science when it states that during this period there was no way at all for the different forms of life to come upon the physical plane.

Ultimately, however, life appeared. And science has gone back hundreds of millions of years into the past and has traced the evolution of the first plant life, the mammoth animals, the huge flying reptiles, the giant birds, and other forms of animal life. But when it comes to human expression, it is the thinking of the scientific mind of today that the ancestor of modern man only dates back barely a dozen million years ago at the earliest. However, I differ in this opinion, but the time element is merely a figure of speech because it is so far back. If we were to use the figure of 25 million years ago, it would be far closer to the truth. Therefore, in reference then to the beginning of the evolvement of mankind or human expression upon this planet, I have used this figure in your classes. It is the approximate period when human expression first began upon this physical plane—25 million years.

To illustrate this point further, let us now go back some 25 million years and study your own planet Earth. There is no human expression in manifestation at this time. All we can find is the prehistoric animal life. However, swarming around the planet is a great sea of germs, a great sea of the germinal kingdom that is desirous of coming into manifestation. Now the higher teachers of Immensity, working indirectly in conjunction with the great Pillars of Light through the Intermediaries, are in a position to observe these germs. They are able to study them and reach the inner consciousness of this oncoming form of life.

Now what do they find? Let us say that they find that this vast sea of the germinal kingdom has the potential of bringing human expression into manifestation. Let us further state that this particular sea of germs has been directed to your planet by some of the great Intermediaries of Intermediaries. Thus we find that these great teachers from Immensity are desirous of enabling human expression from another planet that can now no longer sustain life to once more have the chance to grow, expand, and evolve on a new physical plane. The higher outer consciousness of these previously evolving souls is of course experiencing a lapse of time during this transition period.

This germinal kingdom will now gradually intermingle with the elements of the earth. It will remain there incubating while it is in that element. Then over a period of time these germs, who mind you are both of the male and the female force, will gradually take on other forces of nature and be able to bring tiny bodies into manifestation. These bodies will eventually expand and then die out and revert back into the etheric state while still hovering very close to the planet. Then it becomes possible for the evolving force to eventually take on other bodies, larger bodies, as it returns through the process of very quickly reembodying itself into these various tiny forms.

Over a long period of time the bodies will grow into still larger bodies until eventually the evolving force will function in the animalistic state. This is the identical process, disciples of the earth plane, that enabled you to first come into manifestation on this planet Earth. Then after roughly a million years, or even much longer than that in some cases, it becomes possible for a suitable body to be created whereby the oncoming souls can then awaken to the new world that they will find themselves in.

Now you might ask, "Are these newly created souls?" and of course the answer is absolutely not. They are not newly created in the sense of the word. They are only souls whose outer expression had been lying dormant for perhaps millions or even billions of years since having had physical expression on some other planet. Now, through the efforts of the Pillars of Light working through the germinal kingdom, they are able to come into outer manifestation and have experiences on the physical plane once more.

Awakening the God Consciousness

Now let us say that you and I had returned to the physical plane, and we found ourselves evolving from a lower form of life on this planet Earth. We had taken on an entirely different physical body from what you have today; yet we had gradually evolved, developed, and unfolded our faculties as we returned back into various physical bodies from time to time.

We could say that in the beginning our brain was dense. Consequently, we had to depend greatly on the inspiration of the soul without even knowing it. We were motivated by the soul mainly because the brain did not function properly. It did not conceive or receive the proper impressions of things which we observed. However, as we returned back onto the physical plane from time to time, the brain was able to expand in each of the various bodies that we had. Then gradually we were able to notice things, recognize them, and eventually even give them a name and refer to them with that name in a guttural language. Sometimes it was a sign language or whatever else it might be to convey the thought. Perhaps it could be said that the brain was even larger then than it is today, but the size of the brain is not a criterion for wisdom. A larger brain can sometimes become a curse.

Therefore we recognize the fact that as we reembodied ourself, as we became more attuned to the God Consciousness, we then became more spiritual-like in our actions upon the earth plane. The physiognomy changed. Eventually there was a complete metamorphosis of the body structure, but of course this covered a long period of time. You see, disciples, as we returned onto the physical plane, we were awakening the senses within; but awakening the senses within is merely awakening the God Consciousness. Yet at the same time that the God Consciousness expanded, as it unfolded, then each nerve in the physical body also responded harmoniously, with the result that we were gradually impressed with the finer aspects of life.

It was only after we had unfolded to a sufficient degree that it became possible for us to create the beauty that was to be created upon the earth plane. True, out of the earth came all that was ever created and brought into manifestation; but it was through the senses or the power of the brain, that we were able to exercise and use, that these things were made possible. It is the God Consciousness within that does the work, and it cannot do this work until it has become awakened. It is only from the Great Awakening, the unfoldment of the Spark of Divinity that lies within, that man starts to truly live and not simply motivate upon the earth plane. Most interesting, indeed!

The Inhabitants of Other Planets

The same principle also applies to inhabitants of other planets, and should you come in contact with a dweller of another planet, he would perhaps appear very strange to you. Yet on the other hand, the inhabitants of some of the planets in the various solar systems might appear exactly the same as you. How can this be? The answer is that the similarity could exist not only because of the climatic conditions, but also through the desire of the soul itself. In this case there would be a direct relationship between the human here and the human there, and the desire of the soul would bring the similarities into play.

However, we must remember that even though we have here on the earth plane a species that we call human expression, such an expression on another planet could equally well be called human and yet not resemble earthly humans at all. Here again, it is consciousness that is so all important —not the physical form.

The inhabitant of another planet could have large shoulders, it could have a large head or a different shaped head, it could have this, or it could have that. To you it would be odd; to the inhabitant of the other planet, you might also be odd. These humans might have organs in their body that you do not have; yet the action of their coming into life would in all probability be the same as for individuals of this earth plane.

We must realize that these other forms of human expression are going according to their particular stage in evolution. They are adapting to the climatic conditions existing on their planet. The gases that they might have to take into their lungs may cause them to expand and be much larger, or smaller, or whatever the case may be. These varying conditions will be found in all aspects because we are not embracing only one planet in our study of evolution, but we are embracing all planets. And again I say, the important thing is consciousness when we study human expression.

It is generally believed by occultists today, in some circles that is, that there are people, human expression, who have never had a physical body to contend with. It is believed that in the etheric realms, beings are still existing who have never taken on the flesh. I will answer that statement in the following manner: If I were to say that there are such people, I would be telling you the truth—but in one aspect only. Basically, I could not make that statement. I could not say it intelligently, nor could I well authenticate it. I would have to qualify the statement by saying that if we were to take into consideration all manifestations of planetary life, going back into the past if necessary, we would find that they would have had expression through the physical channel at one time or another. How else could they be what they are today, no matter what state of consciousness they be in at this time?

The Germinal Kingdom

We find that the germinal kingdom becomes an absolutely essential factor in allowing life to manifest in any physical plane. Now let us for the moment endeavor to analyze a particular germ and try to get to the origin of that germ. This germ that I bring to your attention is one of the countless germs that composes the physical body. Let us try to reach its consciousness. We are able to do that because we are a part of everything that is. This you have learned in your classes. Therefore, we must be a part of that germ which we are to study. By going into a particular state of consciousness we can then become attuned to that germ by visiting its own individual germinal kingdom, that is, the germ kingdom of its particular species. We can enter its consciousness, and what do we find? We find that that particular germ is as active and as conscious of its work in bringing bodies into manifestation as you are conscious of yourself going about your daily activities. Think of it! This little germ that is so minute indeed is as active and as conscious of itself as you are of yourself. And their numbers are countless.

Now we must strive to bear in mind, beloved disciples, that we have to take every element into consideration before we can fully understand the human body. The reason for this is that you are an integral part of everything that is. I know this to be true. This means then that you are also an integral part of the God Consciousness, that same God Consciousness that is the driving force that motivates every form of body that you had ever inhabited. This is called the Spark of Divinity, as you have learned in your classes. It is also within every element that is known to mankind.

Now I have made the statement in the past that every one of these elements has been placed within and has become a part of the physical self at one time or another. Therefore it is reasonable to state that your body is a part of everything that is upon the physical plane, as it has been formed out of every known element of the earth. And probably one of the most important elements, or compounds rather, is water, for all life originally came from the sea.

Therefore we must recognize that in our most minute form of germ expression, we had to first come from water. We had lived in the water before we had ever lived on the land. This law is applicable for all species of life on the earth plane today. Now, is that most minute form of germ that eventually brought forth human expression a special species? I never want to claim that we are any special species, yet we today as human expression have dominion over all. Therefore you would say that we would be considered a special entity, and yet this is not basically true. We should realize that the only reason that we do have dominion over much that creepeth upon the physical plane is that our particular species had evolved to the human expression level back in the eons of time. Yet we are not, strictly speaking, a special species. Our form of life, both in the germinal kingdom as well as when it evolved out of the water in the beginning, appeared no different, on the surface, than any other form of evolving life.

The Creatures of the Sea

All forms of life eventually evolve to become greater than what they are today. This includes the millions and billions of creatures that exist in the sea that have never been discovered, as well as all of the other forms of life that you know of today. They will all in time become something other than what they are at the present, in reference to their outer casing or body. However, the Spark of Divinity within the soul never does evolve. It was already perfect in the beginning.

Let us study the whale. We see that he is mammoth indeed as he swims and plays within the deep waters of the sea. Now what does he think of the human expression that he has come in contact with? Can we tune in on his thoughts? Perhaps we can in time. Being so huge, and also being a nervous animal, he has been known to cause much damage at sea by capsizing boats and so on. But he is not deliberately going out of his way to destroy humanity. He is only responding to the nature of his own being. Will he become any greater than he is at the present time? Perhaps not any greater when we speak of his size, but he most certainly will become a more highly evolved expression of life.

Now I mentioned some time ago the fact that in the great depths of the ocean there are innumerable species that have not been observed or studied by human life. There are many that even have intelligence, and they express themselves quite intelligently. The same applies within the darkest parts of Africa, the jungles of South America, or any of the various other isolated areas away from civilization.

I can bring to your attention certain species in the animal kingdom that have such a remarkable sense of intelligence that if you were to compare it with the intelligence of the average man today on the earth plane, you would say that it is almost equal. Why do I make this seemingly ridiculous statement? The answer is, blessed disciples, that they have an amazing ability to recall their previous lives. Thus they can use the lessons learned in the past in finding a solution to any situation in which they might find themselves in their present embodiment.

Your modern scientists call it instinct. I call it conscious recollection of previous life experiences. Perhaps it is routine with them as they do it instinctively, having apparently inherited it from their ancestors, and I quite agree with this point. However, I will qualify that by adding the fact that in their own divine state, or in their own consciousness, they can and do recall. This is their way of expressing themselves or protecting themselves.

It is most interesting to observe that everything that is in the ocean, everything that moves in the great sea, has its own means of protection. If we study some of the creatures of the sea, it becomes not only amusing but also very interesting. Each has its own enemy; each feeds upon the other. In other words, one will eat the other, and the next one will eat the other one, and it goes on and on indefinitely. In fact, we can extend the thought further by stating the fact that everything that moves, every creature that moves on either the land or in the sea, has its enemy as well as its means of protection.

Now let us go on to an even higher form of expression. In the great stories of mythology, you may recall some that are not only picturesque but are also very educational. They are ofttimes romantic and inspiring. It was for this purpose that the originators of mythology, the great philosophers of old, brought mythology into manifestation. All mythology originated in the great consciousness of Atlantis and, before that, in Lemuria or some other great civilization buried in the vastness of time and space. Who can say where lies the true beginning? In any event, mythology is basically a symbol of eternal and universal truths. Take for example the fairy tales given children today. They are simple and amusing and the children love them. But back of these apparent fairy tales and folklore, there is a great significance and they hold a great deal of truth.

Let us study the mermaid, that beautiful siren of the sea. There she is: half human and half fish. Now it is not that I am saying that we have such creatures at the bottom of the sea, but I am saying that a future form of human expression is there. It is not there in the form that you or I are in at this time, no indeed. But it is there just the same. There be the truth behind the fiction of the mermaid. It is gradually evolving to become greater than it is today, and eventually it will come to the surface.

It has been found that over a period of hundreds of thousands of years certain species that originally could not live out of water have been known to come to the shore and live for days before returning to the sea. We have definite proof of that, for as we go back and study their ancestry we learn that there was a time when such creatures could never exist out of water. Then too, there are certain forms of life in the sea that cannot even go down to any great depth. They don't know what the depth of the sea is like. As a matter of fact, some of them cannot be under water for any great length of time before they must be up breathing in oxygen again so that they may survive. Then there are those that can never come above the surface to receive the oxygen, and they must always remain in the water as most fish seem to do. This all becomes most interesting as we observe it and study it.

Shall all of these creatures of the sea become greater than what they are? Yes, of course; the law is universal. They all have even now become greater than what they were in the beginning of their creation. How did they come into the form that they have at the present time? How did they attain their peculiar forms, their peculiar shapes? You might say that some of the creatures do not look like anything at all, or perhaps they might resemble a peculiar little bush, or a little flower, or whatever the case might be.

The answer is, disciples of the earth plane, that it is not only life itself that is ever evolving to become greater than what it was in the beginning, but it is the life within its "self" that is evolving. There are many, many millions of forces in the germinal kingdom that help to move that creature who in turn is a part of the collective whole. Please understand that that creature which you have brought to the surface to study is an integral part of the collective whole, and the collective whole which represents that creature is also the God Consciousness. A very beautiful thought, indeed.

The Versatility of Life

Now you see insects all around and about you. You see them in the garden; you see them in your home. Some of them you have never seen before. There on that leaf is a peculiar-looking little creature and you think, "Well, what is that?" It is a bug. You call it a bug and you think that it is the most peculiar-looking bug that you have ever seen. True, perhaps you have never seen anything like it before. Any day, if you are looking for them, you can go out and you can find insects that you had never seen before. They seem to be quite plentiful. Now then, you must realize that each bug or insect has a reason for being the insect that it represents itself to be. Now just think of the billions of insects that have become extinct, those that you will never see, never see at all. And just remember that this little bug that you have just now become aware of is only a minute part of the billions that do exist at the present time. All are taking their active part. They are all playing their role, whatever role they have to play in life.

Another very interesting point that I would like to bring out in our little talk on evolution tonight is that not only are forms of life gradually surfacing from the great depths of the sea, but going further and putting aside the water kingdom for the moment, we must realize that still other forms of life are gradually coming to the surface right here on earth. There are forms of life within the great caverns that could not see a thing if they were to come out into the sunlight. There are other forms of life within these caverns that can also see in the light, but they venture forth only occasionally. They usually stay within their own kingdom, for they can actually see in the apparent darkness.

If you were to enter into their caverns you could not see a thing, yet they could see you clearly. Some do not even possess the physical eye, yet they can still see. "What do they see with?" you might ask. The answer is that they see through the powers of their own soul. Physical sight is only one method of becoming aware of your environment. Now God has not shown partiality; God has not favored them necessarily. It is only that the laws of evolution have provided an alternate method of seeing to those forms of life that must evolve in total darkness. Yet they are all evolving and becoming greater than what they are today.

The Consciousness of the Flowers and Trees

Now let us move on to the lighter side of the subject, which in my opinion is rather romantic. You have beautiful flowers around and about you, and you notice how beautiful and fragrant they are. You love a rose because a rose portrays beauty and it throws off a perfume that is very pleasing to the nostrils. So you love the rose. You love flowers in general but you especially love the rose because of its color, its splendor, its design, and so on.

You look at a tree and you say, "There is a beautiful tree." You love the tree because you simply love the tree. You don't know why you do, but perhaps it is because it is so noble and high. It has beautiful branches and it is shaped most beautifully. You seem to love this particular tree more than any other tree for some strange reason. And so ofttimes you may go and visit that tree. Perhaps it is in the woods, or then again it might be in your own back yard. You go to the tree and you reverently admire the tree. You wait for its foliage to come in season, and you feel rather sad when the leaves begin to fall. You know that the tree is only going through its seasonal process so that it may live and regenerate itself much the same as when we slush off the elements in our own kingdom, but at the same time you still feel rather sad when autumn comes around. So the tree is before you and you may want to sit under the tree.

Now what I am about to say may sound fantastic, but nevertheless it is true. Did you know that a tree is conscious of your admiration? Did you know that, children? A tree is actually conscious of your admiration! You see, you are a part of everything that is, are you not? And Nature is what? Nature is God, as I have said innumerable times in the past. Therefore you are Nature, and inasmuch as God is also Nature, you are likewise God. Isn't that true? Now what is a tree? It may be an oak tree, it may be a weeping willow tree, it may be any kind of tree, but it is still a tree. And being a tree, it represents Nature which is God. We are all interrelated. I believe research has been done recently relative to plants which tends to give validity to some of these statements.

So when you come close to your special tree, it is not surprising when you feel that it seems to radiate something to you. It gives you something. It doesn't give all people the same, no, but because of your feelings it responds to your presence. You sit under the tree; you love the tree. It is a landmark for you, but you love it and you reverently send forth love. You do this unconsciously while you are in that special vibration that you feel when in the presence of the tree. And at this same moment the consciousness of the tree, which is also a part of Nature or of God, thus becomes conscious of your radiation of love. It is this universal love which is absorbed into its branches and into its roots that enables it to feel your pulsating presence.

Yes, you actually are pulsating rhythmically in the Consciousness of God and so is the tree in its own respective state. It is pulsating in rhythm with you and therefore you are momentarily working on the same frequency that the tree is on. Consequently you feel the radiation that is sent forth from the tree, you feel that invigorating power, and you feel renewed by sitting under the tree or by merely admiring its branches and its beautiful leaves. Do you see what I mean, children? The tree cannot speak to you and greet you in the way that you would greet the tree, of course not. But it still feels and it senses your vibrations. And did you also know that the tree or the roses or the flowers, once they have become conscious of your admiration, will actually burst forth and become even more radiant? Yes indeed, this is so very true.

Now when the time comes for the woodman to go out and chop down or destroy the tree, the tree seems to sense this and there is a certain something within the tree that does not want to be destroyed. Yet, I can only say that since the tree is an expression of God or of Nature, it somehow knows that it will live again and that the essence of itself will revert back into the etheric realm. The outer part of the tree is going to be utilized for other purposes just as all bodies of the earth plane eventually go through the same process. But it is only the outer expression, the outer casing or shell, that is destroyed. The inner essence continues to live in the etheric realm. This law is applicable to all, and it makes no difference whether it be tree, flower, animal, or the human body.

The Balancing Aspect of Nature

Let us now consider one other important point while we are still discussing this facet of Nature. Your tree that stands so very noble and high, your tree that radiates such beauty when it bursts forth with its fruit or foliage each season— that very same tree is eventually going to be attacked by a certain germ, beetle, or insect. However, these other forms of life are not attacking the tree to destroy the tree. No indeed, this is not their motive. They attack the leaves only insofar as something within the leaf enables them to survive. They partake of that which the tree lends or gives to other forms of Nature. Perhaps it is the gum, or a secretion from the tree, or an element within the leaf itself. A worm will often nibble upon the leaves, and then survive by having done so.

Now then, there comes along another form of life, a bird perhaps which will partake of the worm that is destroying the leaves. Or it might be some form of insect that sustains itself on the lesser forms of life. Here we see the balancing aspect of Nature at work. If this were not so, then you could not have flowers on the earth plane; you could not have beautiful trees on the earth plane, for nothing could survive. Thus stronger forces of Nature prohibit and curtail the activities of the lesser forces from going too far and getting out of hand.

We must also realize that the destruction that a particular insect had brought about is likewise going to bring about another form of expression which will in turn lend something more to creation and thus to the advancement of human expression. On the surface perhaps this does not make sense —life eating life in order to survive—but that is only on the surface. If you dig deeper you will find the reason. You cannot escape all that moveth upon the physical plane, disciples; for the moment that you deny this or deny that, then you are denying that you are a part of the collective whole.

Therefore all forms of life revert back to the collective whole. Each be a part of all that is. We live with Nature; we are Nature; we are God. All that is, is God. And in embracing and admiring Nature in its truer sense, we can thus realize the importance of each facet of Nature. Always remember, disciples of the earth plane, that we are the God that was and that we are the God that is. We have only to realize it.

The Great Wheel of Life

All of the activity of Nature, then, is vital for us to understand at this time if we are to get to the origin of life. Or at least we must understand it in its broader aspects. Down through the years there have been any number of theories, both scientific as well as occult, expounded by the adherents of their own particular theory or philosophy. Yet it would seem that no definite conclusion has been reached pertaining to the evolution of mankind that is acceptable to all. Men on the earth plane are limited and have only a small amount of conclusive evidence; therefore they can only speak theoretically.

But on the other hand, the teachers in the higher orders of the Consciousness of Immensity do not speak theoretically. They are in the knowing, for they understand fully all of the laws of evolution. The workings of these laws have been symbolically expressed from time to time by the motion of a wheel—the great wheel of life. In speaking thus, I am only trying to employ your common expressions in passing on to you disciples the basic elements of the evolution of mankind insofar as it is understood and known to be true from this side of life.

It would seem to some that after we had broken from the great Core of Life, we were then on our own. However, we were not on our own, and we have never been on our own in the sense of the word. Each form of life is given different duties to perform, and every facet of Nature is necessary for life to continue. Thus we are constantly being aided by Nature in more ways than you would know.

Now, there were definite laws set up for the evolution of mankind. Man does not evolve by happenstance; man evolves through effort. Yet we were all given an equal opportunity in the beginning. Each one was placed on the earth to go through these cycles. I faltered and you faltered; I arose and you didn't; you arose and I didn't. Then you went ahead, and I would seemingly retrogress or remain stagnant. And the reason that you went ahead was that you had simply put forth more effort than I had.

When one man karmically passes out of the physical body, he then gives room for others to come in and play their role in life. Each has his own turn to learn his lessons and pay his karma. The wheel of life is continually revolving, over and over and over. Each rides for a while and then steps off to give his place to another. Yet this wheel of life is ever in constant motion.

What is the ultimate end to all of this? The answer, disciples of the earth, is to learn your lessons and graduate from this wheel of life. You do not have to ride it forever, physically speaking that is. No indeed, once you have ascended from the physical plane of life, you need no longer evolve the physical vehicle or garment. However, this has been the process for all who are still on the earth plane, and it has been going on for billions and billions of years.

The Desire Body

What will be your appearance once you have graduated from the wheel of life? You have had many, many forms of outer expression since you first began your evolutionary spiral from that great Core of Life. But before we can take up this point, we must first realize that each of the many lives that we have lived has always been the result of previous actions. When you think of bodies, you can very well think of them as many suits of clothes that you used for a time and then discarded. In the case of returning each time to the earth plane, there is bound to be a change in your physical appearance, genetically speaking, because of the father and the mother.

As you are reborn in each life, you move into a family of a different environment and very likely of a different extraction, sometimes even into a different race. The pigment of the skin has nothing to do with the soul, other than explaining biologically that you are of the black race, the white race, or whatever the case might be. If you should be born into an Italian family, you would naturally find that you would resemble those of that extraction.

Then too, the incarnating entity is of course either male or female. We have all had many lives in both of the sexes, and the very fact that we are either male or female also affects our physical appearance. One may have had a series of male lives and be on the turning point to a series of female lives. This then would explain the occasional masculine tendencies dominating the feminine body or vice versa. All these factors must be taken into consideration when we attempt to ascertain the appearance of the physical vehicle in any particular life.

All this then brings us up to the question posed a few moments ago: "What will be our appearance after we have once graduated from the wheel of life?" The answer is simple, straightforward, and most joyful. At the conclusion of its earthly experiences, the soul can look forward to living its life in the Consciousness of Immensity and in the higher spiritual realms in a body created by the soul and which is called the "desire body." The action of your previous lives through your spiritual growth and through the good that you had administered unto others assists in creating the future desire body. You will have earned it in every sense of the word. It is determined completely by your desire and the dictates of the soul.

Over a period of countless incarnations, many, many factors can color our thinking regarding this spiritual desire. Our spiritual growth, the progress we had made in unfolding, the different pigments of skin that we had experienced, the hue of the hair, the eyes, the face, the different features we had admired over countless lifetimes—all these will have their effect upon that ultimate desire. The desire body then will be the final body that we will manifest in, and this embraces all of the degrees of higher consciousness in the spiritual realms.

This body is not in manifestation during your stay in the astral world in between earthly incarnations. You appear during these periods exactly as you had appeared during your previous physical life. This you have learned in other classes. If this were not so, recognition by your parents, friends, loved ones, and others would be impossible. And of course the reverse is true also.

In astral flights a disciple could possibly, in a very rare experience, be aware of being in his desire body. There are some who have brought back such a memory. It is also possible for the advanced disciple to inhabit his desire body when accompanying his teacher in a visit to the great temples within the Consciousness of Immensity. This can be the case but it would be rare. However, the memory of these visits is seldom retained by the conscious outer mind. It is also possible for a replica of the desire body to be in manifestation for a particular physical incarnation. Of course, these particular incidences are completely under the jurisdiction of the soul. In any event, your desire body is the ultimate body which you, through your own efforts and through your understanding of the Oneness, the Divine State, have created and will inhabit in the higher degrees of consciousness.

Thus for all of the reasons that we have discussed in the class tonight, we must strive to understand our purpose upon the earth and our relationship with every form of life that is. It is only then that we will begin to grow, expand, and become so attuned to the Infinite Consciousness. Do you think we are getting there, blessed children? I think we are. I know that sometimes these talks are a little heavy for you, but I think that they are good for you to hear. They do arouse you; they do help you.

Rub your hands together, sound the A-U-M, and call out your teacher's name. One . . . two . . . three . . . AUM.

FOURTH DISCOURSE

THE ASTRAL WORLD

By Dr. Navajo

Good evening, friends. Let us say the affirmation, please.

> *I am master of myself.*
> *I am all powerful,*
> *And nothing can come to me*
> *Of an inferior nature.*
> *I am peace.*
> *I am power.*
> *I am all there is.*

WELL FRIENDS, here we are again to continue our activity as usual with our blessed Agasha when he descends to control the channel. It is always a pleasure to take the opportunity preceding Agasha to bring forth a bit of information relative to your life, your unfoldment, and what we have over here in the astral world awaiting you.

I know that most of you are striving to go beyond the astral consciousness when you expire, but on the other hand we do know that the average person does have to come here to the astral world. We might call it somewhat of a depot.

It is a temporary station where the many come to get their bearing and to find out where their soul is going to take them after they have met their teacher, or perhaps I should have said, met their loved ones.

It is usually their loved ones who meet the person entering the astral world, because you understand, friends, all people who come to the astral world do not have a teacher awaiting them. We know that there are a lot of folks over here just waiting for their loved ones, and this is a good thing to bring out to you tonight. The simple fact is that when someone is to be freed from the physical body, a relative usually knows that that person is to be freed from the body, and he also knows the approximate time.

You Arrive in the Astral World

You know, it is quite interesting to observe the family. They are so anxious and excited in their respective category as they prepare for and plan to meet Mary or Father or whoever it is to be freed from the body. These preparations go on for days, and they talk about it and carry on long conversations about what they are going to do and where they are going to take Father when he does get here. They literally go about planning just like you would plan for Aunt Mary to come out from the East to visit you. Yes, it is very interesting to note the interest that people in the astral world take in awaiting the arrival of their loved ones on earth.

Now I know that most of you folks are also eager to make contact with husbands or wives, brothers and sisters, fathers and mothers when your time comes to leave the flesh. Of course, the many of you have already had the opportunity to make contact with them through the channel, or perhaps you have had that good fortune through other sources.

But just for instance, let us suppose that you came over and you had no one to meet you. Well, that's not usually the case. It has been known, however, for people to come over to this side of life with no one, absolutely no one, there to meet them. It would be like being in a strange land or in a strange country. Perhaps you would not know which way to turn, and that would not seem fair inasmuch as there are millions and millions of souls over on this side. You would think that *someone* surely would be waiting for the one who had just arrived from the material plane. Unfortunately it does occasionally happen that no one is waiting; however, that is not the case for the most part.

The thing that I am trying to point out is that it is most interesting to observe families ushering in their relatives from the material plane. But whether they are there to meet you or not, in either event we know that they do anticipate the arrival of their loved ones. Now this is just a part of it. The entire astral world experience is far greater in scope than merely making contact with your loved ones. Indeed so! However, for the moment, let us say that the average person goes to the astral world to prepare himself to be sent to the division that he had rightfully earned for himself.

Now a lot of people ask the question, "When I pass out of the physical body, if I am an advanced individual, will I be in the presence of my teacher and will I be able to live in his atmosphere and environment?" No, not necessarily. We must not be of the impression that all who seek in this direction shall immediately go into a teacher's kingdom to live, move, and have their being. However, this could apply to the advanced one who had earned the right to live in a particular atmosphere, according to the degree of consciousness attained. We must understand that we have to earn the right to live in that atmosphere, or to be among the exalted, or to be among the advanced ones who had preceded us in learning.

The average person then is likely to go to the atmosphere of his relatives, such as his grandparents, or his mother and father, sisters and brothers, or friends he had known upon the earth plane. You encounter a goodly number of people because the word spreads rapidly—in the particular division over here which is your division, we might say—that you will be arriving soon in the astral world. And they will certainly be there to meet you, that is, in all probability.

You understand that the average person who has a lingering illness slips in and out of the body for several weeks prior to his departure and visits with his loved ones. They have discussed the departure, and it is not new to the loved ones that you are coming for the reason that they have been watching you very carefully. They have been coming to your bedside, and during the moments that you were out of the body you have conversed with them. You may have said, "Now, I don't think it will be very long." And they in all probability then replied, "I don't think it will be very long either." Now that is the way some people talk, and they are not necessarily people who have thought in the direction of the occult.

We find then that the interesting thing about these conversations, to bring you a little closer to the subject, is that the average person has so many unusual experiences just before he takes his last breath. Oftentimes he will tell relatives that he had just seen Mother, or that he had just seen some other particular person. Of course, people in the home usually say that he or she is having hallucinations. That is about all they can say because they don't know anything about the spirit world in the manner that this particular patient does. Although a patient might think he is dreaming, these are actual experiences. Ofttimes there are a number of them just a few hours prior to the departure.

Now you might very well ask the question, "Is the patient, the person who is to be freed from the physical body, able to see these things and to have these presentations because he has slipped in and out of the physical body so many times that he has become ever so close to the astral world?" And the answer is yes. The constant repetition of slipping in and out of the body has enabled him to familiarize himself with the atmosphere that he is going to find himself in. Now you don't have to be an occultist to have these experiences because this applies to many people upon the earth plane.

However, each and every individual has a different experience upon entering or being ushered into the astral world. Therefore it could be said that no two persons have an absolutely identical experience. The experiences may be similar, yes, but in reality they be not the same. This is because your academic backgrounds are different. You are of different parentages, naturally, and you have had different paths among your fellow men. Therefore your exits from a particular life will also be different.

I have seen fliers go down—you know what I mean—to lose their lives. Their plane crashed and they were so confused. I saw this happen some years ago and one fellow cried out, "Jim, Jim, are we dead?" The other one then replied, "Well, I don't know. Huh, by golly, I think we are!" He didn't say it just that way; he used a little stronger language than that. And they kept on with that conversation for some time. I didn't interfere, but the person with me went up and talked to them and verified that they had indeed come over to this side of life. But there was no one else there to take care of them. You might say that it was only by a coincidence that we were there.

Then on another occasion many people were killed in an automobile accident. Some were out of the body and standing there quite conscious of the situation. They saw the car upside down. They saw the bodies there on the pavement, and they knew good and well that they were dead.

Sometimes after a man is saved from drowning, he will tell the story of how his whole life came before him—absolutely everything that he had ever done appeared before him in a split second. Agasha explains this phenomenon as resulting from a sudden shock to the soul whereby it brings everything in a given life right to the surface where it can be viewed at one and the same time. In other words, there is the time element again. Ordinarily it would take months, and even years, to recollect all of the events that had ever happened to us, but it is possible for the soul to compress all of this time into a split second.

Ofttimes the ones who are freed from the physical body will go into a state of oblivion for, let us say, several hours or perhaps two or three days. It varies. Then after this interval of time is up, they will open their astral eyes, which are comparable to their physical eyes, and they will see their loved ones and it is a great and a very joyful reunion. It is just as if you had not seen your people, your friends, or your relatives for a long, long time—and then suddenly you were with them! You would be so very, very happy, and you would make it known that you were happy.

These ones are cared for in what is known on this side of life as a "rest home". This is an expression that we use for lack of a better name, I suppose. We have individual names for them over here but we refrain from confusing you people with too many proper names. A rest home can be any suitable place that can protect the astral body of the newly arrived entity until it is fully awake. Sometimes it is a parent's home, or perhaps the home of some other relative who had been over here for fifteen or twenty years prior to your arrival. Who takes you to the rest home? Well, if you have not a teacher, then relatives who had anticipated your arrival will see to it that you are taken to a rest home. But this is not applicable in all cases. Everyone who be freed from the physical body does not necessarily go to a rest home. However, this temporary lapse of consciousness, even though it be but a short period of time, is an automatic process brought about by the motivating power of the God within.

Then there is the case of some people who come over here who don't even believe that they are here. They will be cared for while going through this automatic process, and then when they open their astral eyes they think they are dreaming, and it distracts them. They look at their mother, or their father, or their loved ones and they actually think that they are dreaming. Many remember saying to themselves, "Well, if I am dreaming, this certainly must be a very vivid dream!"

But they can see that in this so-called "dream", everything is as normal and as rational as it could possibly be. However, it may mean that the relatives will have a good deal of trouble in attempting to convince those entities that they are out of the physical body. Many of them will flatly refuse to accept it. I have seen some awaken in a state like that and carry on something frightfully—just as if they were having a case of hysteria. And the first thing that they think of when they finally realize that they are actually out of the body may be their children, or their financial affairs, or their fortune on the earth plane. It may be this or that or any number of things that will then come into their minds.

Where Are You Going to Live?

Eventually every soul arriving in the astral world will gravitate to the level that it had earned for itself through its actions and deeds upon the earth plane. But this does not necessarily mean that you will join your wife, your father and mother, or whoever it might be and then live permanently with them. You do not necessarily live in the same home in the astral world that your people have lived in for a number of years. Why is that? The answer is simply because of the fact that you are now going to live in a consciousness that you have earned for yourself, and your vibrations quite possibly will not harmonize with the vibrations those who had preceded you have already built up. Now this certainly doesn't mean that you will not eventually join them, but you are going to have different interests over a period of time. Your interests may be completely different from their interests.

For an example, let us say that you have married three women on the earth plane and that you have three wives. They are all in the spirit world. Now when you come over here, which one are you going to go to? You may not go to any of them, and maybe they don't want you either. Then too, they may fight over you. Who knows? Let us hope it is the latter. But all joking aside, folks, I am merely trying to point out that all four of you may have grown in completely divergent directions, and that your interests, both intellectually and spiritually, may be completely different.

However, you will visit with all three of them from time to time, and your people are satisfied. You will carry on long conversations. They will show you their gardens, their houses, the villages where they live. Some of these homes would be called a country estate if they were on the earth plane, but this does not mean that that is where you should live. There are plenty of places and more than enough room in each division to take care of the inhabitants. There is no shortage of buildings in the astral world, you understand.

Then too, you do not move into a dwelling just because you like that particular dwelling. You have to first earn the right to live in that atmosphere. And how do you do this? You have to serve, but you do not serve laboriously. Yet you still have to earn your way in the astral world just the same as you did here on earth. Why should it be any other way? You serve by serving humanity through your individual efforts in helping to create whatever it be of a creative nature. But this is not accomplished by just wishing for things in the astral world, and thus thinking that the force sent out will then materialize them for you. It is not so simple as all that.

Another point with regard to where you will live is that those of you who have a teacher, those who have learned and grown and advanced in the occult field of thought, are in all probability going to be working out of a different plane of consciousness, a different region, a different division of the astral world from that of the more orthodox individuals.

Therefore, you will always gravitate to your own level and be among your caliber in much the same manner that water will seek its own level. But you will not always have to remain in that particular consciousness if it is not of your liking. You will be given the opportunity of taking the initiative and aspiring to the higher. Thus through concentrated effort, you may then attain a still higher state or plane of consciousness if you so desire.

With the criminal mind it is the same; like attracts like. The criminal mind is relegated to the consciousness of similar criminal minds. And never can that criminal mind ascend to contaminate a higher state. It can ascend only when it has redeemed itself and literally earned the right to live in that higher state of consciousness. Whereas in the physical plane of life all states of consciousness function seemingly in the same world, in the astral divisions each state gravitates to its own level.

After a suitable cleansing period, the average individual will then usually find himself in a higher state of consciousness, whatever that state may be. And in all probability, he will be among old friends or perhaps even those that he had not previously known upon the earth plane. In any event, he will be in an atmosphere a little more to his liking. It appeals to him and he remains there for some time. He may be there for twenty years, or thirty, or fifty; he may be there any number of years. Then eventually, if he so desires to go on to still another plane of consciousness, another community, or another division, it is up to him to take the initiative.

The Many Astral Divisions, Regions, and Planes

Now then, what constitutes a division? Before we answer this, we must first refer to regions or zones that separate the various degrees or planes of consciousness so constituted by the collective group. Therefore, these many planes of consciousness, along with their associated regions or zones, are what constitute a division of the astral kingdom. These divisions are independent worlds. They are like a world within a world within a world; and yet each is independent, you might say. Each division does not interfere with the world that is around and about it. It is a world within a world. Thus we come to realize that when we refer to the term "astral consciousness," we are referring to a truly vast consciousness, indeed.

There are many books written to describe the various planes of consciousness in the astral kingdom, and they vary in their interpretation to a great extent. Some, in attempting to describe the various planes of consciousness, will go on to tell you that there be a hundred and seventy planes or some other particular number. They will attempt to inform the reader exactly how many planes there are in the astral kingdom, but we have learned in our classes that this information cannot be determined so readily.

Thus we find that the many, many statements made relative to the astral world can sometimes be very confusing. I say this in all sincerity and not to make light of any person who had attempted to describe the astral world because we are all going to describe it differently. By the same token, if we were to go to New York and then return to tell the Californians what experiences we had had in New York, we each would have a different picture. Perhaps one would have only visited the slums, another only the subway, and still another only the Statue of Liberty as seen from a low flying aircraft. Each of us would have a different picture of New York. The same analogy applies to any particular division of the astral world.

Many people have often asked just how high up or how far out into space does the astral kingdom extend. We cannot measure it in yards or miles but we can state that it surrounds the material plane. Agasha claims that it extends out for several hundreds of miles if we were to view it in a "space" sense, but again this is a misnomer. We cannot put in mileage that which cannot be measured in mileage. Vibration is the word that we should use. We refer to the *frequency* of the rates of vibration of the various planes of consciousness that surround the material world. An astral world is, therefore, the world that is created through the thoughts of men and by the actions of men from any given planet—and it immediate-

world. It is constituted by the thoughts of men, and it is then a world of reality to those who inhabit it and whose senses are attuned to it.

Now can it be said that these worlds or divisions interpenetrate? The answer is not necessarily. They might interpenetrate in a space sense but not in a vibration sense. We must remember that the astral world is all around and about us. For instance, let us take this auditorium you are in. You are aware just who might be in this room; you are aware of the furnishings, the number of seats, and the like. But it can become a large auditorium to us in the astral world, which in turn would enable us to pack in thousands of entities as they come here to listen to Agasha. This is a supposition, of course. I am not implying that there are that many who are here tonight, but certainly there are many, many more from the astral world who attend these classes than those who are in the flesh. And why is this? It is that many of us here want to come to hear Agasha, to see Agasha, to observe him as he manifests, and also to watch how the other teachers come through the channel. So the atmosphere of this auditorium changes for that very reason.

In summary then, we can say that you are going to get a pretty good picture of what the astral world is like if you would only just compare it with the material world. But it is very difficult to describe the sensation and the feelings that you will likely have the moment when you come over here for the first time. We can give you some idea of what to expect but we cannot do justice to it.

You are "sharper," we might say, in the astral world for the reason that your mind is clearer. You are not contaminated. You are not held down and you do not have the pressures or the headaches; nor do you have the sensation that you cannot think properly. But you do have a sense of freedom—a sense of lightness in the astral world that certainly is not experienced while moving that physical body around. In other words, the astral world is very similar to the material world but it is brighter, finer, and keener in all of its aspects.

Everything Is Created Mentally

Let us say that you have just arrived in the astral world. One of the first things to learn is the art of creating whatever it is that you are supposed to create or that you can create. Then you can help in many, many ways. But if you didn't create anything on the earth plane, and you had not the ability to carry out such activity, why then is there any reason that you should suddenly be able to create something in the astral world? The answer is obvious. You are not any more talented in the astral world than you were when upon the earth plane.

Of course, there are extenuating circumstances. Agasha has said that in reality you do not ever really lose anything that you had once learned in a particular lifetime. It follows then that if you can raise yourself back to a state of consciousness whereby you can remember that which you had previously known, the art of creating would then be yours once more.

Each kingdom of the astral world has been set up by a group of people who were desirous of creating that particular atmosphere. They accomplished this through the thought power of the collective group. It makes no difference whether it be comparable to the Pacific Northwest, or to the desert, or to wherever it might be; the process is always the same. The trees, the flowers, in fact everything that is there that enhances the beauty of that particular atmosphere was created by the many souls having one common thought.

Therefore the great deserts, seas, and mountains of the astral world were not created through the power of cataclysmic forces in the same way that the mountainous countries were brought forth here upon the earth plane. No indeed. All that is apparently nothing more than a reflection from the earth plane was in reality created through the great power of the mind, through the concentrated thought processes of billions of souls bringing all of these things into manifestation. Thus everything is just as it was intended to be: a replica of that which exists on the earth, but created out of a more sublimated or finer material.

The Picturesque Astral Communities

I have gone into some of the most beautiful communities here. I have seen streets that were just as clean—why, they were probably cleaner than your table tops—and as bright and shiny as any street could possibly be. And the buildings were just beautifully carried out architecturally. Many of them were very similar to the buildings on the earth plane today, while others reflected the great classical beauty of the past. In the higher planes of the astral world we find large cities comparable to London, we will say, but without commercial or industrial areas, for none are necessary. We also never find any filth because filth has been eliminated. We never have to use any soap and water over here on this side, incidentally. Filth comes into manifestation only by evil thoughts.

In the astral world there is no monetary exchange. There is never any commercial activity, but things are created and then put on display. They are displayed in what would be the equivalent of shops, and we have what might be termed bartering. This action, of course, falls right in line in the astral world because people are always creating things. I create something and you create something, and then we might exchange them. But then suppose that you do not create anything and you want something. Well then you will be given an opportunity to earn your way and the law of compensation certainly does work here in the astral world. However, there is no such thing as the monetary exchange.

Let us go into a little Dutch colony, we will say. There you will find people very much the same as they are on earth in little Dutch communities in Holland. They go about their activity here and have the same customs as they would probably have in those little communities. Here you can see the little wooden shoes just like those you would find in the back parts of Holland. They carry out that activity in the astral simply because of the fact that they feel more at home. You can go into a home where it is very comfortable. You step into it and you see a fireplace. The fire there is burning just as comfortably as if it were right there on the earth plane. Or you might see two elderly people and they are sitting there talking. You might see them carrying on some sort of activity. You notice that the furnishings are carried out in the old Dutch Colonial style or perhaps in some other comparable decor. You go into another home. It is a little bungalow and you enter that little bungalow.. There again, you will find that it is carried out in pretty much the same manner as when upon the earth plane.

That is why I say that if you have a home on the earth plane that you love very much and you like it architecturally, you can have the same in the astral world, but it is going to take time. It may even be created for you by the time you get here, but if it is you will have earned it. Perhaps your folks have created it and it is waiting for your arrival. Remember, you have had long conversations with them while out of the body during the so-called sleep state—conversations of which the mortal mind is in all probability not aware—and you may have expressed the desire that living in that environment would fulfill your deepest wishes. Thus it may be possible for you to move right in when you come over here to live and be in that general atmosphere.

Many of you will ask, "Well, how could I have had a conversation with Father or Mother last night and not even remember seeing them at all?" The answer to this question would be the subject of an entire lecture, but I will say, however, that an out-of-the-body experience is just what it says it is—an out-of-the-body experience. There is no connection with the physical brain whatsoever. Practically every night you folks have visited in the astral world and have not been aware of it at all, that is, your conscious self has not been aware of it. Occasionally though, the memory of these astral experiences does filter back into the dream state. Thus, what many people would consider to be only an extremely vivid dream is in reality the memory of an actual astral visitation.

Let us say that you wake up some morning and think, "Well now, I was certainly in a strange city last night—and that home! Goodness, I have never been in a home like that on earth that I know of!" Your mortal mind thinks that this be only a dream, and yet in truth you are bringing back memory. This is because you had been in that atmosphere or that community, and probably you had met your folks or some other astral being that you had been going around with in the astral world for years. I have often heard people say, "You know, I had a dream the other night of going to a particular cottage surrounded with beautiful trees and flowers, and I have had that dream many, many times." Sure you go to it. It is not a dream; it is an actual fact. But since people do not know the law that governs what is termed "astral flights," they quite naturally attribute everything to dream life.

Climatic Conditions—Light and Darkness

Another interesting point that people have often wondered about is that we have climatic conditions here in the astral world that are comparable with your weather conditions upon the earth. Now if you were to ask the question, "Do you have to contend with storms and the like such as we have here upon the earth plane?" the answer would be no. For the elements do not go on the rampage in the astral world in that respect. The atmosphere is always that which is desired by the collective group, I repeat.

The Eskimo has snow, the same as you have snow on the earth plane. He feels at home with snow. He feels more comfortable with it because he is of the same temperament in the astral world. It is only natural for him to feel more comfortable in the atmosphere that he was accustomed to live in when upon the earth plane. Thus there is a division of the astral world that is the equivalent to the Arctic. It be just the same. In a like token, we could say the same for the South Sea Islander, and so forth.

Now the sun, we do not depend on. We do not depend on your sun in the astral world, but we have light that be the equivalent to your sunlight. We also have darkness that be the equivalent to the darkness on the earth plane. Now since we do not have to depend on your sunshine, we likewise do not have to be concerned about the moon coming around seasonally and moving life. The light and darkness that we have over here is constituted by another thing entirely.

"What is that?" you might ask. There again, it is by the power of the mind. Well now, you certainly couldn't say, "I am tired of it being dark, therefore I am going to turn the sun on." Speaking as an individual, that would be a ridiculous. But our environment or atmosphere can be set up so that at certain periods of the so-called day, we may also have the evenings and the mornings the same as you have upon the earth plane, if it is so desired. However, if this were the case, it would have nothing whatsoever to do with your sun.

Etheric Clouds: The Source for Precipitation

We look out into space. We do not necessarily see the stars as you do from your point of contact. No, we see other things. We call them "etheric clouds." These etheric clouds are formed out there in the ether, and we can draw from them. These clouds then enable us to precipitate the equivalent of the physical elements. Thus you might say that we precipitate astral matter. We can then bring into manifestation things that are not necessarily valuable to us, but to you they would be very valuable if they were on earth.

If you have uranium on the earth plane, then we likewise have uranium in the astral world. You see, every element that is on the earth plane, every diamond and every jewel, is also in the astral; only we do not mine them in the astral world like you do there on earth. That which you so laboriously take from the earth below, we precipitate from the etheric clouds above. If you can have a two-carat diamond on the earth plane, we can also have a two-carat diamond over here, if we have earned the right for it, and if we think it is necessary for us. But everything here is brought into manifestation through the anim; whereas on the earth plane everything comes from the atom.

The higher planes of the astral world are certainly not lacking in beautiful jewels, no indeed. We have the equivalent in diamonds, precious jewels, or whatever they be; and you could see these jewels on your teachers if they were to come within the range of your vision. I have seen some of the most exquisite rings and jewelry beyond compare. Some planes of consciousness are literally studded with glittering diamonds, and gold shines here and there in great abundance. In this respect, these higher astral planes have a grandeur that is beyond comparison to the most magnificent palace of the earth plane.

Music and Religion

The same thing can be said with respect to music. There are vast musical consciousnesses where entire operas, symphonies, and the like are in constant production. Everywhere, it would seem, there is music. Even though we usually refrain from employing proper names in describing specific temples in a particular degree of consciousness, we make an exception with respect to the Temple of El Don. This musical center is a very beautiful structure, and it would be very imposing if it were to be erected on the earth plane. Those on the earth plane who have been interested in music have often gone to this consciousness during the so-called sleep state, and their experiences there have enriched their musical endeavors upon the material plane. This beautiful temple is located in one of the planes of the higher astral consciousness and is known to the many who had studied there by its rightful name—the Temple of El Don.

Of course, we cannot leave out religion. Every known religion is practiced in the astral world. Over here in one plane, we will say, is the Salvation Army. The souls living here are the same ones who devoted their lives on earth to this cause, and they are carrying out the same activity today in helping people in the astral world to be saved. Over there in another plane is the very heart of the Red Cross organization—devoted souls bringing light and mercy to those unfortunate ones caught up in the mire of their own ignorance.

All denominations of Christianity, both Catholic as well as Protestant, are well represented in all appropriate planes. Likewise all other religions have established their individual houses of worship. Many of the temples, mosques, synagogues, and cathedrals are truly magnificent. And strangely enough, there are still those who are endeavoring for other "lost souls" to come under their own particular religion.

The answer to all of this lies in the fact that when people come into the astral world, they do not know any more about religion or God, in the sense of the word, than they did when they were on the earth plane. Let us take the so-called atheist, for instance. Agasha has said that we inwardly know that in reality there is no such thing as an atheist, not even an agnostic. An agnostic is only one who has an attitude on the physical plane of not caring one way or the other because he believes that the nature of God is unknowable. But the atheist states that there is no such thing as God. "When you are dead, you are dead," he says. Now when that atheist comes into the astral world, he has a rude awakening. But when he finds himself alive and realizes that he still lives, he doesn't know any more about God than he did before. And in all probability he still doesn't believe in God. He has not changed overnight simply because he comes to the astral world.

Educational and Recreational Activity

Then what does he do? But this question is not limited to the atheist, necessarily; it could apply equally as well to anyone else who comes over to this side of life. At first the average individual will explore, walk around, and get ac-

quainted with his new surroundings in much the same way
that one would act in moving into a new community on the
earth plane. Then, if he is a well-thinking individual and not
too enmeshed in atheistic attitudes, he will eventually enter
one of the great halls of learning and endeavor to find out a
little more about life.

These halls of learning that we have over here in the higher
astral consciousness may be compared with the great univer-
sities of the earth plane. They are truly magnificent structures
and are usually laid out in much the same manner as a college
campus. It is here that the many come to study and learn.

This is the reason then that the usual answer that a relative
might give, after being asked the question as to what he is
now doing, will be something like this: "Well, I am going to
school and, as a matter of fact, I am learning a great deal. Of
course, I do a lot of other things over here other than just go
to school. We can always find plenty to do in the astral
world. But basically, I go to classes. I am learning and I am
understanding many, many things."

Much of the activity over here is also recreational. It is all
not work or study in the sense of the word. In some communities a group of men have created replicas of particular
models of automobiles, and they ride them around· and
about for sport and pleasure. In other communities there are
lakes, and there are boats on the lakes, and the many get in
the boats and sail around in the same manner as if they were
right back here on the earth plane. Sports such as baseball
and football are also not an uncommon activity. Some of
the parks here have facilities for these purposes.

The Astral Relation

Now the main point that I wish to bring out is that the
astral world is not an independent world. It is not severed or
cut off from the material world. It is just as much a part of
this earth that you live on as the material world is. That is
why we sometimes term it the "astral relation." We might
say that the inner life is the astral life and that the outer life

is the physical life. But it is all the same life! Your life in the astral is just a continuation of your life in the physical. Therefore the two worlds are very definitely interrelated.

For this reason then, those in the astral division are constantly working with and helping those in the material division. If an astral being wishes to enjoy a major sports event such as the World Series of baseball, for instance, he watches it through *your* eyes—through the eyes of his loved ones on the physical plane—by accompanying his loved ones to the sports event and being with them. They are certainly much more aware of you and your activities than you are of them and their activities.

Thus we see that life relative to this planet Earth is divided into two basic categories: the outer and the inner, the material and the ethereal. All that is of a material nature—such as industrial activity, commercial activity, and the like—is delegated to the material world of the atom. And all that is of an ethereal nature—such as creative activity, spiritual activity, and artistic activity—is delegated to the ethereal world of the anim. Now the mental plane that separates the two is also of the anim. But these thought anims are used only by those in the physical world. The astral beings have their own mental kingdom.

We find then that the two worlds, the physical and the astral, are basically the same and yet different. They both are populated by beings who tend to congregate in large cities, or small communities, or even in isolation at times— but the activity being carried out in these communities in the astral is usually, though not always, entirely different from the activity in the physical.

Inasmuch as mechanical transportation is not necessary in the astral division, we find the automobile, the train, the aircraft to be almost entirely missing in the astral environment. The asphalt congested highways are replaced with beautiful streets or pathways. The groups of factories, tall buildings, skyscrapers, and the like which so dominate the average city of the physical division, are replaced with beautiful temples, mansions, halls of learning, and beautiful surroundings and countryside. Each division then, the physical as well as the astral, thus fulfills its own individual purpose unto the life of the planet Earth.

Now the astral world, even though we refer to it as an ethereal world, is just as solid to us as the physical world is to you. We certainly do not see through objects in the astral world. If I am sitting in a chair, I am sitting in a solid chair. And when I am talking to John Jones here in the astral world, John Jones is just as solid to my senses as he was to your senses when he was in the physical plane and you spoke to him there. You do not see through spirit when you exist in the spirit world.

But if I go beyond the candic ray and return back into your atmosphere, then I become a spirit to you. Likewise when you project yourself to our side of life during the sleep state, and you are in our atmosphere with the silver cord of life still attached to your body, then you appear as a spirit to us. But it is all spirit, and the solid aspect is determined only by the vibration that you are in. Therefore, you can pass through what is solid to me in the astral world in the same manner that I can pass through what is solid to you in the physical world.

Traveling from Place to Place

If I were to walk down an astral block in a city or community in the astral world, it would take the same apparent time that it would take you to walk down an equivalent block in your world. This would be so because I would *walk*. I would not simply skim down the block, or float down the block, but I would walk in a very normal manner. I would be conscious of the time element because I would be localized in that particular consciousness or that community. And I would remain conscious of the time element as long as I would remain there in that locality.

However, if I were to travel from one community to another, then neither the time nor the space consumed in going from one given point to another would be considered. And it would make no real difference to me whether it would be an adjoining community or a consciousness far removed from the community that I had been in. But with you people both time and space have to be considered because you are going at a lower rate of speed. But then when I would finally localize myself again, when in other words I would set my astral feet down in that new atmosphere, I would walk again normally and feel and sense and hear just as I had done before. And I would also be aware of time once more. Thus when the teachers use the expression that there is no time nor space to be considered, they are using it in relating one degree of consciousness to another.

Now what process do we use in traveling from community to community? How is this accomplished? The answer is that it is done through the power of *will*. We have to learn how to will ourself there. Some people on the earth plane have the idea that when they are out of the physical body, all they will have to do is to will themselves to anywhere on the face of the earth. But after they have come over here, they soon find out that it is not so easy to do that. Now why is this? It is because you have to train yourself in using the power of will, pretty much as when on earth you have to learn to crawl before you can learn to walk.

We travel at a greater speed than you do on earth. Our velocity is many times faster than the velocity that you are functioning in. When your thoughts reach us that we should be at a certain place, or when we suddenly desire to be in another community, we merely focus it in our mind, very much the same as you would line up the lens of a microscope or a telescope with the tip of a finger and then focus it. When the point of contact is reached, we are there.

Now all who come to the astral world do not have the ability to do this, not by any means. There are some who have been over here for as long as 200 years; but they have remained in the same plane of consciousness all this time. Have you ever thought about traveling to another part of the country where everything is supposed to be so beautiful, and yet you stayed where you were, as you could not go because you did not have the money? Well, that is just the way it is with some of the people over here. They want to go; they hear about these other planes. But they have not earned the right to go there, and so they stay where they are; yet it cannot be said that they are in prison, no indeed.

The Lower Astral Hells

The real prison is reserved for the lower planes of the astral world that be comparable to Hell, or the Inferno, or Purgatory, or whatever you want to call it. There are planes in the lower depths of the astral, for instance, where just swarms of people, thousands and thousands and perhaps even millions of souls, seem to be literally swarming over one another. This scene is truly a frightening and terrible thing to behold. It is just as though they are possessed with something. They seem to be going over the same thing, repeating the same action, over and over again. It is obviously some crime that they had committed on earth, and they are in their own hellish state. They are in their own purgatory that they had created for themselves. And yet they have all been brought together into the same plane of consciousness because like attracts like.

Some are dressed in uniforms of the Civil War and the various other wars of the earth plane. Others are dressed in civilian clothing, and it doesn't seem to make any difference whether it be of the rich or the poor. The similarity lies in the fact that they are all carrying out an activity of hatred, as if they are going to kill one another. Of course they cannot do this, but they merely go through the motions of it. Don't they ever get tired of it? That is not the point. The point is that it is all automatic with them. They just live out an incident in their individual life, one in which they were obsessed with intense hatred or revenge, and they repeat this over and over again because they cannot within themselves break away from the crime that they had committed. You might say that they are in prison, but no one put them in prison for they are only locked in the prison of their own mind.

And it does not stop even here! In extreme cases, observers have reported coming upon what might be called a pool, perhaps thirty feet across. There was steam rising from this pool and in it there were faces. There were all kinds of faces and these faces would also rise up from this pool. And as they would rise up, some would have an ugly grin on their face and others would have some other horrible looking expression. Then these faces would disappear once again into the pool, and it would seem just like some horrible dream.

But this was all created by the mind! The soul was forcing its outer consciousness to live in that state in order to go through a purification and to rid itself of the evil that had been committed on the earth plane. However, this scene that I have just told you about would only apply to extreme cases where hideous lives had been lived and where the mortal mind had simply refused to accept any compassion whatsoever for his fellowman.

A keen observer, one who had descended to the planes of the lower astral consciousness, will always report seeing white forms above the sufferers in these lower hells. These white forms sometimes come very near and then go away; then they return again with outstretched arms as if they want to help. These are the teachers, the angels of light, and beings from the higher astral planes who are trying to reach those in the lower astral consciousness and trying to help them. But many of the sufferers cannot be released from this condition until they have first completed a certain cycle or period, and while they are in that state they can only see the helpers as lights in the distance. Then, after this cycle is completed and *if* the lesson has been learned, the opportunity is there for them to grab ahold of the power sent forth from these helpers and literally raise themselves out of the lower depths to the point whereby they can then be free.

How long will this take? This again is an individual

thing. There is only a certain allotted period of time for this to take place, and if the individual has not raised himself out of this condition during the period set aside for his total astral experience, the law of reincarnation will then bring him back into a new physical embodiment without his knowing a thing about the higher astral degrees or planes of consciousness.

So then what is the result? The result is that he will simply go on acting out the same condition of hatred, violence, or whatever it was that he had failed to learn or overcome. But now he will be in a new physical body. Thus we can account for the hell, the confusion, the filth, the privation, the starvation, and so forth that some people have to endure upon the physical plane. But here again they have the opportunity to redeem themselves. And if they do not take advantage of it in this new lifetime, there will be another and another and another until the lesson is finally learned.

Let us suppose that you were a swindler, a racketeer, a trafficker in dope, and that you tried to push this habit unto others whenever you could. Or then again, perhaps you were the victim and you thus became a helpless alcoholic, a drug addict, and you went about accomplishing no useful purpose in life whatsoever. You were then a frequent visitor of the so-called dens of iniquity, and by so doing, you completely submerged any redeeming qualities that you had originally possessed. You lived in that atmosphere for years and years and years, knowing nothing else and having no other experiences. In other words, you lived in an atmosphere where you could cut the smoke with a knife and the stench of filth was all around and about. And then when it came time for your departure, you passed out of the body gambling, stealing, cussing, and the like.

Now you certainly would not be a shiny angel in coming to the astral world! Your environment would be the same as it was on earth. I have actually gone into dope dens in certain regions of the astral world that were very similar to those of the earth plane. The participants used what they thought was dope or other narcotic drugs just like they had done while in the physical body. They really believed that they must have this type of astral environment in order to go about their business. In other words, their consciousness had not changed in the slightest.

Now let us multiply these individuals by many hundreds of thousands, and we have the situation that exists in some of the astral planes of consciousness consisting of under-developed souls from all of the races and continents of the earth. This embraces not only the common coolie of the Orient, where opium dens used to be so prevalent, but it also embraces every other race where this type of activity has become the challenging factor. Yet we must remember that these individuals that we speak about are human beings precisely the same as you or I or anyone else upon the earth plane.

These rather extreme situations are examples, then, of what goes on to make up the lower astral divisions. Now this certainly does not mean to imply that these souls are going to remain in that state. Agasha tells us that all will eventually aspire to the higher and arise. And even though there are those who, knowing nothing else, might now be living in an atmosphere that they deem to be quite comfortable—and they may even think that they are enjoying themselves while they carry out their present activity—it will not always be so.

Eventually all will learn of the teachers, the higher degrees, and the great beauty that awaits those who aspire to the higher. When this will occur, we do not know; but we do know that sooner or later they are going to arise. And the immutable law of reembodiment will see to it that nary a soul is lost.

The Middle Astral Divisions

Now between the lower astral divisions and the higher astral divisions are a vast number of planes or degrees of consciousness which make up what is termed the middle astral divisions. Many of the planes in these so-called middle astral divisions are very beautiful, indeed. Though they cannot be compared to the higher astral divisions, they still offer much that be pleasing to the earthly senses.

For instance, one can often hear the chirping of birds, and in looking around you can see beautiful trees, flowers, brooks, and streams. The air is sometimes like it is after a light shower, where everything is so fresh and so very wonderful. And the scent from the flowers as it hits the nostrils seems to perfume the air, or the ether rather, in a most fragrant manner. So let us not underestimate the sensuous pleasures that can be yours in these middle astral divisions.

What About Food and Sex in the Astral World?

This then leads us up to the question of eating, drinking, and the other bodily functions. Now in the astral world, you don't want food, necessarily, unless you would think of food and then desire it. You do not have to have food or drink in order to sustain the astral body. You never get hungry or thirsty. Therefore these are not natural functions of the astral body.

But there are beautiful fields of wheat, corn, and the like—or rather we might say the essence of wheat or corn—that the astral body unconsciously draws from in order to replenish itself. The bees extract the nectar from the flowers; the astral body extracts the prana or the life-giving force from the atmosphere. You breathe in this life force every time you take an astral breath in order to sustain yourself. But you never have to eat in the sense of the word.

However, let us say that you would come upon an orchard in the astral world. There are apples on the trees and many other fruits dangle delightfully from the limbs. The thought might then cross your mind that you would like to partake of these fruits and taste the various juices contained therein. You could then pull an apple from the tree and bite it in precisely the same manner that one does on the earth plane. It would taste ever so delicious and you could even finish it if you so desired. You could taste this fruit and that fruit and each and every one of the fruits for that matter. But there would not be that hunger; you would not retain the desire for any length of time, that is, in all probability. And if you should not finish eating the fruit, it would simply disappear from your hand.

Inasmuch as there is no gross feeding in the astral world, the process of elimination is also different from what it is on the earth plane. And the same thing can be said for the sex act whose basic function on the physical plane is to bring children into the world. However, a man is still a man and a woman a woman in every sense of the word. You absolutely retain every component part of the human anatomy and you are the same in nature, appearance, and physique as you were upon the earth plane. The only difference is that the young grow to maturity and the old grow young, the norm being that which is usually called the prime of life.

Thus we find that the sex act is not normally used in the same manner that it is used on the earth plane. To say that it is "different" is actually a very inadequate description. It has been said that this sexual action and reaction between the partners in the physical plane is nothing more than a pale imitation of or a feeble attempt at duplicating a very intimate spiritual state of ONENESS. Lovers can then know the inner and deeper satisfaction that is peace itself. Therefore it is reasonable to believe that passion is only a part of love and ecstasy is that state which is only induced through love. There is no word in the English language to adequately describe this spiritual experience. If you were to make the statement that no mortal love can equal the pure joy that is experienced during "union" in the higher planes, you would be coming somewhat close to the truth, although it is not strictly "sexual" in the sense that the average mortal would understand the term.

Another question that is frequently asked is relative to the population of the many planes of the astral division. You must understand that we have many more spirits over here than you have on the earth plane in the flesh. This is quite understandable when we realize that the average life in the physical division is perhaps only sixty years, more or less. Yet your life over here will be for at least a hundred or two hundred years in all probability. Thus it readily follows that our population here in the astral division must of necessity be several times greater than yours, inasmuch as until you ascend from this physical-astral relationship there is simply no place else for you to be. Yet it is all spirit life and it makes no real difference whether you be at the moment in the material or the ethereal division.

The Animatical Force

All of the foregoing then leads us to consider now the basic force that ties these two divisions together. The Hindus call this great life-giving force by the term *prana.* It permeates the atmosphere of all planes where life can exist; be it astral or material, it makes no difference, for it is always present where life is in manifestation. However, Agasha has a different name for it and he calls it the *animatical force.* You would not get the value or the benefits out of the food that you partake of daily if it were not for this particular force or energy which is the basis for all life. Everything that is capable of supplying energy to either the material or the astral world is intermingled with this force.

These animatical forces are constantly passing through the astral body and replenishing the various divisions of the astral world. They are to us what oxygen is to you. Sometimes they can be seen by the spiritual eye as flashes of light that dart hither and thither in the atmosphere like tiny shooting stars. They are very colorful and each color that is produced has a certain chemical affinity. The length of their flash can be as short as perhaps three inches, but sometimes these flashes have been observed to cover a span of six or seven feet in length, and then they are gone. Of course, we only see them seasonally or periodically, but these animatical forces are all important unto both your life in the physical as well as our life here in the astral world.

Why is this so? Why are they so all important? We must understand that these animatical forces that are constantly going through the bodies of the inhabitants here are helping to replenish that body in much the same manner that oxygen and the vitamins in your food are helping to replenish your body in the material world. As we move about in our astral body, we are also losing a certain amount of energy that must be replenished, the same as you are losing energy. After all, there is a law that governs us here the same as there is a law that governs you. When you are deficient in some particular chemical or vitamin, you become weak and anything can happen. We realize that. Now then, knowing that we have the same thing to contend with over here on this side, we also cannot continue to function properly if our atmosphere were to become null and void of certain necessary animatical forces.

But this is a two-way street. Please try to understand that every division over here must be supported by the inhabitants. Even though the inhabitants need the animatical force to survive, the division likewise needs its inhabitants to survive. For the minds of the inhabitants are constantly creating and recreating the animatical forces which in turn pass through the spiritual bodies. Thus if a division were not supported by its inhabitants, if the inhabitants were to abandon it, it would become what is termed a dead division and be null and void of the animatical force.

The Abandoned Astral Divisions

If we were to come upon a division that at one time had been inhabited by the souls of the astral but is now abandoned, we would be conscious of a dead division. Or then again, it might be only a region and we would call it a dead region. We use the word "dead" to let you know that the division or region has become null and void of the necessary animatical forces required to support a group of souls or any other inhabitants. So when it is null and void of these forces, naturally people do not live there. In fact there is absolutely no way for the people to live in that division or region at all.

Perhaps it had been abandoned for generations, or then again at least for a considerable length of time. Now this certainly does not mean that it must always remain in that state, being unable to support life. No, not by any means! The Ascended Masters from the Consciousness of Immensity could very easily replenish that dead division. They could direct their power into that region or division whereby a group of astral souls could then go into that area, draw in the power, and recreate a division of liveliness.

Now what caused these inhabitants to abandon this particular division? Was it because it had become null and void of the animatical forces? No. As long as there were sufficient souls living in that consciousness, the action of their minds would automatically activate the animatical force. The answer is that the collective whole of that division had striven for a higher understanding. They had all started out at first pretty much along the same line of thought. Then a few would gradually drift away. These would be the ones who desired to climb higher, to reach a still higher state or degree of consciousness. Then others would follow and gradually the population would decrease. Undoubtedly there were more souls aspiring to the higher and leaving than there were those returning from the earth plane. Eventually there were not enough souls remaining to support a division, and then these, too, had to leave.

Thus this previously thriving astral community is now nothing more than a corpse—an abandoned, dead, no-man's-land utterly devoid of life. Yet, this abandoned community or plane of consciousness is still there. Let us make no mistake about that. It is a certain numerical division of the astral world and it will always be so, that is, until the earth itself disintegrates. The mark is still there; the division is still there. But it has become null and void of all life and is like an empty shell.

Now the Ascended Teachers from Immensity go into these abandoned divisions from time to time to observe what remains. But they will not try to make them inhabitable again because there is not enough space in the astral world. No, not at all. There is plenty of space in the astral world for all of its occupants. But they will endeavor to observe as much as they can for their own information.

Yet it would be an impossibility for me, as an astral being, to safely enter one of these dead divisions even for a moment. I have neither the power nor the necessary protection, for there is no available astral source for the animatical force. However, a Teacher of Light of the higher orders can lower his vibration and investigate such a region by drawing upon the reserve power that is within him. It is much like a diver who descends down into the ocean depths to observe a wrecked ship. He can stay under for only a certain length of time, and then he must come up for oxygen. So therefore the Teacher of Light can only remain in that consciousness for just a few moments or perhaps minutes of earthly time.

What is it like in these abandoned divisions? What would the observer find? Agasha has told us that he personally had explored some of these dead zones many times. In fact, just a few months ago he mentioned that he had visited one of these planes for just a few moments while he was slowing down his vibration in coming to earth prior to class. He said that everything was hazy and it was like being in a fog. The colors were rather dark—dark greens and dark browns with occasionally a tinge of burnt orange. He found all that had previously been created and brought in there, in the form of furnishings and so forth, to be deteriorated but not completely disintegrated. He could see the remains of the plants and the trees and everything like that, that is, to a certain extent. A certain portion of everything remained; it had not disintegrated completely.

You see, when a division is abandoned it will take time for all that was in that kingdom to completely disintegrate and vanish from sight. Everything just gradually melts away. The process is very similar to that of the earth plane where we find metal objects rusting away and organic life withering away. So it is not surprising to find remnants in the average abandoned division of that which at one time was important to the inhabitants of that kingdom. However, Agasha said that in some divisions he had found nothing at all. Everything, absolutely everything, had disappeared from sight. The entire division was null and void of anything that might produce animatical light. Now that kingdom may have at one time housed thousands of inhabitants. In fact, they could have ranged into the millions—in just one division alone.

Now let us leave this subject for the moment and take up another very interesting aspect of astral life. You know friends, when you come over here you can do pretty much as you so desire. There is no one here who will tell you that you cannot do this and that you cannot do that. In fact, your only limitations will be your own personal capabilities. You will find that you will be able to do anything that you are capable of doing. This is pretty much the same as it is on the earth plane, where you may travel anywhere that you wish provided that you have the money and the means of transportation. However, if you do not obey the laws of the land you will eventually be apprehended, and then you will not be able to travel anywhere you wish because you will then be behind bars. So it is the same way here.

The bars in the astral world are the barriers that separate the various divisions. Even though one had eventually learned how to project himself, how to will himself to any destination that he so desired, he would find that he would be incapable of projecting himself to a plane higher than his own division. He may go lower but not higher.

Thus we find that there are many spirits over here on this

side of life who are just wandering about without any particular aim or purpose. They may be compared to the hoboes, tramps, or vagrants of the earth plane. They are here one day and there another day. Sometimes they walk as they did on the earth plane, and at other times they project themselves if they had learned the use of the will. Thus they find themselves in these different divisions, and they move about because they had not been taught any differently. We call these stray individuals by the term "wandering spirits."

Now let us go back in our thoughts once again to an abandoned, dead astral division. You see what I am now coming to, do you not? Danger always lurks in the background for the wandering spirit. At any moment he might find himself crossing the border into an abandoned division and thus be caught up in a current which would be null and void of the animatical force so necessary for the sustenance of the astral body. If this occurs, there will be trouble for that individual. If he discovers it soon enough he will cry out for help and perhaps get assistance. Or if he still has sufficient power left, he might be able to escape through his own efforts. But unfortunately the realization of his predicament by such a wandering spirit usually comes too late. It is much the same as getting caught in quicksand when you are all by yourself and there is no one around to help.

What will then happen to this individual? This is a good question and the answer is not a pretty one. Of course, you know that there is no such thing as death in spirit. Not death in the strict sense of the word. But over a period of time, these unfortunate ones will sink into a state of oblivion and merely drift along in unconsciousness. And all the time that they are in that state they are not dreaming. They are not contacting anything else and they are completely oblivious to life itself. And what happens to their body? Like everything else in these dead divisions, the body then also begins to deteriorate. Agasha has said that eventually it becomes rather formless, or let us use the word *shapeless.* That seems a better way to describe it. And these unfortunate ones will remain in that state sometimes for a long time before anyone will discover them. And some are even never discovered. But, of course, that great law of reembodiment will finally intercede and thus save them from annihilation. As we stated earlier, nary a soul is lost.

This then is the reason that so many Teachers of Light visit these dead regions and zones. Astral beings cannot help, for lacking sufficient power they also would be caught up in the web. Now there are not a great many of these stray spirits entrapped in this manner, but now and then one of them will be found. Sometimes there will be more than one, perhaps an entire group will be discovered. In any event, once these shapeless bodies are found they are then removed from the dead zone and placed in a suitable rest home where the astral body can then be nurtured back to its normal state. Over a period of but a short time, it will form most beautifully once more to be the same way it appeared prior to the time it became entangled in that web, as we might say, or in that abandoned kingdom.

Once they are revived they become conscious once again and they are well taken care of. What have they lost from having gone through this unfortunate experience? They have really lost nothing other than the time that they could have spent learning. Or then again, perhaps they have gained a great deal. Perhaps they have learned the great lesson that the unpurposeful life of a wandering spirit has its own just reward—temporary oblivion. But the purposeful life of the spirit that aspires and strives for the higher is ultimately rewarded in time with the very opposite—permanent, continuous, conscious awareness. And the reward to the Teacher of Light who was able to bring this unfortunate and now fortunate one up to this understanding is great indeed.

Well folks, Agasha has given me a lot of time tonight in this period before he manifests, and we certainly have covered a lot of ground—I will grant you that. But I think it has been worth it. I know many of you have not had a clear, concise understanding as to the nature of the world that awaits your arrival after your departure from the flesh, and if I have been any help whatsoever in adding to your understanding, I am gratified. At any rate, perhaps you have a better idea of the vastness of the astral world—absolutely immense according to my concept. Truly, the average person does not comprehend the vastness of the astral consciousness.

The Happy Hunting Ground

You know folks, it was not too many years ago when I was in your shoes. Of course, I was never really in your shoes, not by any means, for I was just a simple Navajo Indian. But what I mean to say is that I was in the physical world and giving much thought to the nature of the Happy Hunting Ground that I was so accustomed to. When was this? It was in the latter part of the 1700's, towards the end of the 18th century.

I had visited that beautiful land many times during sleep, and I often brought back the memory of it. Many of the Indians did this, and then they talked about it and described this other world that they had often visited during sleep. We were quite psychic and we lived very close to Nature, as you undoubtedly know. And we wanted to take our belongings with us to the Happy Hunting Ground upon our departure from the flesh.

Of course, and more recently during the past hundred years or so, the white man came to influence the Indian's consciousness of the Happy Hunting Ground to a very great extent and to bring many changes to it. But in our day we were quite familiar with this beautiful consciousness, and this is especially true for those of us who were medicine men of our tribes. It meant to us exactly what the English words imply—the Happy Hunting Ground.

Now this consciousness is still there today, and it takes in a rather large division of the astral world. It is a beautiful consciousness with its many forests, streams, and plains where the herds of buffalo do indeed roam about in a very natural setting. Why an Indian, or a group of Indians, certainly would not feel satisfied living in downtown New York, as a supposition. No, they have their own particular consciousness in the same way that the Eskimo and those in the little Dutch colony have theirs. All of the various communities have their own individual consciousness.

Now what will be the eventual fate or future of this particular division? We must remember that many of the Indians are not returning inasmuch as many of the souls have incarnated recently in other races and countries. Many an Indian is now living today in the white race as an American. And of course these souls will certainly not gravitate to the Happy Hunting Ground upon their departure from the flesh. No indeed, they will have become accustomed to other environments and climes in this more recent earthly embodiment.

And then again, many an Indian has long since left that division as he aspired to the higher and sought after new degrees of understanding and consciousness in the higher levels of the astral world. Your own Indian guides are perfect examples of this! I can even look at myself and hardly recognize the Indian that I had been not too long ago. Therefore, it would seem to me—but of course I am no authority on this subject—that somewhere in the distant tomorrows our own beloved Happy Hunting Ground could quite possibly become still another abandoned division, since its many inhabitants are gradually moving out of the past, we might say, and into the future.

But in the few moments we have left until Agasha arrives, let us focus our attention on a less somber note. Picture then, if you will, happy youngsters at school romping and playing during recess just like they do right on the earth plane. Look at the sparkle and the happiness in their youthful faces. You know, babies and children have to be cared for and watched over here the same as they are cared for on earth. In your mind's eye now picture a group of women, young women, as they are singing and dancing in an atmosphere where the most beautiful music rings forth to touch the ear. Some of the women are painting, some are dancing, some are singing and humming, and still others are busily engaged at playing some stringed instruments. Each and every one is doing what he or she desires to do in this beautiful consciousness that awaits your arrival.

Agasha's light is building up pretty fast now. I think I just barely got those last few thoughts out. Oh, oh, goodbye . . .
. . . .

FIFTH DISCOURSE

THE ETHERIC PLANES

By Agasha

MY BLESSED CHILDREN—Manzaholla and bless each and every one. If we did not have to consider the time element on the earth plane, it would be a very wonderful thing, wouldn't it children? And yet I realize that we are all doing the very best we can in striving to learn that one basic lesson in our philosophy—patience. Think of the astronomer, for instance, as he gazes through his powerful lens out into fathomless space. To him, time apparently stands still. Some celestial bodies seem to be stopped right in the midst of an explosion. Except for the slow motion of the few planets within your solar system, some seemingly at a snail's pace, all is still. All is quiet. If it were not for the incessant turning of your earth on its axis, there would be no apparent motion whatsoever. Yet as we observe the astronomer making his deductions, calculating, and endeavoring to learn through the higher calculus more about fathomless space—we find that he knows patience. In fact, even the span of several million light-years does not even phase him.

We must realize, blessed disciples, that there are many things which the human ear cannot hear. It is also incapable of hearing noises and sounds that would be terrific if your ear were to be attuned to these vibrations. Yet they are constantly going on, and there is no letup as far as that is concerned. These sounds and noises which are created in the etheric vibration have been going on for generations, and yet they have no particular reaction even upon us in spirit, upon our spiritual hearing, that is. They also do not affect the eardrum on the earth plane. They are of a much higher pitch than even the dog can hear.

These sounds, these terrific noises, are the cast-off, or the slush-off, of the vibratorial waves in the ether which cause reactions in the form of explosions—a literal chain of explosions which seems to go on and on and has no real effect on the individual nor the eardrum. If it did, you would not be able to hear. It would burst the eardrum. These explosions are also invisible, and they have no connection whatsoever with the etheric force itself which brings forth pure light.

The Invisible Worlds Around and About Us

It is the same with the physical eye as with the ear. You perceive with the physical eye only about one tenth of what actually is within a radius of eight feet of your body. Now that may sound extremely strange, but it is true. And I am not referring to objects so small that they could not be seen, such as atoms, dust particles, and the like. I am referring to "solid objects" in the etheric vibration within just eight feet of you and within the range of your view. You will find that there are many thousands and thousands of things which your eye cannot pick up because you only see within a certain small range of the vibration scale.

You see distances, you see miles; you see things in the distance, perhaps not clearly, but you see them. You can see for miles, indeed you can. After all, you can gaze out into space and see the star out there, and as you do this you are seeing millions and millions of miles away; you are seeing light-years away! But between you and the particular destination that we so choose, the star, there are billions of things that cannot be seen with the physical eye and never will be seen with the physical eye. There are no instruments employed today that can detect what is out there in this stage of your growth.

So then as you look out in space—not up in space but out in space—you are not looking out in what might be termed "space" because it is not space at all. Why is this? It is simply because everything out there is sectional or regional, and space is not space per se. If you were to have the spiritual sight to see what is really out there in that so-called space, you would see layer after layer, division after division, region after region. But to you, from here to the moon or from here to the sun is space. You can take your spaceship and travel through space for many millions of miles, but in reality you will pass through zone after zone, region after region of gases, elements, solids—anything, you name it, that be unfelt, invisible, or unaffected by your physical sight or touch.

Each of these zones contains matter of the etheric vibration, matter of a different frequency than your physical plane matter. But it is still matter. Though it is invisible to your physical eyesight, it is nonetheless real. So therefore in your travel through "space," you will actually pass through worlds, planes, divisions, or regions of what might be termed the *spiritual consciousness*—worlds within worlds within worlds. But you will never realize that by looking through the lens or even penetrating these worlds with your spacecraft, for that matter.

Now it has never been adequately described to the satisfaction of the average individual who seeks in the occult just where the spiritual world actually is. He has usually been told that his own individual spiritual consciousness is within himself, and that is true. Yet some will say, "Well, it is out there somewhere." The average person will look up; he feels that heaven is up there. He does that automatically. He does not look down; instinctively he knows that it is not down there. So he will usually roll his eyes up into heaven and then bless and pray unto his God. He simply feels that heaven is up there somewhere, and in one sense this also is true.

So then zone after zone, region after region constitute the universal spiritual consciousness. Therefore, when you are looking out into space and you see a bright star, or the moon, or the sun, or whatever it might be, you are actually in reality looking through the spiritual degrees of man's way of thinking, learning, and conduct after he has left the physical plane. This means worlds within worlds within worlds populated by millions and millions and billions of souls who at one time lived, moved, and had their being upon the physical planets. That is understandable. You have had this lesson before, but I am bringing it to you again for emphasis.

The Various Degrees of Spiritual Consciousness

When I refer to the physical plane, I am referring to that which deals with gross material—the atom, naturally. We have many departments of the physical. We have to break down the physical plane into the various departments of the physical kingdom which deal with the mineral, vegetable, animal, and the different other kingdoms that we are aware of, as a child would learn in school.

But when we step out of the physical we are stepping into the ethereal, and this word relates to anything that would appear on the scene that you could see right through. You seemingly could walk right through it. It would be flimsy to some people, or you might say that it would appear to be shallow. There are various ways to describe it—ethereal. Therefore, as you step out into the next plane you are going into the ethereal, and this means then that we must refer to its divisions or departments also.

Now there are many regions or planes in the spiritual consciousness. Indeed, it would appear that they be infinite. If I could only get you to believe that you are living in the spirit world right now, I would be accomplishing a lot. Therefore I will repeat again: you are now living in the dense body, the dense force, the dense phase of spirit expression. What is the next phase? It is the ethereal phase. The next phase is always the ethereal phase; the ethereal always follows the dense. As you rise in consciousness you are always going higher, at a higher rate of vibration. Everything is relative; what may appear to be solid to you is ethereal to me, or vice versa. Therefore, you are living right now in the dense body. This is the dense phase.

The next phase that you will find yourself in is known as the astral division, the astral relation. This is the next division of the spiritual consciousness where you will live, move, and have your being. That in turn is followed by the Celestial Consciousness, then the Cosmic Consciousness, and finally we come to the Consciousness of Immensity. I should not say finally, because there is always the Consciousness of the great Pillars of Light to be taken into consideration, and of course, the Godhead, the great Core of Life from which we sprang.

The Etheric Worlds

Very well. Let us return now for the moment to the astronomer who is gazing through his powerful lens out into fathomless space. What does he see? He sees countless planets, suns, stars, and other gaseous bodies. Over here is a star cluster of so many stars that it is difficult to even separate them apart; over there is an island universe, a galaxy of stars, and another, and another, and another. But blessed disciples, these all belong to the material; they are *all* atom or physical worlds. The astronomer does not see even one anim or etheric world.

But the etheric worlds are there just the same. In fact, they were there long before the material worlds were even born. The dense material worlds are merely a slush-off of the etheric worlds, the worlds of the anim. Yet if you have a dense material planet over here and an etheric anim planet over there, and if you were to compare the two, you would find that the etheric planet is just merely one degree, we will say, higher in relative position than the physical planet. Of course, the vibratorial rate of the physical planet is many times slower than that of the etheric planet; but aside from this, the basic difference between them is that their frequencies are out of phase with each other.

The physical planet depends on the atom; the etheric planet depends on the anim. It is atom matter as opposed to anim matter. They are merely two sets of opposites; they are counterparts of each other. Yet the anim matter is precisely the same substance that your scientists refer to today as anti-matter. They are one and the same. Thus the anim or finer planet is called the etheric. The word *etheric* relates to something that is finer or starry.

Now then, if you have mountains on the earth, you have mountains in the etheric world. You don't have just flat land in the etheric world. You have mountains, you have seas, you have rivers, you have brooks, you have trees, you have flowers—you have everything that you have on earth. Therefore as it is on earth, so it is in the etheric world. But the etheric world is a world without friction; it is perfection. The earth or material world is a slush-off of the etheric world, a reflection of the etheric world; it is imperfection. It is like what you see when you look into the distance and think that you see something, but then you only learn later that it was nothing more than a mirage. Therefore, the earth or material world is a world of unreality; it is only the image of the real world, the etheric world, the world of reality.

It follows then that if you are living on a material planet, you are living on an unreal world. You had come out of the reality and into the unreality, disciples. The real life is yet to be lived. You will not experience it until you return once more to an etheric planet to move and have your being. True, it could be said that you have more advantages on a material planet because there you have the opportunity to grow and arise and to conquer that which had caused you to return again onto the physical. By living in an imperfect world you have the chance to perfect that which is imperfect.

The etheric world, which is already in a state of perfection, does not offer this same opportunity. But the earth itself will eventually revert back to its etheric state and become once more that which it was in the beginning.

Now these etheric or spiritual planets are also inhabited. They are inhabited by the Arisen Ones, those who had aspired to the higher and who eventually ascended from a material planet, as you disciples are striving to do at this time. So let us then not confuse the Arisen Beings in the etheric planes with the astral beings in the ethereal planes of a material planet. We have to segregate the two worlds in our minds so that we will have a clearer understanding. That is why we refer to the astral as the *ethereal* and to the spiritual as the *etheric.*

The Earth and Its Divisions

Now let us leave the etheric or spiritual planet for the moment, and study a material planet such as your earth. If you were to clairvoyantly see your planet with your spiritual eye from a distance of several hundred thousand or perhaps even millions of miles away, you would see the illumination radiating forth from this earth. It arises, encircles, and engulfs this little planet that you are living on. You would actually see this illumination, that is clairvoyantly you would see it. It would not be visible to your physical eyesight.

But the illumination would partly stem from the gases that surround the earth, and which form a ring around some planets, incidentally. These are the particles of other planets that had long since gone into a state of disintegration. They make a base there, they hover, and they literally swarm around a planet for many hundreds of thousands and even millions of years. These form the layers of the atmosphere consisting of the stratosphere, the ionosphere, and the various other spheres of which you are well aware.

Very well. Our spiritual eyesight further reveals the fact that there is anim matter intermingling and coexisting with the atom matter of your material earth planet. This anim matter, being of a more ethereal nature, of a higher rate of vibration, then forms planes which interpenetrate and extend out from the physical planet itself. It is the anim matter which is the major source of this great illumination that radiates forth from the earth.

Thus we have the physical or material plane with its atom force as well as the astral plane with its anim force. These two forces make up the elements of the earth. But it is the anim force emanating from both the earth and its inhabitants that forms what is termed its astral relation. This interpenetrates the immediate world and carries with it the emotions, feelings, and actions of men and those of the earth itself. Thus we have the astral relation.

But there is still another major division. Separating the material plane from its astral relation is the mental plane with its animatical force. This mental kingdom which emanates from the physical plane is created by the minds of men—mortals, mortal mind. But this mental kingdom which separates the physical from its astral relation does not have anything to do with the astral beings and their mental thoughts, no indeed. The astral beings have their own individual mental kingdom, as a matter of fact. They become precisely the thought that they are actually entertaining, so to speak, and they attract unto themselves precisely what they are thinking.

Thus our spiritual eyesight has revealed three distinct and separate (even though they interpenetrate each other) realms or regions of consciousness: the physical plane, the astral relation, and the corresponding mental planes. This triune relationship exists on every material planet in the entire universe. I am in reference, of course, to planets that are inhabitable. Each and every one has its physical plane, its astral relation, and its mental planes. There is the trinity again: the mental, the physical, and the astral relation. In this case the astral relation corresponds to the spiritual. All is created through the mind (mental), the actions (physical), and the emotions or feelings (spiritual) of the inhabitants as they reembody themselves innumerable times upon that particular earth planet.

The Great Powers of the Mind

We find then that on the one hand we have the dense, rather opaque, material plane of the atom; and on the other hand we have the ethereal, light, tenuous, astral plane of the anim. Now in between the two we have a mental region that houses all of the thoughts and the mental pictures that men have created down through the ages and still are creating in their everyday walk of life. It constitutes a conglomeration of numerous designs and symbols that have been created by the thoughts of millions of souls on the earth plane. The mental kingdom is made up of the animatical force which separates the atom state from the pure anim state. It is anim in energy form.

Another point that I would like to clear up: a mental plane is not an imaginary plane. It is not any more imaginary than the hall of learning that we have created of late is an imaginary hall of learning. It is a hall of learning that is real! It is as solid and as tangible to our ethereal touch as a "solid" object is to your touch upon the earth plane. It is only on a different frequency. Therefore, the mental kingdom of any individual cannot be referred to as being imaginary. It is a reality for it is you who had created that mental kingdom.

Let us say that a group of men and women are concentrating for a time on a certain object. They could be on the physical plane or the astral plane. But that which they were concentrating on would then automatically become a reality on the appropriate mental plane, and one could see clearly what had been created if he were to visit that plane. Do you follow me on that point?

The witch doctors of certain tribes in the darkest parts of Africa had learned this law, and they used it in a crude way. They had learned that by going through certain procedures, or by using various oils, they could place themselves more or less in a receptive state. This would be a mild form of the cataleptic state, and the fumes that they would inhale could put them even deeper into an exotic or intoxicated condition which would enable them to produce extremely potent thought forms or mental images. In fact, these thought forms would sometimes be so potent that they could seemingly become a living reality and annoy those to whom they were sent. It has been well authenticated that on occasions a witch doctor could even turn himself, seemingly, into a hideous looking animal. This apparition would then go forth and annoy the enemies of the tribe. This form of witchcraft had been practiced in that part of the country at one time, and some of it is even being done today.

Now of course we know that these things cannot touch any of you disciples here tonight. In fact, they do not even make sense to many people in the Western world. I am only bringing them to your attention in order to demonstrate the power of the mental plane. You have all seen hypnosis demonstrated at some time or another, and yet hypnosis is a great mystery to a great many people. They cannot understand it; in fact, many do not even believe it at all. But the power of hypnotic suggestion has been demonstrated over and over again. Even the slight-of-hand artist, the magician on the stage, will have you see what he wants you to see. Why were you not observing what he really was doing? The answer again lies in images created in the mental kingdom, either subconsciously or consciously. And if you were to step out of your physical body and function for a time in your mental body in your own mental kingdom, then everything there would be as real and as solid as the physical world is to you at this moment. Thus we should never underestimate the great power of the mind.

The Candic Ray

Now the divisional line between this mental kingdom and the astral world, or actually that which supports the astral world, is a force that is called the *candic ray*. Its frequency is at the extreme, upper level of the mortal mind. And it is at this rate of vibration, either just above it or just below it and sometimes even in it, that we find we are able to project ourselves to the many places of the earth's material plane. Thus the candic ray becomes a sort of "super highway," if I may use the term in this manner.

Scientists today are striving to understand more about this force. But the candic ray is not even understood by the average occultist, nor is it understood by the spiritualist. Therefore it is difficult for the scientist to ascertain more about the anim because he must first penetrate the candic ray. This ray, then, is the ray that immediately surrounds the material plane including its related mental kingdom.

The candic ray enables men to have television, radio, and the like, as it carries the voice and the sounds and everything that is callable throughout the candic kingdom; yet it has no effect upon the eardrum necessarily. It also does not create any great statical force on television or radio. It is a ray that most certainly must be employed in order to send the anims and the animatical forces out into space.

However, it plays no important part for the inhabitants of the astral world with the exception that it must be penetrated before communication can be established with you people in the physical plane as I am doing tonight. Sometimes one becomes inadvertently caught up in the candic ray, which is like being caught in a whirlpool of force. This does not necessarily injure the astral or spiritual body, but it can become very confusing to that individual. He then has to mentally project himself out of it, either to the earth side, the material side, or back into the astral division from whence he had come.

There is one further point that I would like to emphasize before we leave this subject. Many of the disciples would like to place the candic ray at so many miles above the ionosphere or at some other point above the surface of the earth. But the candic ray has nothing to do with distance. It is a

rate of vibration; it is a velocity. The candic ray is everywhere. It is right next to you, right where you are sitting
tonight. But when you leave the physical body, your spirit
will penetrate the candic ray and go right into the astral
world. If you were to have a rheostat, or of the like, and if
you could then raise your vibration at will, you could be in
the candic ray without even leaving your seat. So let us not
say that it is out there somewhere. The spirit world is all
around and about you.

Consciousness: A Vast Honeycomb of Cells

If we raise our vibrations still higher, we can then find
ourselves in that vast region of consciousness known as the
astral world—the many, many planes which constitute the
lower, middle, and higher divisions of the astral consciousness. Each degree of each plane, each region, each community is on a different rate of vibration.

In other words, here is a world where children are at play
and they are busying themselves with a lot of things. They
are going about with laughter and joy in their hearts as they
go to school, or as they do something else of a similar nature.
Right next to it, over there in a different rate of vibration,
is another astral consciousness that perhaps would be just
the opposite from that of the children. These people might
be studying and learning more about themselves, or then
again it might be something pertaining to the earth plane. It
could be a class of any kind, or whatever.

Now this applies all up and down the scale. Everything is
a series of vibratorial waves, and we must meet its equivalent, reach the same frequency, or else we do not function
in that state. Thus all can be accounted for by the vibratorial
rates of the various degrees of the planes of consciousness
that we might find ourselves in.

Planes of consciousness could then be said to be honey-
combed. Let us use this as a mental picture. Then each cell,
each bee cell, would constitute a degree of a particular plane
of consciousness. Now let us say that there are two cells

together. These two bee cells would represent two degrees of the astral world. It might represent two degrees of any plane of consciousness for that matter; the analogy is the same. Now let us say that I am in one cell and you are in the other cell. You can easily see how near you are to me. My vibratorial rate would be just slightly higher or slightly lower than yours, whatever the case may be. You and I would then be localized or conditioned to that particular degree. You might say that we had become astrally acclimated to it. Therefore I am conscious of you as an individual and I know your vibratorial rate. I know your location, so to speak.

Now let us say that I am desirous of contacting you. Then I would have to send a message in the vibratorial waves that would reach or leak through to you. Then you could respond to the call if you were able to recognize the equivalent of my rate or my particular frequency. Or then again, I might be desirous of communicating with someone near me in a degree a little further away. I might not even know him as an individual, but the procedure would be the same. I would send out the call with the hope that someone would pick it up and respond to the call.

You must strive to understand that when you step out of one degree and into another degree, it is like going into another world or another community altogether. The new community would be solid to the spirit touch as all things are tangible in spirit. It would simply be going at a different frequency.

Now this applies to the different *planes* of consciousness as well, although the difference in frequencies is much greater. Let us say that the inhabitants of the lower astral divisions are functioning within a particular range of the lower frequencies. Then those that are in the middle astral are going at a more rapid rate of speed in a higher frequency band, and those in the higher astral are going at a still faster rate. This is applicable to each division of the spiritual consciousness, and it makes no difference whether it be of the astral or the divisions higher than the astral. The law is the same. Yet each frequency band is independent in its own category. Let us put it that way. Each plane of consciousness is independent; yet all are more or less interrelated and play a very important part unto one another.

For a better understanding, let us try to liken it to your earthly television frequencies. You are tuned in to Channel Two, we will say. It is a beautiful travelogue about Spain, and you become so engrossed in the program that you are actually there, mentally that is. Then you suddenly remember that there is something else that you wanted to see or do on Channel Seven. So what do you do? You simply turn the dial to a higher frequency, and in the twinkling of an eye you are in Tibet, perhaps climbing the slopes of Mount Everest. Now this is only a two dimensional picture with your television set. In reality you are only watching it.

But with the spirit world it becomes three dimensional, and you are not only just watching it mentally, but you can actually step out into the consciousness physically. Therefore as it is on earth, so it is in the spirit world—only more so. We have the same here in its finer state whereby it enables us to pass out of one rate of vibration and into another rate of vibration. We immediately become attuned to the new atmosphere then, and we become cognizant of what is around and about us.

The spirit world is also all around and about you as an individual. But your rate of vibration is tuned to the physical plane, and let us say that it is somewhere within the range of 1 to 100. It would have to be here or otherwise you could not be in the physical body. Now I could be right here beside you, and yet I would be very far away vibrationally speaking. I would be in an entirely different world than the world that you are in simply because my rate of vibration would be so much higher than yours. And the reason that it is higher is that I am a spirit, an entity, who had advanced far from the earthly consciousness. Yet I could be right here beside you and still be entering degrees of consciousness far removed from you as an individual.

But my vibratorial rate must always be the equivalent of the vibratorial rate of the plane or the element that I am in, or I could not function in that consciousness. Each individual must always go through a series of degrees in each element or plane as he progresses upward. This too is the law.

Each Cell Is Like an Electric Fan

For a further illustration, let us liken each cell of each plane or region to an electric fan. And let us further state that each fan is turning or running at a different speed, from the very slow to the very fast, all up and down the scale. Now you—or your body, rather—are also an electric fan, but you have a rheostat. This is only a supposition, but it is a good illustration of the principle involved. You can adjust the current running to your electric fan, your body, and thereby increase or decrease its speed. But you cannot change the speeds of the fans in the individual cells; they are fixed and constant. Let us suppose now that you approach this honeycomb of cells, each with its fan running at a different speed, and what do you see? You can see through all of the fans because the blades are turning so fast they seem to be nonexistent.

But wait! There is one cell, and one cell only, where you can see the blades of the fan. Indeed, this fan seems to be stopped. But this is only an illusion in that it is actually spinning at the same rate you are spinning. Therefore, you can take your body, your fan which is now running at the same speed as the fan in the cell that seems to be stopped, and enter into that cell in complete harmony for the blades of your fan will mesh with the blades of the fan in that particular cell.

What if you had attempted to enter one of the other cells where the blades of its fan were invisible? If it were running at a much higher speed than your fan, it would tear your body apart. What happens when you step into the propeller of an airplane? You know the result. Then again, if the fan of the cell that you had attempted to enter were running at a much slower speed than your fan, you would have in turn torn the cell apart. But suppose you were to use your rheostat and lower the speed of your fan, reduce the rate of vibration of your body to the point that you could see the blades of the fan in the cell that you were desirous of entering. If you were to do this, you would then "materialize" to the occupants of that cell from out of the nothingness so to speak. You could then enter into their kingdom in complete harmony.

However, there is a limit to the point that you could safely reduce the speed of your fan, your body. If you were to reduce your vibratorial rate down to a certain point, if you were to slow it down to where it would lose its momentum, then destruction would be the result. A child in school knows that if he whirls a bucket of water around and around, the water will stay in the bucket. But as soon as he slows his whirling down to the point that there is no longer any centrifugal force, the water will first fall from the bucket, and then the bucket itself will fall to the ground. This is why the teachers of the higher orders of Immensity must reduce their rate of vibration before they may safely enter this instrument's body. This is also why a medium or a channel of the earth plane must in turn raise his own vibration at least to the minimum safe vibratorial rate of the communicating entity.

A Journey to the Rim of Immensity

Therefore, it would be impossible for an individual on a lower plane to vibrate on a higher plane. The only way that an individual on a lower plane could go to a higher plane is by advancing and growing, and this advancement then automatically raises his vibratorial rate. When he has thus earned the equivalent of the vibratorial rate of the plane he is striving to reach, then and only then can he function in that category.

When a disciple visits the higher planes of Immensity at night while out of the body, he is accompanied by his teacher. He travels on his teacher's ray, his teacher's rate of vibration, and the visit is only temporary. He may only remain there permanently when he has conquered the mortal, passed his initiations, and thus merited the higher vibratorial rate by his own actions.

Progressing in spirit life is like climbing the stairway to the stars, disciples, and each pinnacle that you reach is a higher step on this stair. Indeed, life is a series of rates of vibrations, a series of forces, and these forces are created by the vibratorial waves from the actions of Man and the reactions of Nature. Nature, of course, is God.

But this stairway is circular, disciples. In reality, everything in life, seen or unseen, could be said to be circular or cyclic. You will find then that as you arise from one zone to another zone, you will be literally whirling through that zone to get to the next zone. But you would not be conscious of this motion because it would be so rapid. You would be whirling in a circular manner at an extremely rapid rate.

Even at this very moment you are moving so rapidly in a circular fashion that you do not even realize it. Everything within your body is whirling around in a circular form. Everything outside of you is also whirling and revolving. The earth is revolving, but to your state of awareness it seems to be going very slowly. Indeed, the further you gaze out into space, the more it seems to appear to you that the universe has stopped, that time is standing still. But this is only an illusion. The astronomer will tell you, or you can read in your books on the subject, that the galaxies are actually moving at a tremendous speed. But I say in reality they are in circular motion. Even things that are growing on the earth are growing in circular form. Therefore, as we whirl ourselves out of the ethereal and into the etheric, out from the unreal and into the real, out of the astral and into the higher planes of the spiritual consciousness, we are in reality moving ourself in what could be termed a perfect circle.

So now disciples, come with me as we mentally whirl ourselves out of the physical and into the mental kingdom, then out of the mental and into the astral, and then finally out of the ethereal altogether and into the great etheric consciousness which be the Kingdom of Reality. We pierce these previous planes of consciousness like you would pierce anything hurriedly. You are not even conscious of having pierced them because it is so immediate. Indeed, it is accomplished in the twinkling of an eye, as I have said so many times in the past.

First we find ourselves in the great Celestial Consciousness where we stop for a moment as we absorb the beauty, the harmony, and the love radiating forth from Donna and the many Angels of Light. Then as we raise our vibratorial rates still higher, we enter the great Cosmic Consciousness, a consciousness so filled with light and inspiration that it boggles the mind. This is the highest consciousness known to the average student of the occult on the earth plane today— Cosmic Consciousness, or as some would say, the Consciousness of the Cosmic Christ.

But we can even go higher. Increasing our speed to the ultimate, it would seem, we will eventually find ourselves on the extreme, outer rim of fathomless space, which is called the Rim of Immensity. Yet if you were to observe the vastness of what you had just passed through in arriving at this point, it would seem to be an impossibility. But you were not even conscious of it, and so here we are in the great Consciousness of Immensity.

What is the Consciousness of Immensity? We could answer this by saying that unfathomable space represents Immensity. It embraces all that is. It embraces the countless galaxies, the countless clusters of stars and planets forming countless solar systems. Now let us say, as a supposition, that there is a given end to all of these planets and gaseous bodies that I am in reference to, and that out there some-where, wherever it be, lies the outer rim of fathomless space. Therefore the outer crust of all the planets that be, that great outer force, would represent the outer rim of the Conscious-ness of Immensity.

The Analogy of the Railroad Track

But the Consciousness of Immensity is not just way out there somewhere. It is also right here where you are sitting. It is everywhere; it embraces all that is. Whereas the Con-sciousness of Immensity could be said to be the plane of consciousness containing the outer rim of fathomless space, it likewise interpenetrates all of the other planes of conscious-ness as we travel inwards towards the great Core of Life.

To illustrate this point further, let us draw a circle. Let us say that the circumference of the circle represents the rim of a wheel, or the rim of the Consciousness of Immensity. Then the center of the circle will represent the hub of the wheel, or the Core of Life. Now let us draw spokes on this wheel connecting the hub with the rim. Let us say that these spokes represent roadways, or better yet, let us say that each spoke is a railroad track leading from the outer rim to the inner hub. Then as we stand on the rim and gaze into the distance along one of these tracks, the rails seem to converge to a point which would appear to the mind's eye to be the hub or the center of the wheel. This is logical.

Now let us actually start to travel along one of these tracks to the hub. Let us "whirl" ourselves to the hub, as it were. But we would never get to the hub. The converging point of the rails, or the hub of the wheel, will always seem to remain in the distance. No matter how far we travel, we never seem to arrive at our destination. Why is this so? Why can't we reach the center? What is the meaning for all of this?

The answer, disciples, is that you are being fooled by your outer senses, by your outer mind. You think that you are remaining the same *size* as you travel or whirl yourself inwards towards the center. But actually you are becoming smaller as your whirling velocity increases the closer you get to the hub. In fact, the vibratorial rate of your consciousness is inversely proportional to your distance from the hub. Therefore as you whirl yourself faster and faster and faster, you are in reality becoming smaller and smaller and smaller. Thus you would have to apparently be whirling infinitely fast before you could ever reach the hub or the Core of Life.

You can see very easily from the diagram of the wheel that we drew a moment ago that the rails of the "railroad track" in the Consciousness of Immensity are not really parallel. The rails may appear to be so as far as your outer consciousness is concerned, but you can see that this is only an illusion. They actually *do* converge in the center and they are not always at the same distance apart. This is the reverse of your railroad tracks in the physical plane of life.

Let us say that the distance between the cross ties of the track represents a cell. Each cell then, as we travel inwards from the rim, is slightly smaller. Each is at a slightly different rate of vibration. If we were to say that the size of each cell, as a supposition, were to be one millionth of the distance from it to the center, then as long as we traveled along the track, no matter how far we went, there would always be the equivalent of exactly one million cells the same size as our present cell ahead of us—no more, no less.

Therefore from our understanding of the higher calculus, we could place all of the countless planets in the Consciousness of Immensity within the cells of our railroad track, from one given point to another given point, and we would still have an infinite number of vacant cells remaining from the inner point where we were, to the center. All of this may explain but very little to the average disciple, but if we simmer it down and study the principle involved, we can realize that Immensity be infinite. It is a consciousness that is or was before anything of a gross nature was ever brought into manifestation.

The Infinite Universe

This then is the Consciousness of Immensity. Then as you find yourself out of the body among the Arisen Ones of a particular spiritual planet—and you disciples have done this on occasion while being accompanied by your teacher—you are mingling, conversing, studying. But you become so attuned to the atmosphere that the human element usually stands out. By this, I mean that you will usually have a desire to continue to live in that atmosphere. Of course, this does not apply to all, but it does apply to the majority. Some might have an entirely different reaction, but these would be in the minority. Everything over here in the etheric worlds is so indescribably beautiful, so real, so tangible to your spiritual touch that you simply do not want to leave.

The average disciple usually says unto himself, "This is what I always want; this is where I want to be forever." You become so relaxed in that blessed atmosphere, in that wonderful atmosphere, disciples, that you are human enough to want to stay. "What is the use of my going back to the physical plane when it is so wonderful here?" you might ask. Yet your higher self, your God Self, answers that you must return unto the physical plane because it is the *only* way that you can learn your lessons and thus earn the right to live here in this consciousness permanently. Therefore the soul will automatically bring you back whether you want to return or not, but you are just human enough in your outer consciousness to want to stay. I certainly do not blame you because everything in the etheric consciousness is so restful, so peaceful, so beautiful!

Tonight then, for your better understanding, I have endeavored to bring to your attention and cover the basic planes of consciousness up from God's kindergarten, the physical plane, and then through the ethereal realms and into the higher planes of the etheric consciousness. Of course, we have not really covered them; we have merely touched upon them. But perhaps this talk tonight might bring a little more light into your mortal consciousness relative to the vastness that lies ahead. There is simply no way for me to adequately describe or tell you about the peace, the calm, and the force that does prevail in the higher consciousness of the etheric, but perhaps you will gain a glimmer of it anyway. And there are even no words that I may employ to fully describe the beauty that awaits you in the higher consciousness of the astral, for that matter.

Of course, tonight we have not even touched upon that blessed Consciousness of the Pillars of Light, nor of the Core of Life, as far as that is concerned. To adequately describe these states is quite beyond me as an individual teacher of the Higher Order, and even beyond the Intermediaries that you have heard from time to time; but I will cover them, or rather give you as much information as I can, on a future evening. Yes indeed, disciples, God's universe is truly infinite. But in the long run, it all simmers down to one thing: always know that we are definitely on the path, that we are going home, so to speak. We are now returning unto that consciousness that the Teachers of Light have wanted us to return to for such a long period of time.

Rub your hands together, sound the A-U-M, and call out your teacher's name, if you please. One . . . two . . . three . . . AUM.

SIXTH DISCOURSE

KARMA: THE LAW OF CAUSE AND EFFECT

By Dr. Navajo

Good evening, friends. Let us say the affirmation, please.

I am master of myself.
I am all powerful,
And nothing can come to me
Of an inferior nature.
I am peace.
I am power.
I am all there is.

Well friends, we feel tonight that we are going to receive the great power from Agasha and the many teachers who are present; and we are going to receive not only that, but we are also going to receive wisdom in its simplest form. We believe that and we have found it to be true. So then tonight as we listen to Agasha, we know that everything that will be given unto you is in order so that you may have a better understanding of your life and the things that are to come.

How significant is it actually that we come together? Is it

just because we are striving and trying to hold on to something? Is it just that we want to believe in something in life? Is that the idea? I don't think so—not in this case. We have all striven for an understanding in the past, and we have sought in various directions for our spiritual education. We have been told many things, and it makes no real difference whether we studied in the orthodox faith or whether we were students of occultism, spiritualism, or other kindred subjects. Perhaps we can say then that as we enter the Agashan consciousness, we find that all that we had in the past in a spiritual way were but stepping stones to the real understanding of life. And the real understanding of life embraces all there is.

We have asked in recent months, and particularly since we have come into the Agashan classes, that we be shown the way. We have asked for assistance. And the many of you who have stayed with Agasha during these past months and years know that it is ever so significant that we stay together and learn. We listen carefully because Agasha eventually proves himself in a most remarkable manner.

Agasha often tells us that if we have a smattering of any one thing, it is dangerous. By not knowing a subject in its entirety, we may misconstrue it and then undo all that we had heretofore done in a spiritual way. If it is true that we had arisen at one time and then literally became fallen angels insofar as we have had to return innumerable times to redeem ourself, and Agasha claims just that, it would seem to me then that today we stand in the same manner as we stood prior to the fall. Not that we are going to lose what we had learned previously, no, I do not mean that. I am only bringing out the point that we might close the door on this information, and then we would not continue to learn.

In that case we would have to go through many more trials and tribulations and literally bump our heads against a stone wall all over again. We would miss the cue and then fall once again into the mire of ignorance and confusion. That is why Agasha states that a smattering of knowledge on a subject can be quite dangerous, insofar as by not knowing it in its entirety, the possibility of a misconception of the ideas expressed is always present.

I have listened to Agasha for many years now; I have had that great pleasure, and every time he comes it thrills me no end as I listen through the astral wave. I like to quote him; I like to refresh your memory of things that mean a great deal to you as an individual. I do this because I think that it helps to break down the barriers that surround the average person. All of the entities, as you call us, come through and say, "We are trying to break down that which is of an inferior nature which surrounds the average individual." It has been no easy road for us, and most certainly it is not an easy road for you because you on the earth plane are contaminated with a lot of material problems. Agasha says that you are to be highly commended simply because you are in the Western world where your temptations are greater and where materialism is greatly expressed in this highly commercialized world.

Society demands more of you here than perhaps in the backwoods or in a far-off place such as India or some other foreign land. The people in these areas (some of them at least) have not been accustomed to all the niceties of life of a material nature. You people have not only become accustomed to the material things, but you have also come to accept them as your rightful heritage. It is only natural then that when you are deprived of them, some of you are going to be miserable because you had not learned to adapt yourself to present prevailing conditions. This naturally takes away a great deal from your spiritual endeavors and only adds to the stresses, strains, and tensions that combat the average individual of today.

Karma: Its Basic Aspects

Why are a good many people on the earth today miserable individuals? Why is it that many have been deprived of the niceties of life? And even going further than that, why is it

that many hundreds of thousands have not even the necessary food, clothing, or shelter to sustain themselves? The
answer to these questions lies in understanding the great law
of karma.

"What is karma?" you ask. Karma is a word which is used
to indicate the reaction or the result of an action put forth,
either for the good or the bad. There is good karma as well
as harsh karma; each is brought into being by the quality of
a previous action. It is this great law of karma, the law of
cause and effect, that has placed you in the position that you
find yourself in today, be it good or be it bad.

Agasha says that karma, in itself, is the absolute and
impersonal action of this law of cause and effect. This same
law, as relating to individuals, indicates that many of the
problems that we encounter are the direct result of wrong
action in lives past, and you people in this incarnation are
given a new opportunity to bring these previous violations
into adjustment, balance, and fulfillment. This is not only
applicable to those of you in the physical plane of life; it is
equally applicable to those of us here in the astral world
as well.

There is a time for everything: a time for sowing and a
time for reaping. There is also an end to every cycle that is
started by any individual. A small pebble that is cast into a
pond starts a series of ripples that move out until they seem
to eventually blend into the body of water. This action is
precisely the same when we plan and then start an effort,
whatever it might be. This, it can be said, then becomes the
start of a particular cycle which moves out and then embraces everything relative to it. No matter how minute the
action is that is started, that action is always interrelated,
but not necessarily directly related, to the major things that
are so important in your lives at this time. Thus we are in
evidence of everything being interrelated in the final analysis.

When we make a step in the direction of that which we
wish to accomplish, this marks the beginning of a new cycle;
and even though the cycle may be short lived, we can at that

time only estimate the results that will occur when the cycle is completed. We never really *know* the results until we arrive at the end of the cycle, for our intermediate actions or efforts are constantly changing the final picture. And these efforts could be numerous in the course of a lifetime. But they can also be contributing factors to compound a karmic condition.

Let us say that in looking back upon a particular effort, we see wrong action, action contrary to God's laws. We then know that the end result will invariably be negative, although its ultimate effect can only be estimated. But even at this late date we can still initiate a new positive action to counteract it. Thus any karmic condition, a condition which eventually must be paid for as a karmic debt, may be either compounded or lessened by our actions right here and now.

Often we refer to karma in a manner that indicates that karma is a dreadful thing. But this is not always the case. We may make the statement, "I'll be glad when this karmic condition is over," which indicates that we are going through something unpleasant. Agasha has emphasized that when we employ the word *karma*, we must not fail to see or understand that this word also applies to the good karma that we enjoy from time to time. For as we live each day, walking in the light of truth as we know it, we will at times become aware that our heavenly state has come into manifestation, or at least seemingly so, as the light enshrouds us and then reflects unto those we encounter. When manifestations of good karma such as this occur, oh what gracious living is then yours to enjoy in the years to follow! Therefore we should put each statement that we make about karma into its rightful category—good karma or bad karma.

You see, the person who you are today and the position that you are in today—whatever you are doing or whatever you represent yourself to be in this life—is the result of a series of lives in the past. What you are today is the result; this present life is your reward. Whether you are now living in riches or living in poverty, whether you are lame or whether you are this or that—that is your reward and that is the position in which you have placed yourself in this life.

All of the people that you meet in life, all of the people who pass in and out of your life, come for a purpose. And the most important people who come into your life—those whom you are strongly attracted to and with whom a strange force seems to exist—are all a past relation. This is what we call a karmic relation. There is a past connection in each and every case; and in this life of yours that you are now living, you are to work out certain things that are very vital and very important in this present embodiment.

When is karma over? When do we cease paying karma? Agasha explained this years ago when he said, "Be it known unto all in the hearing of my voice that there is one basic statement in regards to karma that I wish to make. That is that karma is always in evidence in every life that you live, for in the final analysis, karma is the result of actions in lives past." So then one cannot say, "I have not any more karma to pay henceforth, for I am impressed that I have paid my karma." This is a false statement; this is a statement of a mortal without a clear understanding. Karma, being the result of a previous action, is always in evidence.

Now this is not to say that we cannot, temporarily at least, cease paying harsh karma and start reaping the rewards of the good karma that we have built. But it would seem that harsh karma would be not entirely over until one would have his ascension and graduate from the earth plane of existence. Then the scales would have tipped in the other direction, and all future karma would be good.

Everything Cannot Be Attributed to Karma

We should ever be on the alert in the usage of the word *karma*—it is used loosely and too frequently. Everything cannot be attributed to karma. Every little thing that comes to us is certainly not a karmic condition. Then, too, we could very well be placed in an environment that would bring on conditions which, in themselves, could be very difficult; yet this would not necessarily be a particular problem that we should overcome. Many are born into a home or a community where poverty is rampant; but this does not imply that poverty in itself is the condition to overcome, that this poverty is a punishment for wrong action. No indeed, it may offer a tremendous opportunity for soul growth.

We may have been placed in those circumstances so that we could arise from that environment and excel, perhaps in a profession, or then again so that we could do something helpful for that poverty-stricken community. Or perhaps the lesson might be that material wealth is not a prerequisite for spiritual enlightenment. Or an even greater lesson might lie in the fact that the individual is at a point in evolution where he should now begin to chip away the corrosion that surrounds the soul and embark upon the path which states, "Seek ye first the Kingdom of Heaven, and all these things will then be added unto you."

It is difficult to indicate any one thing as karma; it is always an individual thing. But there are many incidents arising in our everyday life where one in the occult field might interpret these actions as sowing the seeds of bad karma. We do create karma in our everyday life; this is true. We create many things that we will have to face eventually, or that we will have to pay for eventually. But on the other hand, we also create many things that we will never have to pay for. Instead, it could be said that because of them we will even be reimbursed, for they be the good things that men create.

Therefore, we must strive to understand that we must learn our lessons, and learn them well. We must be patient and never take anything for granted. Agasha says that the soul will eventually reveal unto us that which is a karmic condition and that which does not need to take place in our life. This comes through discernment, tolerance, patience, and learning the art of adaptation.

Abortion is another highly controversial subject when we try to place it within the framework of karma. Agasha has pointed out to you that here again abortion is an individual thing and that there could be mitigating circumstances. It could be said to be not "wrong" if the birth would impair the mother's health or even bring on more distress, economically or otherwise. We must also understand that if this action takes place shortly after pregnancy is recognized, one is dealing only with the germinal kingdom—a form of life, but not yet a human form of life.

But if abortion takes place after life is felt, this means then that the soul has taken over and that the mother is denying life to a particular soul. Therefore this might be an action that could bring forth an unpleasant karmic condition.

Harsh Karma: A Punishment for Wrong Action

If we are in evidence of working out some harsh karma because of some action of the past, we must be mighty sure not to contribute some new wrong action or further violate the law, because these new actions will most certainly be an added factor to the karma that we came to work out. The action of this compounded karma will usually indicate itself quite decisively and rather quickly. This we must pay for, sooner or later, either before we leave the flesh or after we leave the flesh.

If you do not fulfill the karmic debt or make amends while still in the body, then you will have to do so either in another lifetime or in the astral world after you leave the flesh. Yes, you can even pay karma in the astral world in between earthly lives. Moreover, it is well to know that karma, being the result of an action, can also be built in the astral world the same as it can be built on the earth plane. But in any event, we cannot escape punishment if the debt is still to be paid. Ofttimes the reason that a debt is not paid is because we have not learned. We find ourselves continually making the same mistakes over and over again; and this, in its compounding action, means that we have all the more to work out. There is not one mistake in our life that we escape paying for eventually.

Yet it can be said that while you are in the flesh you can do many things that may be contrary to man-made laws, the same as they be contrary to God's laws. And until you are apprehended, you may continue to violate these laws against society and mankind. Yet eventually you are going to hang yourself by your own rope. The God kingdom will see to that. Even though the punishment is meted out by the courts, on the surface, it is in reality the God kingdom who is meting out the punishment in the final analysis.

The God kingdom metes out this punishment, basically, because of our refusal to learn certain necessary lessons. Of course, there may be many reasons why we refuse to learn. Perhaps we do not see ourselves in the same light that others gaze upon us, not that we are referring to those who be hypercritical or those who bring forth judgment when it is not necessary—no, we are not in reference to that. But we are referring to the cases of false pride or the times when we might harbor a false illusion of ourselves. Or there might be many other reasons why we refuse to learn. In any event, until we do learn we will go on suffering. We may pray unto our God for forgiveness, but we cannot bargain with God, the God within, for the God within knows our behavior and will give us an opportunity to make amends—but only after we have given in to the God-Self and realize that which it would have us to learn.

Agasha is always referring back to this action of earning and learning. When you are going through a dilemma of any sort and you cannot avoid it, keep in mind that the more you murmur, the worse it will be; the more you complain and condemn, the longer you will stay in it. He says that it is only when you stop complaining and condemning that you will arise from that category and be on your way to achieving or to conquering that which you had suddenly found yourself a victim of. It could very well be that this particular problem was the very thing that you were sent back to the earth plane to overcome.

Calling Your Karma

Some disciples, in their eagerness to unfold and walk more quickly in the light, will make a demand upon their soul that all of their harsh karma be meted out to them in this present life. This is called "calling your karma," and it is a hazardous thing to do. Karma is absolute and impersonal in its fulfillment, and rarely will we find one in life strong enough to bear the combined karmic conditions of many lives precipitated into this one incarnation.

If we are to advance ourselves spiritually and overcome that which we were sent back to do in this life, it is easy to understand how an individual who has "called his karma" in reality has only magnified his problems. It is difficult enough to move forward even with limited karma, and just imagine the efforts of one deluged in a mass of chaotic, puzzling, and hurtful episodes! In this situation, when would the time come to cultivate the positive attitudes so necessary for advancement? When would the time come to bring forth love to our fellowmen? It would seem that one making this demand is actually bringing unto himself greater karma which can only mean added problems. He is also asking for something that he is possibly not in a position spiritually to handle properly.

Then too, what are the motives for this action? Is the one who is making the call asking for or seeking aggrandizement? Is it that he wants to display some personal wisdom? Or is it that he simply wants to demonstrate to the others his spirituality? If it is for these reasons, his soul will undoubtedly even chastise him further. However, if through some misguided logic he simply seeks to sacrifice himself unselfishly for the love of God, the result could be entirely different. All action put forth unselfishly is eventually rewarded.

Therefore a great deal of thought should be given to this

desire before making such a request. Let the motives behind such a demand be crystal clear. For the action of "calling your karma" definitely usurps the careful, thoughtful, and wise decisions of the soul, and it indicates that we as mortals consider the soul's judgment inferior to our own.

Race Karma

Not only individual life, but entire races of human expression are subject to karma. Every race has its karma to pay and this is what is known as race karma. And we could carry the point even further. It might be said that you as an individual are helping pay the karma of the entire human race of the planet Earth. And this karma has been building up over millions and millions of years! But it would seem that this is in order, for who were those ancient peoples of the past? They were you and you and you, and of course I cannot exempt myself or anyone else for that matter. This is where Agasha points out that in the final analysis we are all responsible for the actions of our fellowman.

You say that you are a victim of circumstances, and perhaps you are. This is not necessarily of your making, but you are the victim of it because you are in that particular community which is having to suffer many trials and tribulations. Therefore you must be alert and you must be continually on guard because of the contamination, the impregnation, and the many things that emanate from the minds of the unlearned or whatever they might be called as they bring forth the confusion that we are in evidence of at this time.

Study the histories of mankind. Think back, as Agasha had pointed out to you, and you will see clearly and be able to understand the many things about the behavior of mankind that be thus on the written page. First of all, Agasha says, men of today be fundamentally the same as men of the yesteryears. They fought, they resorted to violence, and they carried on their chicanery just the same as it is being carried on today in all societies. It can be said that we can

point to any society and find that there be those who have
larceny in their heart, those who be insidious, and those who
be ever so unkind unto their fellows. And if one were able
to go back and study the akashic records of those who are
acting in that manner today, one would find the causes, the
temptations, and the challenging factors buried therein.

If the soul brings you back into a particular race or country to overcome one thing that you must conquer before
ascending, then let us find out what that one thing be. Usually your karma has to do with a goodly number of things,
but let us say as a supposition that there be one thing that
you are to conquer in this embodiment. You are brought
within the general environment of others who are also to
conquer this same thing. And let us say that that one thing
be selfishness. Now if we are selfish to a fault—and certainly
selfishness is not going to be dressed up in any other word
or package so that it is going to appear beautiful in the eyes
of any well-thinking individual—then selfishness is something that will hold one back. By the same token we may
apply greediness, or prejudice, or intolerance. And as Agasha has pointed out so many times, these sins or vices apply
equally as well to nations, races, or individuals.

Race karma indicates itself in many environments. Let us
take the case of Hitler and Nazi Germany. If Hitler was the
direct cause of millions of people losing their lives, one could
question, "How could any one person pay the penalty for a
crime such as that?" The answer is, of course, that this was
not the action of just one person. Many people were involved
because this was race karma, and this again brings us back
to the individual and the awakening of each. For race karma
is the karma of a group of souls going through the same
learning process.

So then as we go through this movement of evolving
through negative conditions, let us always endeavor to remain in the light and rise above the consciousness of those
with little understanding. Agasha says that if we will do

this, we can then assist the Masters of Wisdom who are continually working in this field to eliminate the hate, the prejudices, and the suspicions between peoples, classes, and governments.

Everything in Life Is Recorded

Another very interesting point that should be emphasized in our little talk on karma is that everything in life is recorded. This includes every blink of the eye, every movement of a muscle, every cough—absolutely everything that be part of the human system. All of this is recorded. The TV eye of the camera of the soul, as you would say, is ceaselessly recording every action of its outer self. This in turn then becomes a part of the individual Akashic Record.

To the mortal, this recording procedure of the soul may seem quite unnecessary. "Why should everything be recorded?" you might ask. However, when we accept the theory that every action made by mortal relates to the fulfillment of some endeavor by the entity, the answer is forthcoming. Indeed, if it were not for this basic law which permits all action of mankind to be recorded in the God Consciousness, the very laws of karma itself—justice, retribution, punishment, reward, and the like—would not be able to manifest. Thus each and every action becomes a contributing factor or an added force for the eventual fulfillment of a cycle to be completed. And then a particular problem or karmic condition can be analyzed in its entirety.

All in the flesh are subject to karma. We must ever be aware of our actions and our statements, and we must be careful about making laws for ourselves. Remember, the laws for our kingdom were established long before we came into the body, and it is not up to the mortal to change them. Many of us bring new laws into our kingdom by making idle statements, and it is said that we have to account for every idle word we utter.

Agasha emphasized this point a few classes ago when he

said, "Nothing should ever be said, whether it be spoken in jest or simply as a statement, but that it be said with some purpose in mind." We should always remember this. Let each of us ask himself very carefully before speaking, "What is the motive behind these words that I am about to utter?" If we do this, many thoughtless and hurtful words will not be spoken.

Therefore, we can readily see that all on the earth plane can very easily add karma unto themselves. So let us make mighty sure that it be only good karma that we build for ourself.

The Karma of the Avatar

Inasmuch as karma is built according to what we say and do, the same must be true even with the great souls whom we refer to as Avatars. An Avatar is one who by his own decision returned to this earth consciousness to complete a great mission. Yet, regardless of their understanding, these great Initiates were still of the flesh, and consequently subject to material trials and tests. This law holds true for all on the earth plane.

The Avatar, however, because of his greater sensitivity, can sometimes bring unto himself quite severe reactions by uttering one little word indicating annoyance, or by having one thought of anger, or by doing whatever it might be that is contrary to that which they know is the law. Therefore the greater the understanding, the quicker and more severe in its consequences is the karmic law of adjustment.

But great understanding and knowledge also brings with it the power to rise above the consciousness of the multitudes. The great Avatars of the past have demonstrated this principle over and over again. And in doing this, they were able then to transform an extremely negative condition into a great positive lesson for mankind. Now the average scholar of the earth plane has learned considerably relative to the history of these Avatars, or their fate as some refer to it; and if a great message had been brought forth through the lips of one who was called the Avatar of his time, his words have then lived down through the history of mankind, and many to this day are motivated by the philosophy uttered by this one.

But how was all this accomplished? What single action was the basic motivating force that enabled his words to be left to posterity? The answer is that he *demonstrated* the philosophy thus taught. He became the living proof of his philosophy through a completely selfless action at a time of great duress. Had he acted in a different manner, his words would have been long since forgotten, having been swallowed up in the negativity of the day.

This then is the reason that an Avatar had to meet the fate he did or why he was taken out of the physical body so abruptly as indicated by the records. It seems that if one has a great message to give to the struggling people of any land, there always has to be that demonstration—something strictly mortal that that person, the Avatar bringing the message, has to endure. He must always set the example through his actions of that which has been uttered through his lips. This is the answer then to a question that has puzzled many people down through the years.

In the final analysis, it is well to remember that the one and most important factor in the life of a great Avatar, or in the life of a higher Initiate who is embarked on a spiritual mission, is the carrying out and completion of a definite action for the betterment of humanity. The nature of the manifestation is not always the same; it varies according to the individual karma of the one carrying out the mission. This is a basic law on the earth plane and all up and down the scale of life—to perform an action for the express purpose of bringing about the advancement of humanity. It is the desire to spark this advancement that brings those individuals, those who have left so much to posterity, back to the earth plane for their own particular effort.

Even the Higher Initiate Is Challenged

There are those, down through the evolution of mankind, who did not have to come back into the physical body; yet they did return to fulfill a special mission through an individual desire. Now these souls are most certainly in the minority. Agasha says that when a person reaches a certain stage of advancement—a stage far removed from the astral strata—the decision whether or not to return to the earth plane will then be the entity's own individual responsibility.

However, when one does not need to come back, the "I" within knows that if he does return, after conditioning himself to that which is mortal, he will then be faced with the possibility that he may be prosecuted, persecuted, or confronted with such great trials or tribulations so as to even endanger the successful accomplishment of the mission. Just because you chose to return is no guarantee that your mission will be accomplished, because as long as we are on the earth plane we are subject to building more karma. And to make matters worse for the individual returning through his own desire, he quite often (the outer self, that is) is even oblivious to the fact that he did so choose to return to the earth.

Rare indeed are those high souls who have so chosen to return to the earth plane. Even though they infinitely know their mission, the moment they return to the earth body and the material world they are challenged. Agasha has told us that Kraio was one of those who did not *have* to return. Yet he returned as Jesus of Nazareth and was limited precisely the same as any man today inasmuch as he was dealing in the flesh. He dealt with mortals who even tried to rob him of that which he came back to accomplish. Using that as a focal point we can readily appreciate the limitations of a soul, one who is an advanced entity in the higher planes of life, when he descends from his high state and returns once more back to the earth plane.

In other words, we might picture a highly evolved soul expressing the following thought: "If I return, am I willing to stand all that may be meted out to me by my mortal mind? For it will be a test and I may be oblivious to that of which I am now aware, and when I come into the earth consciousness I may not have it revealed unto me." Now this is confusing to the average individual. How could a soul who had previously ascended from the flesh be put into a position where it would be possible for him to blunder?

The answer, Agasha points out, is that any soul, no matter who it be, upon entering the physical body has to first deal with and then overcome the mortal mind. And the mortal mind can certainly get you in trouble! Even though, basically, we are infinitely intelligent, the mortal mind can close the door to this intelligence. And even though this intelligence be tapped, never can it be said that in the life of mankind we can point to any one particular person who actually was aware of or displayed the Infinite State in its entirety. We cannot name one.

Let us again refer to Jesus, for he is the great Avatar embraced by millions in Christianity and yet he too at times gave indications of being mortal while he was in the flesh. It can be authenticated, according to the books of the Bible, that he became angry on at least one occasion and threw the moneychangers out of the temple. He also was involved in politics, not appreciably, but he had spoken out politically to assist the politicians of his time. Of course there is nothing wrong in all of this; indeed it is commendable in that he was endeavoring to correct the situation and set things straight. But I am merely trying to point out that even the very highest of Masters, once they have descended and taken possession of the physical vehicle, must first overcome the feelings, the negative emotions, the negative thoughts of the mortal self. After this is accomplished, they may then ascend once more unto the higher consciousness.

How to Modify Karma and Complete Your Mission

Agasha says that it is always in order for us to try to learn how much we can eliminate of a karmic nature so as to avoid harsh karma. How and what must we do to lessen it? Here again it is an individual thing; nothing comes to us that is not earned. It seems to me that the way to go about changing conditions is to first realize and accept the fact that we are here to learn the lessons most needed for us at this time. Then we will not be in the position of refusing to learn. Agasha says that regardless of all the adverse conditions around us, if we hold firm in a true desire to do right, we will then move into a path of modified karma.

The first step is the clarification of the situation. If we do not first realize the scope of the problem, how then can we go forth to solve it? The next step is the balancing and the adjusting of all that needs to be adjusted. This is accomplished according to our talents, according to our academic training, according to our awakening. But we must first comprehend where we stand in our own particular category. We must understand the individualism of the matter; the things that are needed to be carried out in this way always vary with the individual. This clarification and adjusting will enable us to fulfill our mission in this life; whether it be my life here in the astral world or your life in the physical body, it makes no difference. The problem is the same. But your mission is that for which you came to the earth plane in this generation.

Well folks, the light is building up in the center of the room and I am going to have to leave pretty soon. Agasha's light is a very beautiful thing to behold. It always focuses right in the center and then builds up and gets stronger and brighter. Yet it is rather difficult to describe. Did you ever see the full moon shining in the window? It is something like that. I can usually gauge when he is ready to take over by the brightness of his light. He seems to have given me a little more time tonight to talk about karma, and perhaps it is in order as this subject has needed to be clarified a little more for some of the disciples. Anyway, I love repeating his simple statements about life and all of its ramifications. He still seems not quite ready to take over the channel, and so therefore I shall continue on with my thought.

And that final thought is that their understanding of karma enables Agasha or your teacher to say that it is possible for you to complete in this life that which you are meant to complete, whatever it might be. Generally speaking, this is not always known by the average mortal, for one could be oblivious to his or her real mission. Therefore the teachers come to awaken the mortal self to take the initiative to find out what this mission is and then to complete it. Agasha has said on a number of occasions that it is possible for the average person attending the Grand Finale to complete that mission—your own individual responsibility—in this incarnation. There is, however, no promise or guarantee that because one attends this class or other classes of a like nature that he will surely overcome. But this is the way.

Let us strive then to live each day as though we were going to live forever and perform each task as though it be our last. Let us strive each day to make the Divine Will our will, and we will never be overwhelmed by the hell and general unrest around and about us. Let us keep on thinking positively, and perhaps each day then say to ourselves, "I did not start it; I cannot finish it; I will not contribute to the mortal confusion of the world."

The vibrations are getting stronger now and I am going to have to step aside. Oh, oh, here he comes . . . .

SEVENTH DISCOURSE

THE ANIM: THE SOUL OF THE ATOM

By Agasha

My BLESSED DISCIPLES—Manzaholla and bless each and every one. It is my desire tonight to discuss a little further the subject of the chemical worlds and the vibrations necessary to keep the chemicals alive, so to speak. We have learned in our previous classes, and we accept it to be true, the fact that everything that is brought unto the earth plane had first come from the etheric state. We believe that and we can prove it unto ourselves. Every known chemical upon the physical plane is also known on the spiritual side of life and is utilized the same. The spiritual side of life is of course the etheric side of life—life on the etheric planes. Therefore the same chemicals are utilized there that are utilized on the earth plane, but basically we must understand that all originally came from the etheric plane. The chemists and physicists today are studying much in that direction, and it is only a question of time before many things shall be revealed.

The atom of the etheric plane is called the *anim*, which is the spiritual counterpart of the atom. This is what the scientists are doing today: investigating that ghost-like something that they refer to, and which in turn has puzzled them to a

161

considerable degree. They have since given it a name somewhat similar to the correct terminology, which is *anim*. I am
in reference to the words in your scientific vernacular, *anti*-
matter or *anti*-particle. The ghost of the atom, so to speak,
is the anim in reality. This is what they are investigating,
and many have come out and said openly that they think it
is reasonable to believe that there are worlds within worlds
invisible to the sight of men.

However, anything that has to do with the earth plane,
the physical plane, the flesh, and all that be involved, cannot
go into the ethereal kingdom any more than oil will mix with
water. We must try to understand that. Not one particle of
substance that has to do with the atom world can go into
the ethereal world which deals with the anim. Atoms have
slowed down to a much lower frequency than the anim, and
they have become a complete contamination because of their
ever mixing and intermingling with the forces of nature.

Anims are pure in character and are not contaminated.
They are vibrating on a much higher frequency and are more
sublimated in nature. The anim is pure in state; it is the inner
core of the atom. The anim is the very *soul* of the atom.
Therefore the anim soul is bringing forth light unto mankind.
The anim is also furnishing power for the atom, its outer
expression. But the outer shell or crust of the anim, which is
the atom, is too coarse in character to enter the higher vibrational rates of the ethereal planes, the inner planes. Therefore we say that anything that has to do with the earth plane
cannot enter the ethereal kingdom without first leaving its
atom body behind.

But not all anims have slushed off and thus created an
atomic counterpart around themselves. Indeed, the vast
majority of the anims still remain in their pure inner state.
These anims could then be said to be the cousin of the atom.
Why do I say this? Let us remember that the basic particle
of the element is the atom. Isn't that right, children? In the
same way then, we may also say that the basic particle of

what you people call anti-matter is the anim. But the relationship between the element and this anti-matter is the same as that existing between a positive force and a negative force, or between a brother and a sister. Therefore we may say that their children, or basic particles, have the same relationship as cousins. The analogy is rather crudely put but it does tell the story.

Now then, we recognize that the physical plane depends on this outer portion of the anim, which is the atom. The anim is feeding it at all times as it whirls at a great rate of speed thus producing a radiation. An anim never becomes what we call dormant. Its constant motion is what gives the atom its power as it turns incessantly upon its own axis, spinning like a top. It is constantly pulsating, gyrating, and we might say even dancing in a most beautiful manner.

All of the time that it is going through its gyrations, it sends forth a radiation called the *animatical force*. This in turn is the instrument which brings the atom into play. There is your trinity again. We have the animatical, the atom, and the anim: the mental, the physical, and the spiritual. The animatical (which is the intermediary between the atom and the anim) corresponds to the mental, the atom to the physical, and the anim to the spiritual.

The Anim Will Eventually Claim the Atom

Thus we understand that everything in the physical plane came into manifestation basically through the anim stages. But everything that is of the atom must also revert back to the anim because the anim is going to claim the atom. Do you understand that, disciples? Always remember, as I have said in your previous classes, that the anim will eventually claim the atom because the atom has to go back into the anim. There, that which had been the atom will be intermingled—the positive and the negative or the natural polarity becoming a part of the Oneness—and become part of the whole, so to speak. There within the Oneness, it will wait to

be created once more by the directors of a collective group
or through the thoughts of any one individual who may
desire to bring into manifestation whatever he may so desire
at the time.

We know that before anything came into manifestation,
it had to be created out of the mental kingdom. It had to be
in the minds of men before it became a reality in the physical
world. There is not a thing upon the physical plane that you
use today, be it garment or be it machinery, that had not
first been in the minds of men. It was in the mental world
before it came unto the physical plane, and the same thing
applies to all particles of the earth, even the earth itself.
Everything, absolutely everything, was in the other world,
in the anim stage, before it was sent into the vibration that
it is in today, before it came into what we might term the
atom stage. And it was the etheric forces of the collective
force of the universe itself that enabled this earth to come
into play.

The atom today can be dissipated, but after its apparent
dissipation it does not disintegrate and be no more. It merely
reverts back into its original consciousness, its original state,
and there it waits to be reutilized over and over again. Let
us take a single atom, if it could be so defined in this direction, and let us then dissipate it to its ultimate point. It
becomes ever so minute, and a certain point will be reached
where it cannot be dissipated any further. It becomes a
minute speck in the Cosmos. At this stage any further dissipation would merely revert it back automatically to the
anim.

So we must try to understand that anim was before atom.
Before atom came into manifestation, there were no worlds
as you have today. There were no gaseous bodies out there
in fathomless space, so called. There were no stars, moons,
and so on, as you have learned in previous classes. Before
all planets came into manifestation, everything was in the
anim stage. The soul of the atom was completely unfolded
and fully expressed.

Now then, it is a bit confusing to the average mind to try to understand too much at the moment relative to the atom. Many years ago when I first spoke of the atom, before it was brought to the attention of the average lay mind in the manner that it is today, you learned that the atom plays an all-important part in the lives of men. We know that this is so. You are a part of the universe; all that is you are. Therefore, a single atom is just as much a part of a life cell within your body as the life cell is a part of you. Likewise a single life cell within your body is just as much a part of you as you are a part of the earth. We may carry this analogy on further to the solar system, then to the seven solar systems, then to the galaxy, and so forth.

Let us take the earth. Now the earth itself may be likened to a single atom. A single atom represents an earth plane. Therefore, within a single atom is the equivalent of that which is within the earth. But on the other hand, its cousin the anim is in the consciousness of the spirit. Yet all are related. All are of the Oneness.

Now let us take your physical body. The physical body is composed of what? It is composed of atoms. But the anim is the equivalent part that we employ to motivate in the various other bodies that be called sublimated. Therefore, it is the anims that produce the outer appearance of each ethereal body that we find ourselves in, in the same way that atoms produce the physical body.

Therefore you have the atom on the earth plane. But that atom is always to be attracted by the anim. And it is the animatical force that attracts the atoms and enables them to become the particular atoms that form the outer crust of the physical life. The anim is always there attracting its counterpart. Does this mean then that a single anim is always following the atom wherever it be? Not exactly in the sense of the word; but we can say that the anim is always in direct accord or direct relationship with the atom, because the anim is very definitely individualized unto the Consciousness of God.

Thus the anim is in reality a part of the integral force of the Universal Consciousness God. Do you follow me on that point? We may say that it is a single entity, and yet it is a part of the universal whole. An atom or molecule of water is likewise a single entity, and yet it is a part of the sea. You, we will say, are individualized. You are a single entity. But you are also completely absorbed in the Divine State and a part of the collective whole. This means then that if you are to understand life, you must understand a single atom.

A Single Atom Is as Powerful as the Universe

The atom is not independent. The individual is not independent. They are all a part of one and the same. Therefore we are dependent; we are dependent on the God force within. The atom is dependent on the anim for its force, its power to revolve, its ability to intermingle and become fused with other atoms. It is the collective whole of a certain force within the atom itself that produces the outer crusts of the material, whatever it be. It might be a stone, a grain of sand, a high mountain peak, or even the mountain itself. Then we are going into "illions" of atoms, but let us not go into that subject at this time.

You and I, in observing the result, cannot single out any particular atom that was the creator of all because one single atom could not be the creator of all. Yet when it reverts back to the anim, it is the equivalent to the great power of the universe that it once had, or that it once was, when in the anim stage. Thus it could be said that a single atom is as powerful as the universe is itself. For it *is* the universe in miniature form; yet it is still a part of the collective whole. Do you follow me on that point? It is confusing to some but very interesting to the majority.

Therefore that mighty, powerful, most minute atom is actually the equivalent, relative to power, of the power of the whole of the world. This is a very difficult point to understand, but it is so. It is so powerful that if it were misused, in conjunction with the higher animatical forces, there would be an explosion causing a chain reaction that would lead to the disintegration of this earth in the twinkling of an eye. The atoms would go wild and thus cause a tremendous inner explosion. That inner explosion would then cause even further explosions to the extent that it would be a chain that would be endless as far as that is concerned. Anything that had body to it would explode—anything, everything that had body. Therefore there would be no earth.

However, you understand that nature provides the anims which modify, rectify, and govern their outer counterparts. You follow me on that point. Therefore the explosion to the extent that I have described it would never occur, in all probability. We can see then that if it were not for the anim, you would have no earth. You would not be able to function upon this earth plane because there would be no earth plane in the first place. Thus the inner laws of the anim, the natural laws, require it to modify the atom. The anim then is vital to the human mind, to the human body, to everything that is.

The anim kingdom is what we use exclusively. We do not consider the atom in the same way that the atom might be recognized on the physical plane. We use the word "atomic" in the various degrees of the Consciousness of Immensity simply because it signifies that which is powerful, that which is universal, and that which embraces all—the atom. Yet we understand that that which we call the atom is simply the outer crust of the anim.

If it were not for the atom, the pebble would not be a pebble at all. It would be in a state of disintegration. If it were not for the atom, the highest mountain could not be in existence. Nothing could come into physical manifestation in the light in which it is now. There would be no form of physical life whatsoever. But you see that all the time the atom is working to sustain you, to sustain the physical, it is being fed by the real powerhouse, its counterpart the anim.

The anim then must always be reckoned with if we are to get to the source of the energy produced by the atom. This anim energy source that is always back of the atom may be either positive or negative, whatever the case may be. It is these positive and negative forces, the male and the female principle, that enable the most minute atom to be the equivalent of the universe itself.

Worlds within worlds within worlds! There within that most minute atom is a world within a world. That is something which the average person cannot fully comprehend, but the space between one element of an atom and another element of an atom could be the equivalent of the space from here to the sun. Of course, that really doesn't explain anything; it only gives you a general idea. I might add that the same applies to the anim, for before atom was created, anim was in existence.

Spiritual Chemistry

Now let us leave this subject for the moment and turn to what you would call spiritual chemistry. This is a term used by the alchemists on the earth plane. It means to bring into manifestation or to precipitate any desired material or object. This is accomplished by bringing the atom into close relationship with its spiritual counterpart and by knowing the exact frequency of the object to be precipitated. In reality there is nothing mysterious about it. It is just as scientific as any other science on the earth plane. No matter what is to be precipitated, the law works the same. Be it gold, be it anything of a metallic nature, be it moisture, be it fruit, be it anything you want it to be, it makes no difference. Then it can be consumed, or be employed for a building, or be employed for jewelry, or be worn as clothing, or be employed for any desired purpose.

The same law is applicable to apportations, which means the translocation of objects from one place on the earth plane and their reappearance at some other place. This is an intricate subject but it is demonstrated occasionally, usually by your close friends from the astral, or sometimes by your Indian guide. More than likely the apportation will be demonstrated by your Indian. He would use the same law of precipitation through the anim kingdom.

Let us say you have an apple in your hand. You are on the physical plane and the apple is made up of billions and billions of atoms. You know that the apple in your hand is eatable and that it is of a certain variety. You also know that the *atom* kingdom keeps the apple in its solid form, helps to bring into manifestation the color and everything that it is, and brings forth the vitamin content that is contained therein. Very well, Now let us say that I am on the etheric plane. I am invisible to you but I become conscious of the apple because I am concentrating upon it. The apple on the physical plane becomes visible to me only insofar as I make an effort in that direction.

Now let us suppose I want a counterpart of the apple on my plane, the etheric plane. What do I do? I know that every atom contained within that physical apple has a spiritual counterpart. Therefore I merely draw forth the *anims* of the spiritual counterpart of these *atoms*, through a certain power of the will, and I have my apple. It is the same variety of fruit and an exact duplicate of your apple. Perhaps it might even be termed to be more luscious because the spiritual is considered the highest, in the sense of the word. So therefore we have the luscious fruit in the etheric realm the same as you have upon the earth plane. What happened to your apple? You still have it. I merely created a duplicate.

However, if that apple in your hand were to be apported to another place on the earth plane, it would literally disappear from your hand, seemingly vanishing into the nothingness. How is this accomplished? By simply breaking down the elements of the apple into their finer, more etheric counterparts, the apple then becomes invisible to your physical sight. The frequency of every *atom* has been raised to its *anim* state. The entire apple is now vibrating on a higher frequency, or higher rate of vibration. In this state it can be sent or transported to any other point on the earth plane at the speed of thought. Then, after arriving within the atmosphere of its designated location, the Indian or one directing the apport merely lowers the rate of vibration of the apple once again to the physical frequency. Thus it suddenly reappears on the table, on the floor, or in the lap of the one to whom it be sent.

Creation in the Etheric Realms

So it is that when you have a green leaf in your hand, the green leaf has its counterpart in the etheric realms. But only insofar as I become conscious of the green leaf can it become visible to me, or can it become usable in my particular kingdom. Now I am not concerned about a green leaf necessarily. I am only using that as an illustration to bring out the point that everything on the physical plane can also be produced in the various regions on this side. And they can be reversed, back and forth, created first in the etheric kingdom, then brought to the earth plane, and finally reverting back again as its counterpart.

Likewise a speck of gold on the earth plane that is hardly detected by the physical eye can be duplicated over here. We take the anims of the atoms within the speck of gold, and we have its spiritual counterpart. The speck of gold has now become gold in the anim kingdom, having reverted back to its original state in the etheric consciousness. Now that most minute speck of anim gold—not atom gold, mind you, but anim gold—can be multiplied and multiplied and regenerated until it becomes usable in the spiritual consciousness, until it becomes a solid form or becomes whatever we desire it to be. This creative principle applies to anything that we so desire in the spiritual consciousness.

Therefore in your studies of occultism, you realize that when you come into the astral world you can have a counterpart in the ethereal realms of that which you possessed upon the earth plane. If you desire to have a certain garment in the astral world, you can have a duplicate of the same garment that you once wore upon the physical plane. If you had some article, perhaps an heirloom of no intrinsic value, and if you would still like to have it, then you can have its counterpart over here on this side, and it is yours to keep just the same as if it were right there on the physical plane.

Of course *all* things that you have on the earth plane are not duplicated and brought with you to the higher planes. There would not be the necessity of duplicating all that you have on earth. Therefore, we need not go into that. The men who were able to build whatever it be, and to bring it into manifestation, would not bother to bring all that be on the earth plane into manifestation in the astral because much that is on the earth would be an oddity in a typical astral community. We have the advantage, as you know, of controlling our environment and not contaminating it with much that is on the earth.

Each community in the higher realms is first created by the collective whole, now follow me carefully—by the collective whole with a single thought, with a single desire. This would be more or less an automatic precipitation and not by any one individual. After this has been accomplished, individual members of the community, those who have attained the power of will, may use their force and their knowledge and their artistic ability to carry out the designs and to carry out what we would call the interior decorating. They would complete the atmosphere of the furnishings and provide the beauty, indeed, of its completeness. There we have established a residence, many residences, a community; and when we bring forth the flowers, the trees, and all that be comparable to what you have on earth, all be then complete. All is thus precipitated in such a way that it is as we desire. All becomes a reality through the great power of the soul of the atom, the anim.

Objects Take on Your Personality

Returning again to the earth plane, let us now examine all of the objects that be in your home, your apartment, your room, or wherever it be. You will find that your garments, the rings that you wear, literally everything that you possess of a personal nature are absorbing your personality. They take on your vibrations. Therefore we are often influenced by articles. We are influenced not only by material things belonging to ourselves, but by material things belonging to other individuals as well. If it be a negative vibration, burning sulfur will often eliminate the anims surrounding the article. But aside from this, any article in your possession gradually takes on your anims and becomes almost a part of you. You are constantly clothing it with your thoughts, your emotions, your anims.

Let us say you have a jewel box. It has been in your kingdom for thirty years, and prior to that time it belonged to your grandmother. It had been handed down to you and you have had it for thirty years. You also have jewelry in it, and you have whatever little trinkets you might want to put into it for a keepsake. They may be of no intrinsic value but nevertheless you are fond of them. You use this heirloom and you put articles into it that you have worn for five years, ten years, or perhaps only for a few hours.

Very well. Now all that material is inanimate or lifeless as far as you are concerned, but as far as I am concerned, as I scrutinize it from the higher consciousness, I see it alive, vibrating, and very animated indeed. You see, disciples, I do not necessarily know what you put into the box, but whatever it be, the anims surrounding each object are all mingling with one another. Therefore the box with its jewels becomes actually alive and extremely animated. The animation is caused by the force that goes through the ether and produces the anims, which in turn cause it to become alive. That gold ring is alive. Yet it is not animated as far as you are concerned. Still it is alive or else it could not be in solid form. It is the anim that gives it life—not the atom. This is a very important point to understand.

Your Aura and the Teacher's Light

Now the anims that you have around and about you, in your immediate atmosphere, compose or make up what you would call the aura. These are the anims that you have absorbed, your rings have absorbed, and your clothes have absorbed. This is your aura. Now these anims are always modifying the atoms within your immediate vicinity. They are keeping everything around you alive, which in turn enables you (your body, clothing, et cetera) to be seen from the higher consciousness.

Anims can also at times be seen by mortal in the form of light or color. Sometimes they are red, sometimes blue, purple, or white. Golden anims can very often be seen by the advanced disciple. Of course, when I say that they may be seen, it is the light or energy produced by the anim that can be seen.

When a teacher shows his light, he is using the power of the anims. He is drawing the anims from the immediate atmosphere of the room to produce the light. Do you follow me on that point there? The teacher will also, in all probability, eventually materialize or etherealize to the advanced disciple. And when he does this, he will be drawing the sympathetic vibration, or simply the very high force that is there, from the immediate atmosphere. Then he can begin to clothe himself, and he can become visible to you by slowing down his rate of vibration to reach the vibrations of the anims that are then in existence in that particular room, home, or wherever he is to appear. It could be out in the backyard, it could be out in the street, or it could be anywhere that would provide the right vibrations at the right and proper time.

However, he will never stay long. He cannot stay long. He may stay a minute, a half minute, or just long enough for you to see him before he fades away. You never know a teacher, one who is no longer in the flesh, to stay any length of time unless that individual is definitely drawing from a full-fledged materialization medium who is throwing off anims to produce the necessary ectoplasm. The ectoplasm then draws the anims together and thus produces the form so that it may be seen. But this becomes an intricate subject, and I don't want to get into it this evening.

Your Thought Anims Are Like Carrier Pigeons

Now everything that is upon the physical plane was first created in spirit, as I have said before. Therefore, you who are here on the physical plane, as well as all else that is of the physical plane, are in reality a part of the spiritual life. You are simply in a denser vibration, or in other words, in the dense phase of spirit expression. The link between the dense phase and the ethereal phase is the anim. It is the anim that brings to you the etheric vibrations. It is the anim that enables you to live in the physical body. It is the anim that becomes your spiritual food, so to speak. Anims also enable you to move about, to send thoughts across the country, to heal. Therefore if it were not for the anim, you could not be in the flesh. But the same could be said for the atom. Both are necessary for you to manifest here in the dense phase of your spiritual life.

It is the magnetic attraction of the physical plane that attracts these anims unto you. They were there at the time that you came into this life and took your first breath. They are there now. You then clothe the anims with your thoughts and your emotions and your desires, and they stay with you—usually for a long period of time. As a matter of fact, a great many stay with you during the course of your life; but as you change your way of living, your way of thinking, then these anims are dissipated and new anims are attracted unto you. By dissipation, I mean spewing them forth so that new anims can be absorbed or recreated back into your own etheric relation.

Anims work in nature, work with nature, and work with

God. They hover around and about your physical body and they do their work for you. You could not possibly send a thought out into space and have it be received by a particular individual were it not for the anims carrying the thought through. It is much like when you send a message with a carrier pigeon to be delivered somewhere, the pigeon delivers the message and then returns. So do the anims.

Then as we send the anims out, we are conscious of those little fellows, as it were, going out and doing their work for us. They are going out and they are doing this and they are doing that. They are colored with our personality. They are colored with our thoughts, our intentions, our desires. They become a part of us. They are specially designed to work with us because we have built up these anims. We have drawn them to us. Therefore they are as much a part of us as a swarm of bees would be to a beehive. Do you follow me on that point? The bees know their beehive in the same way that the anims know us as a beehive. We will put it that way. They belong to us. No matter how far we send them out, they are going to come back to us. Time and space is not considered by the anim.

Anims Create Harmony or Discord

Your anims must be on the same frequency as another person's anims in order to have a harmonious relationship. Then they may intermingle with complete harmony. It is like the situation when somebody remarked to another disciple, "I will mix my anims with your anims anytime." Now I don't think that needs any better explanation. It simply expresses harmony. However, if there be discord, then there is friction among the anims, and the anims are just as conscious of that friction as you are as an individual. What do you think of that?

But now that you are conscious of the anims, since I have brought them unto your attention, you might ask whether the anims themselves are conscious of the fact that you are now aware of them. The answer to that question is no, not necessarily. They are conscious only that a harmonious relationship exists.

You must understand that there are both positive and negative anims. And this causes a great deal of disturbance if they are intermingled with others that are just the opposite. In other words, there is the positive and there is the negative —the male and the female. Does this then mean that the female is spewing off or creating female anims and the male is doing just the opposite? It can be said so. But you must remember that in the male there are both the male and the female anims, and the same can be said to be true for the female. Likewise, both the male and the female anims can be clothed in either a constructive or a destructive thought, feeling, or emotion. Do you follow me on that point? Like attracts like. They must be of a like nature to be in harmony with each other.

If we build up something in our kingdom by entertaining thoughts of an inferior nature, then these anims are there and they are spewed all over the room. They are spewed all over the garments that we are wearing, and thus we are tagged as the individual that we are. But our home is contaminated with negativity. We contaminated it, and this same negativity eventually reverts back and contaminates us in turn. In other words, this is the result if we build up that negative force.

But just the opposite could occur. We could sanctify our home with thoughts of harmony, or of beauty, or of love. It might even be a hovel, but therein that hovel one would still have a very beautiful feeling. The same thing could be said for this very auditorium that we are in tonight. You couldn't possibly come through that door without thinking to yourself, "Doesn't this place have a wonderful vibration!" You say that as a matter of fact, as a matter of habit; yet the average disciple basically does not quite understand what is meant by all that. You think you do, but the truth is that the anims cause the vibrations. These are the very anims that have been created, and are being created, through the manifesting of the teachers and through the harmonious vibrations that you bring into the room. These anims are constantly spewing out into this room. Therefore these four walls are absorbing that wonderful force of harmony which is ever present.

Yet let someone come into this beautiful vibration and spew forth a negative force or, if I may use the term, a bee-hive of negative anims; then you can actually feel it. But it will do no permanent damage. The negativity will soon fade away, but for the time being we will have to overpower it. We do this through our harmony and through our own anims that we have built up in this room. We ignore the negative force and we don't let it bother us. We just try to settle the residual down and send the individual on his way.

Now an individual may come in contact with other individuals whom he distrusts, or who confuse him, or who do not seem to be in harmony with him, and then there is that friction. The friction is caused by a negative thought emanating from the individual himself. The thought colors the anims that are with that particular personality and the result is what? Friction, of course. The anims of that individual are simply not in harmony with the anims of the other members of the group. You follow me on that point, don't you. Isn't this an interesting subject tonight, disciples of the earth?

How Psychometry Works

The final point I would like to bring out tonight relative to our discussion on the anim is the subject of psychometry. As you have learned, your clothing, your jewelry, everything that you possess has taken on these anims. That is why we know that everything about you is recorded right on your own articles. Now these objects can be sensitized to the extent that the vibrations can be picked up by a person who is capable of getting in touch with those anims, and they will very easily tell the story about the individual. By applying the art of psychometry then, it is possible to become aware of events related to the past as well as the present thoughts, feelings, or actions of any one individual.

This is accomplished by simply holding an object in your hand that has been worn by the individual desiring the reading, and if you have unfolded your psychic powers sufficiently, you will be able to receive the message recorded in the anims that have been absorbed by the article. This is usually in the form of very strong mental impressions.

But what about the future? The future can be seen only through the actions of the past, and then by projecting the possible results of these previous actions into the future. You know that as you have had this lesson before. There is no one who can foresee the future unless he can pick up the actions of the past. Therefore psychometry is only a tool or a means towards this end.

Now all these things are extremely interesting and very vital for the average disciple to learn. We now know that we are building up our anims. We are building up our supply. When we become weakened we realize that we need more anims and that we must draw them unto ourself. We do this by becoming conscious of the anims around and about us, by becoming conscious of harmony, by becoming conscious of love, by becoming conscious of all things that are good. When we do this, we are drawing these anims unto us and then we can do our work. We can feel renewed; we have renewed energy; we feel renewed strength.

However, we must understand that we must have love and harmony in our anims at all times. That is all that is necessary. If our anims have love and harmony, then the anims will do the rest for us. They will attract love to us; they will attract harmony to us; they will attract all that is good to us. In this way then, we know that we are going to be able to progress in a most wonderful way. And when you do this, you are expressing God.

Rub your hands together, sound the A-U-M, and call out your teacher's name and your disciple number. One . . . two . . . three . . . AUM.

EIGHTH DISCOURSE

QUESTIONS AND ANSWERS

By Dr. Navajo

Good evening, friends. Let us say the affirmation, please.

> *I am master of myself.*
> *I am all powerful,*
> *And nothing can come to me*
> *Of an inferior nature.*
> *I am peace.*
> *I am power.*
> *I am all there is.*

W<small>ELL</small> F<small>RIENDS</small>, here we are again tonight to continue our activity with our blessed Agasha when he descends to control the channel to bring forth his message. We know that he is working diligently, especially for you. Besides those of you in the physical body, the many of us here in the astral world who have come into the fold also derive considerably from what is said.

However, in the time period preceding Agasha, as you might well know, we have a few moments to spend in

answering questions or clearing up other things that you do
not quite understand. This has been my desire for the past
number of weeks or months, and Agasha has gone along
with it quite nicely. Therefore I am going to take a moment
or two to answer a few questions—not too many, but a few.
If there is something perhaps that you do not quite understand, I would be very happy to try to give you the answer
by quoting Agasha. It does not make any difference what
it is; just go ahead and ask any question that you wish. You
now have the opportunity.

Elementals or Nature Spirits

Question: *Dr. Navajo, I came across a book recently on
fairies and other elemental nature spirits. Do these forms of
life actually exist, or are they nothing but mental bodies
created in the imagination by the mind?*

This is a very good question, and Agasha has covered the
entire subject of the elemental kingdom of Nature in the past,
although not recently. Yes, these elementals—little fairies,
elves, gnomes, brownies, sylphs, or whatever you want to
call them—do actually exist and are in fact a very vital form
of Nature. However, they live, move, and have their being
in the anim kingdom and are usually invisible to the average
man's sight. Children, however, have often seen them and
once in a great while they may even be seen by the adult.
Of course, in viewing them through the adult eye, we recognize that the subject becomes rather fantastic to the average
intellect and consequently much has been accredited to the
imagination.

These little nature spirits may be seen in the woods, or
among the flowers, or wherever it might be. But they are
doing their work. They are not just existing, in the sense of
the word. These little fellows have a job to do the same as
you have your job to do. They assist Nature. You say that
it is the insects, the bugs, and the germs that come along

that are necessary for the growth of a plant. True. If it were not for the little bugs that come along to destroy other destructive insects or germs, a plant would have a very difficult time growing. Thus all of the bugs and germs are either doing their good or doing their bad. You are aware of this, naturally.

But the little elves and other elemental spirits are even more conscious of these bugs than you are. The nature spirit is in tune with the germ and the bugs and such, and in reality he is doing more to keep the germinal and insect kingdom in line than you could possibly imagine. They do their work the same as the bees go about gathering nectar to create their honey. The elemental spirits go about drawing in anims to bring into manifestation the necessary atoms. Of course, they are not doing this exclusively, or all by themselves, but they are helping Nature which is God. Are there any other questions?

The Dark Forces

Question: *Yes, I have a question, Dr. Navajo. If the elemental spirits are assisting Nature, which you say is God, what composes or makes up the dark forces which seem to be in opposition to Nature or God?*

Before I answer your question, let me first state that an elemental spirit is not a human spirit; that is, it does not belong to the human kingdom. It is in a complete, separate kingdom of Nature all of its own. Now the "dark forces" that Agasha refers to from time to time are essentially built up of unlearned human spirits or souls. It is Man himself that makes up the dark forces, and the dark forces have nothing whatsoever to do with the nature spirits or the Deva Kingdoms.

We refer to the dark forces as such because they are made up of individuals who have not the illumination and who are living in darkness. They have not learned and they have not accomplished. They are not in a position to obey the God Kingdom because they are strictly mortal, strictly material-istic. They have come to the astral world unprepared and filled with revenge and hatred for their enemies. These individuals, taken as a whole, are what constitute the dark forces.

Let us say that you would leave the material world under great duress and with absolutely no understanding or com-passion for your fellowman. All that you could think of, after finding yourself over here on this side of life, would be wanting revenge for those who perhaps had sent you over here prematurely. You would find yourself in the company of thousands of others who had similar feelings, and the common thought form sent forth would hover as a dark cloud very near to the material world. Through ignorance, revenge, and lack of understanding your group would be endeavoring to create a new war and cause much destruction in the physical plane of life.

Situations such as the one described are causing plenty of hell all over the world at the present time, and these dark thought forms are seizing people right and left, like a disease, and causing them to react in a very negative manner. These thought forms are what create the evil forces, and indeed at times they become quite powerful. The Teachers of Light then do everything that they can to change the picture, and they stand as a bulwark of defense against these forces of evil which are identified in the field of truth as the dark forces.

We sometimes refer to these denizens of the lower astral consciousness as being unlearned or "earthbound spirits" because they have not yet ascended into the higher planes, although strictly speaking, an earthbound spirit is not neces-sarily a "dark force." In fact, he is usually only the victim. The thought forms created out of his own negative thinking have simply enslaved him. Moreover, until he first gives his consent, he cannot be reached by one who has ascended.

Yet the Illumined Ones are always descending to assist, but many times the earthbound spirit will flatly refuse to be helped and will thus continue on his own way and with the same actions. He is like a person heavily inebriated. He cannot be reached until he comes into what is called his sobriety, and his flat refusal to accept enlightenment will cause the light emanating from an Arisen One to not make any impression whatsoever. It is as though the earthbound spirit would tell the teacher to go and mind his own business.

This might cause one to question, "How is this possible if the teacher is so powerful?" The answer is, of course, that learning and unfolding is always an individual thing, and it is the individual responsibility for each one to take the initiative so that he may learn and grow and achieve that which he needs to achieve. Thus the earthbound spirit must first desire light before he can receive light into the darkness that imprisons him. Is there another question?

The Devil

Question: *Dr. Navajo, some time ago Agasha stated that life on the earth plane could be compared to a battle between God and the devil. I realize that God is the Universal Consciousness, and that sometimes we refer to God as being identical with Nature. But who and what is the devil?*

This is an excellent question, but before it can be answered properly we must first give thought to the three departments of your life—the mental aspect, the physical aspect, and the spiritual aspect. You cannot ignore any one of them. Each one is interrelated and interlaced with the two other components, and taken as a whole they constitute what is known as your soul pattern. Thus you become a triune being, which means three in one, and you are literally a trinity in unity.

Very well. Now please understand that mind, simply stated, is nothing more than awareness of being—awareness of the fact that you are an entity, an individualized ego, a personality. And following the pattern just set forth, this awareness then also takes on three separate and distinct, although interrelated, phases—a mental awareness, a physical awareness, and a spiritual awareness. The inner awareness of each of these subdivisions has to do with the motivating factor that moves you in your respective bodies, be they ethereal or be they physical. The outer awareness has to do with the creative function. Thus the inner awareness acts as the mover while the outer awareness acts as the creator.

Now where is the devil in all of this? The devil is the challenging factor, the opposition, and always in a lifetime it has to do with the outer mind of the mortal awareness. This outer mind of the mortal awareness, sometimes called the mortal mind, is always in opposition to the outer mind of the spiritual awareness which is called the divine mind. Now one has to yield to the other. Being of the outer awareness, they both are creators—the divine mind creating positive and spiritual thought forms as opposed to the mortal mind creating negative or mortal thought forms. The unlearned individual, having not yet awakened to his higher nature, is controlled by the negative creations of his mortal mind. And he not only is controlled by them, but he is also enslaved by them. These thought forms then bring into manifestation what is known as the demon-self, or in other words the devil.

Now the enlightened individual, one who has awakened to his higher God-Self has dissipated this demon-self through starvation; that is, he has ceased to feed this monster with negative thinking, thus yielding the power and the control over his life to the divine mind or the God-Self. His pathway is then illumined with light as opposed to the pathway of the unlearned individual which is enveloped in darkness.

You see, there is no special devil running around causing trouble for mankind, for you know in your philosophy that the only devil that ever existed is the devil that men have created through their evil actions. It is mankind itself who creates the devil, or rather individual devils, through its negative and wrongful thinking and actions. Now this devil that man creates is not another being. No indeed. Man's thinking creates a thought form which then envelops the thinker and takes charge of his very being. In other words, man becomes enslaved by his own thoughts and literally becomes the devil himself.

Every time you lose your temper or become ever so negative in your thinking, it is your own special demon-self that takes over your mortal consciousness, and this demon-self then temporarily enslaves and imprisons the God-Self. Eventually, once you have calmed down and returned to your senses, the God-Self will then once more take over, if you will permit it to do so, and the light from the God-Self can once more illuminate your pathway through life. Thus we explain the eternal "battle" between God and the devil.

The demon-self is very often referred to as the "monster." It is the dweller on the threshold that man has to confront and subdue. It is the dragon that must be slain. Every negative thought we think becomes a mental entity that the monster then draws unto himself to feed upon. So we must burst these mental entities like bubbles so that they will have no potency in our lives, and we do that daily when we go into the silence and become ever so peaceful within our own being. This is what Kraio did when it is said in the Bible that he cast out demons. Thus the monster is dissipated through starvation, and he has then lost control over our life. We must be ever so careful to not give the monster power; then, if we do this, we will not be controlled by the demon-self and thus not be held back from the unfoldment that we are entitled to receive.

However, Agasha says that sooner or later the demon-self will try to defy, and it is then that our monster will confront us and we shall have to do battle with that monster. This apparition or monstrous feeling can be very frightening, mortally. And if this occurs, then you must say to yourself,

"This that appears before me is the monster. Therefore I shall dissipate him. He has no control over me, none whatsoever. It is only my own mental creation. He has followed me long enough, therefore I will not entertain him. I give him no power and no control over my kingdom. I eliminate him and I shall not recreate him or bring him back into manifestation ever again. I shall show him the way out." And if these words are spoken in earnest once you have confronted your own individual monster, what a burden will then be lifted from you! You will then feel so free, and so easy, and you will then truly have real freedom upon the physical plane. Well folks, now that we have dissipated and disposed of the monster, are there any other questions?

The Astral Body

Question: *Yes, I have a question, Dr. Navajo. I have read recently that when one leaves the physical body and enters the realms of spirit, he becomes a part of the "Oneness"; yet, in your talk on the astral world a few classes ago, you discussed the reality of the "individual" astral body. Could you clarify this point a little further?*

Agasha has made the statement over and over again that you must never at any time in your unfoldment allow yourself to think that in the ethereal kingdom you will not have a body. I realize that there are schools upon the earth plane that teach that when you become a part of the "Oneness" you will have no body. They indicate that you become merely a part of the overall picture, the Oneness, and this is confusing to many. There is a lot to be clarified in the field of occultism and the various other "isms" in related fields, but let me say this in answer to your question: Consciousness can exist as a point of light, true. But when you live, move, and have your being in *any* plane of the ethereal or etheric states of consciousness, you must necessarily have a body to function in that is composed of the elements of that particular plane of consciousness. Otherwise you would have no way to be singled out as an individual entity.

Now the body that will be yours in the next phase of your existence, in the astral world, will be similar although not identical to the present physical body that you now possess. It will be a spiritualized version of your present body without its defects and impurities. For instance: the fluid that your heart will pump through your astral veins will be pure and not contaminated. We call this liquid "astral fluid". The blood that is now pumped through your physical veins is impure and can carry disease. You must remember that there is no disease in the astral world. Your scars or other disfigurements will have disappeared unless there were some particular reason that you wished to retain them. Otherwise your astral body will be a replica of your present body with absolutely every component part fully intact.

However, certain functions that you must now necessarily perform in the physical body will not be required in the astral body. You do not have to partake of food and the body elimination is different. You do not need rest as you need it here on the earth plane. The only time that you would become oblivious to your immediate community would be when you had a desire to rest the mind. In that case you would go into a state of meditation whereby you could be said to be oblivious to your immediate surroundings. Otherwise, you would always be conscious and very much awake. The sexual act is entirely different, although sexual attraction is definitely not lost in the astral world. Sex becomes here more of a blending of forces whereby the two blend themselves mentally, ethereally (the counterpart of physically), and spiritually. Sex in the ethereal planes, I might add, is much more intense than upon the physical plane.

Thus we find that there is a great similarity between the astral kingdom and much on the earth plane, even though some of the functions of living are entirely different. But basically, they are very similar worlds. Now inasmuch as here in the astral world we do not have to eat, cook, or earn money in order to eke out a living, one might think that we would be concerned with so much time on our hands. This, I can assure you, will never be a problem to one awakened. We graciously utilize all of the existing periods. We are always busying ourself in some particular effort. No one ever says to anyone in the astral world that he should do this or that or tells him that he must partake in some particular activity or otherwise he will be penalized. No, there is none of that. It is always up to the individual. He may do whatever he pleases, and he is free to do so regardless of whether it is good or bad, but his progress will depend entirely upon his desire to bring forth good. Is there another question?

Mental Imprisonment

Question: *But Dr. Navajo, what if that person who is free to do anything he so pleases infringes upon the rights of others?*

I was expecting that response because it is a perfectly logical question to ask. The answer is that such action in the ethereal world could result in one being imprisoned mentally. And this self-imprisonment would be meted out by your own God-Self. There is no organized police force over here on this side of life. But you would in all probability end up in your own mental prison which would be very similar to being imprisoned behind bars in a penal institution on the earth plane. However, mental imprisonment is possibly more agonizing than earthly confinement.

Now mental imprisonment is also very much in evidence on the earth plane as you well know. Aside from your mental institutions which take care of the many who have closed the door to outer reality, there are also those who even though they are quite "sane" are also in their own mental prison. These are those who flatly refuse to learn their lessons. Many will say, "I am too old to learn," and they thus imprison themselves by limiting themselves with such a very, very narrow vision. Agasha answers this by saying, "You must have a broad vision, a broad scope. You must not be narrow-minded and you must be willing to change. You must adjust that which needs to be adjusted, and you must try to encourage your outer self that it is to your own benefit that you should pursue to advance in this manner. Then, if you do this, you will prevent yourself from blundering as you have blundered before in the past."

Many on the earth plane question and wonder what they had done to deserve some particular predicament that they find themselves in. Or perhaps they are only placed in an unfavorable environment. To answer them, Agasha can only say, "Look within yourself and see the picture: this is why you blundered." He has said on several occasions, "If I could take you into your inner kingdom for about five moments of your earthly time, you could see the picture— the picture that is you. Your soul would let you see not only what you are going through, but also why you are going through it. Then you would realize that there is a just God and that eventually everything will right itself, correct itself, and adjust itself. You would also see what you must do for all this to come about." A few moments of reflection on these words of Agasha will almost in themselves give you the answer to most of your problems. Just meditate on them sometime and see what happens. Are there any other questions?

Bottled Sun

Question: *Dr. Navajo, there is much talk today relative to the so-called energy crisis. Has Agasha ever given any information pertaining to the source of energy in the future, and if so, how it will be utilized?*

Indeed he has! Of course, basically, he has always said that the energy of the future will all be atomic although not in the same way that you use atomic energy today. The secret seems to be hidden within the anim, the modifier of the atom, and when the scientists of the earth plane finally discover the higher occult laws of the anim, the atomic age will then be here. He often refers to the anim as the cousin of the atom, and sometimes he calls it the governor or counterpart of the atom. The scientists of the earth refer to the anim as anti-matter inasmuch as they have discovered that its electric and magnetic properties are completely opposite to the atom.

Specifically though, Agasha has stated as far back as 1950 that eventually the scientific mind would capture a ray from the sun and then bottle it. This may sound strange, but he used the term in your vernacular, calling it "bottled sun." This energy ray from the sun would be captured and then placed within a glass tube where it would circulate millions and millions of times in, as Agasha says, the twinkling of an eye. A current similar to a galvanic current would then be generated that would cause a slight secretion to occur within the confines of the glass. This secretion would never be dissipated unless the glass were to be broken, in which case it would simply go back into the ether from which it came. This intermingling of animatical forces with electrical forces would then produce light and heat. Agasha stated that the appearance of these glass tubes would resemble your modern-day neon lights, although they would be produced in various sizes and shapes. Thus you will have for all intents and purposes "bottled sun."

The lighting that you have now in your homes will become obsolete in comparison with that which will be used in the future. An outgrowth of this bottled sun energy will be light globes or tubes that will always be illuminated. You may place them in your dark closets or anywhere else in the house for that matter. You may take this ball, this very fancy light, and perhaps you may provide a shade over it so that it would blend in with the rest of your furnishings. If you place it over here, for instance, it will be morning every day for many years to come as it will always be illuminated. And when it becomes dark, your house will automatically be lighted.

Agasha also said that this bottled sun energy will likewise be of great therapeutic value. It will be used to bring into manifestation powerful iridescent lights in many different colors which will send out various rays. These rays will be more powerful than your ultraviolet rays and more penetrating than the infrared rays. They may be placed over the eye or over any other affected part of the body and will be of great therapeutic value in healing. There will be the pure white light, the pale blue, the pale red, the dark red, and various other colors to treat the different diseases. In other words, the rays from these lights will destroy the germs and eliminate the bacteria in your body, and these rays will be many, many thousands of times more powerful than the light that is employed at the present time that has been proven to be of therapeutic value.

And before we leave this subject, let me bring out one other point. Even though it sounds fantastic at the present time, Agasha also stated, as I recall, that this bottled sun energy will eventually be mixed with a certain liquid and then taken internally. And it will not only give you energy and strength in its use as a tonic, but the moment that it enters your blood stream you will find that it will become organic. Through this method many of the diseases of today that are now incurable will be eliminated. This takes in cancer and especially leukemia, and they will be very easily taken care of. Are there any other questions?

Raising the Dead

Question: *Yes, Dr. Navajo. It is reported in the Bible that Jesus raised the dead; that is, he brought back to life at least one person who had already died. Is this true?*

Agasha has covered this subject many times in the past, and it is certainly worth repeating again tonight. The answer

to your question is both yes and no, the key being the defi-
nition of the precise point in time that the body is either dead
or alive. Your medical science has observed that the body
dies by degrees; that is, first one organ will cease to function,
then another, and so forth until ultimately all of the organs
and then finally even all of the cells within the organs can be
said to be dead. Even consciousness follows an intermittent
pattern during the time that a patient is in the process of
dying. He will be alternately conscious for a while, after
which he will lapse into a state of unconsciousness, and then
he will return to consciousness once again. So where is the
precise point of death?

It used to be that medical science determined death to be
the point at which the heart ceased beating. Now I believe
the generally accepted theory is that death is the point at
which the brain is no longer alive. But all this controversy
makes no real difference as far as the true occult understanding of death is concerned. You in your philosophy have been
taught that death is that precise point in time when the silver
cord of life is severed from the physical body. Once this
silver cord of life is severed, the spirit can never again return
to the physical body, and this severance can occur almost
any time during the process of death after the patient lapses
into unconsciousness.

Now there was a time on the earth when a certain rare
disease came back into manifestation. This disease caused
the body to temporarily slip into a state of suspended animation whereby absolutely all of the vital functions slowed
down and stopped. There was a temporary cessation of all
of the vital functions of the body. This included the circulation of the blood, the pulsation of the heart, and the breathing of air into the lungs. To all intents and purposes the body
was lifeless. Now in sleeping sickness of today the patient
merely falls asleep. The other disease was different.

Now during the time that Jesus was in Palestine there were
a few cases of this disease. It was very rare, however. Oh
perhaps, within a few years, a case would break out over

here or over there, but they were very few. These were the cases that Jesus came upon. And when he would come upon a case of this type, he could see clairvoyantly that the silver cord of life was still attached to the body. Therefore, from his observations he knew just what to do. Through his magnetic power, through his healing power, he was able then to draw the spirit back into the body and force the vital functions back into operation. Thus the person arose, and so it was recorded in the good book. According to the writings he caused the dead to arise, and that is seemingly just what he did. But they really were not dead. They were merely in a state of suspended animation. There is not a healer on the earth plane who has ever existed, or who will ever exist in the future, who is able to bring the spirit back into the body once the silver cord is severed. It simply is against the law. Is there another question?

Astrology

Question: *Dr. Navajo, astrology is also a very controversial subject today. The scientific society does not accept it at all, and yet there are some very learned philosophers who not only teach it but also treat it as a true science. What does Agasha say relative to the truth or the untruth of astrology?*

Astrology is a very ancient science dating back not only 7,000 years to Agasha's period in Austa, Egypt, but also dating back well into the Atlantean period. Agasha states that there were many learned astrologers during his day, although he personally was more of a student of the numerical influences on life. He makes the statement that basically, astrology is a true and exact science, although he is not aware of how much the astrologer of today has actually rediscovered. But in comparison with the knowledge the ancient astrologers possessed, the astrologer of today knows but very little.

The laws of astrology basically stem from the very structure of the universe. He has told us that we are living in a cluster of seven solar systems that are both interwoven and interrelated. Each of these solar systems depends upon the other six solar systems for its sustenance, and they all have their respective suns and planets. This would be comparable to a gigantic, moving mechanism with each component part working inwardly and outwardly in perfect harmony and rhythm. Now each planetary body sends out vibratorial rays that affect and influence all of the other planetary bodies within the system.

Man, being a spiritual being living within this complex system, is likewise affected by these planetary influences and vibratorial rays that are constantly bombarding his physical body. He is so affected because the glandular system within his body is in direct accord with these astronomical and astrological forces. Each gland and psychic center within his body is vibrating with a particular rate of vibration that is either in harmony with or discordant to these external influences and vibratory waves. Thus all of the different members of his body are affected, and so in its entirety we can say that the planets play a very important part in the life of mankind. As above; so below. Man, being the microcosm of the macrocosm, cannot divorce himself from the universe. This entire subject, taken as a whole, is basically what we refer to as astrology.

Now strangely enough, your date of birth is very important unto you as an individual, both numerically speaking and astrologically speaking. The state of the universe at the precise moment that you are born is somehow reflected into your own psychic pattern. This stamps you and gives you a particular rate of vibration. You would not have to tell certain Ascended Masters your date of birth. They would automatically know it the moment they tuned in on your vibration. They are able to judge an individual who is born under a particular sign, and they are able to tell much relative to the character that he possesses or is likely to develop under such a sign.

Yet perhaps you were born on the same day as your

neighbor, and then, let us say that your characteristics are quite different. How is this? Agasha says that the answer is your spiritual elevation. Your spiritual elevation is either higher or lower than your neighbor's, and thus you would have a rate of vibration in a higher or a lower octave that could be completely different from his. You see, your entire character and personality is not quite as simple as it would appear to be on the surface. There are too many factors and variables involved to make any broad, overall statements.

There is one important point, however, that we should make at this time before we leave this subject. Agasha has said over and over again that if you are being controlled by vibrational rays or planetary influences of an inferior nature, as you advance spiritually you will be able to elevate your consciousness to the point whereby these negative influences will nave no control over you. They will have no effect on you whatsoever for you will have arisen above these negative vibrations. Only those who have not elevated their consciousness become victims of any negative static that might be in their atmosphere as a result of vibrations radiating from a particular planet that is in their sign. True, it might bring a problem into your life, but that problem was not given you to victimize you. It was given you as a challenge so that you could hurdle it and then become ever so much more powerful. Well, let us have another question now.

Symbology: The Language of the Soul

Question: *Dr. Navajo, many times just before the meditational period Agasha will ask us to try to see a particular symbol. And if a symbol is seen in meditation, where does it come from and why is it presented to us at that particular time? In other words, what has symbology to do with our unfoldment?*

Symbology is a fundamental part of your unfoldment. It has a great meaning to you in your organization and in your classes because symbology is vital. It can be said that symbology is a solid language, but it only becomes a live language when one begins to understand the symbols of the past. That is why all disciples of the higher order eventually begin to see symbols, and with the symbol usually comes an impression which takes the form of a mental picture. Then, of course, there is also the vision—the clear vision of an event either in the past or the future. Thus there are three major items in your unfoldment: first the symbol, then the impression, and lastly the vision. Now why are these so all-important? They are important because they all come from the soul.

However, when the disciple first begins to see symbols, he does not on the surface usually understand them. First he will question the experience itself and then he will ponder over the symbols. I know that they were very perplexing to me in my day upon the earth plane, and I would spend many an hour trying to discern the true meaning of a particular symbol. But that is what you are supposed to do—ponder over it, work with it, visualize it, and lastly use it. Your soul has literally handed you a key to unlocking that vast storehouse of memory contained therein.

Now the symbols that the soul brings forth were created long, long ago. Agasha states that we have to go back to Atlantis to find their source, and even that consciousness is not their true source for some symbols are as eternal as life itself. All of the symbols of Freemasonry, I might add, stem first from Atlantis and then from the great Peace Period in Austa, Egypt. The symbols of all of the higher orders are established symbols that pertain to each individual kingdom—first the universe, then the planets, and on and on until we take on the higher vibration and study ourselves individually.

We study ourself in reference to our character or the characteristics that we might possess at the time. And when we do, we realize that there be the action and there be the result. The entire drama then takes on the form of a symbol. It becomes a fixation. It is in your aura; it is in your soul pattern. As the symbol is created it becomes fixed, and there within your aura it is implanted. Then, many generations and many lifetimes later, it will suddenly loom up before the mortal consciousness. Why does it do this? The answer is that your soul is literally handing you the key to reel yourself back to the event, or the act, or whatever it might be, that brought the symbol into manifestation. But first you must pick up the symbol and recognize it! And once you do this, once you have given it the recognition it so justly deserves, it will then enable you to drift back in consciousness to that point in time wherever it be. Thus it can be said, and it has been said many, many times in the past, that symbolism is the language of the soul.

I do not know who first stated that a picture is worth ten thousand words, but whoever it was, he was certainly speaking the truth. Words alone will never do justice to a great work of art or architecture. Can you adequately describe a great masterpiece of sculpture? No indeed, you cannot. But is not that great piece of sculpture, or painting, or whatever it be, actually nothing more than but a symbol of some great event in the histories of mankind? Has not the man Jesus, dying on the cross, become a symbol that may represent God to the average Christian lay mind? Even take yourself. You are known to others by that body that you possess, but is not that body only a symbol of the real You? All down through history we find that men have been inclined to deal with dumb idols. That is, on the surface they were dumb idols, but in reality they represented something much dearer and more important than what appeared on the surface. We have always had the symbols and the dumb idols down through the ages to represent this or that because it was the only way to stimulate the mortal or the outer mind. Today the Catholic church is very much in evidence of this as it keeps these symbols constantly before the minds of men, women, and children. But the symbol itself is not important; it is that great meaning back of the symbol that becomes so all-important.

It can be said that the soul is gradually satisfying itself as it observes the mortal self struggling along with its individual responsibility. Agasha has said that we cannot set aside our responsibility in thinking that we are going to pick it up later. It will never be escaped. It is something that one has to face whether one likes it or not. Yet, if you can only realize this and pay the penalty now, or work out whatever it be, then your soul is going to bring to your outer consciousness that special symbol. Your soul then embraces you as a wonderful individual. It praises you in every sense of the word. The Higher Self is always eternally grateful that the mortal self has finally learned or conquered whatever it was supposed to conquer. Then you are congratulated by the soul and shown that special symbol. But if the soul learns that you are not grasping, or that you are not growing or expanding, then naturally it becomes disturbed. I should not use the term disturbed because the soul is never disturbed, but it merely then goes into a state of submission and waits until the mortal mind is capable of responding to the God call.

All of this then leads up to a question that was asked of Agasha some time ago—way back in 1951 I believe—and the question pertained to the various methods of soul communication, that is, the means whereby the mortal can actually communicate with his or her Higher Self. And his answer was that it can be done through the universal language of symbolism, which the soul can speak so very clearly. Once the disciple is able to understand this symbolic language, to interpret the symbols correctly, then he also will be able to understand the things that are or the things that are about to be. This is what is known as becoming attuned to the Infinite State, becoming attuned to all that is in the great Consciousness of Immensity. He can then very readily understand why men are suffering on the earth today and why they have suffered down through the ages.

But how does one go about finding the symbols to interpret? The answer is that they are all around and about you. Every dream that you have is nothing more than a symbolic presentation of some problem that is affecting or has affected your everyday life. Understand symbolism, and you can interpret the dream. Then there is the symbolism contained within the study of astrology, numerology, and so forth. Some teachers in other organizations highly recommend the I Ching, that ancient Chinese book of divination that is sometimes called *The Book of Changes.* And then, of course, in the Western tradition there is always the Tarot, that ancient and mystical pack of cards that is held in such high esteem by many on the earth plane, even today.

There is one catch to all of this, however. And that catch is that there has been a discrepancy down through the years and down through the generations insofar as knowing the correct meaning of these symbols of the past. Agasha stated on that evening that I refer to that the Tarot cards of today are supposed to be well authenticated insofar as they display the symbols of man's actions on the earth plane. They can also show the results of man's actions and the possibilities of certain things transpiring in an individual life once these cards are played with, worked with, and studied. However, there is still that discrepancy. Agasha said that we have to go back many generations before we can arrive at the true symbology relative to the Tarot cards as you refer to them today. This discrepancy then can throw many people off relative to the correct indications of the future and so forth.

But the truly amazing thing in all of this is that the soul, being infinitely intelligent, can work through a deck of picture symbols and cause the mortal self to so shuffle the cards, or toss the coins as in the I Ching, so that the correct symbols will appear and show the probable solution to any stated problem. This, indeed, is truly amazing. Does it always work? No. But the fault lies in the correct interpretation of the symbology by the mortal, and not with the soul which can express so adequately the things that are, as well as the things that are about to be.

Well folks, this little discourse has dug into the subject of symbology a little deeper than I originally intended, but in discussing it I too seem to now have a better understanding. But one final word of caution—if you have a teacher, please take your problems to your teacher first. Remember he is your best friend, and he is far more capable of reading the symbols pertaining to your life than you are. Is there another question?

The All-Seeing Eye

Question: *Yes, I have one more question, Dr. Navajo. Just exactly what is the All-Seeing Eye, and how is it significant for our unfoldment?*

Going back into recorded history for the past seven to nine thousand years, the All-Seeing Eye has always been a symbol indicating the eye of the soul. Through all of these years this one single eye has been in evidence in one way or another. Many times it has gazed at you from the canvas of some artist, or from some beautiful fresco, and it is even represented in the apex of that great monument of spirituality, the Great Pyramid, exactly as it is shown in the currency of the United States today.

The All-Seeing Eye is a most significant symbol because of its great meaning. It represents the inner soul, the integral part of the Universal Spirit God—the Absolute. It means also the "I" within, and this all-seeing "I", being all-knowing and ever present, then becomes the God Presence—the God within. Many in the field of seeking are privileged to have it manifest before them. When it does manifest, they see this one single eye looking at them. It can be as large as, shall we say, a horse's eye. Some have compared it to the beautiful eye of a camel. Sometimes it appears as the eye of a human being. It can be brown or blue or any of the various other colors. Indeed the student is blessed who sees it, for its manifestation is the finest indication of his unfoldment of the inner kingdom. This living symbol, then, is what is known as the All-Seeing Eye.

It is also the central symbol of the consciousness of Austa, Egypt. Agasha refers to this consciousness as the Grand Unit of the Three. Its symbol is a trinity consisting of a pyramid with a white base and a golden apex. There in the center of the pyramid is the star and crescent. And there in the center of the apex is the All-Seeing Eye. All of the teachers of the Agashan organization belong to this Grand Unit of the Three, and the complete pyramid, along with its associated parts, is its symbol. Now this particular symbol also signifies membership in the Great White Way which was established during the Atlantean period. The Great White Way, incidentally, embraces all of the many Masters of Light who have ascended from the earth. You people on earth refer to it as the White Brotherhood. The Agashan teachers refer to it as the Great White Way. In any event, it is a great organization and indeed it is very powerful.

Returning once more to the All-Seeing Eye itself, let us examine its function. This third eye, as it is often referred to, is ordinarily indicated as being located in the center of the forehead. It comes into being because of two glands that are very important in the activating of this all-seeing third eye. These are the pituitary gland at the base of the brain and the pineal gland at the midsection of the brain. The pineal, if functioning properly, will enable one to see into the various strata of the ethereal planes of life. He is then able to see coming events as all actions in life cast their shadows before them, and in this manner he can then know the result of an action before it is completed.

Now to the one who is able to pick up these visions, it would seem that he is seeing them in the center of his forehead. This only verifies that that is where the reactive forces are, and the gland seems to secrete the necessary fluid for him to see clairvoyantly. Through this action one is actually standing in a dimension that permits the individual to gaze into the past, the present, and the future at one and the same time. It may seem to the unlearned to be rather fantastic, but nevertheless it is so.

Now then if a person is seeing clairvoyantly, he quite naturally sees visions, he sees panoramic views, he sees people's faces, he sees symbols; in fact, he can see almost anything in a clear, concise manner. And it is usually in Technicolor, if I may use that term. This is what is called clairvoyance. On the other hand we have the psychometrist. He is one who from the simple act of holding in his hands a coin or an article belonging to someone else, can then pick up conditions relative to that person who has worn or carried the article for an appreciable time. Now right down through the middle of these two extremes, we have the impressionist. The average person in the class falls into this category. But remember that impressions are never to be ignored because impressions are often just as accurate as visions, and ofttimes they are even far more accurate than the visions themselves because we have a tendency to misinterpret the vision. However, all of these psychic manifestations are the result of the action of this inner eye.

Each of us, to a greater or lesser degree, has the ability to use this third eye. However, there was a time in our evolution on the earth plane when this faculty was developed to a much larger extent than it is today. In addition to what we call animal instinct, we had at our disposal a sixth sense or extended vision which alerted us to danger, storms, or whatever might be threatening. At that time this was very important because it enabled us to survive against sometimes overwhelming odds.

Today, the reason that this sixth sense is dormant in the average person is due to the fact that you now depend upon other means for protection. It is understandable that if you fail to use a member of the body, it will in time become atrophied from lack of use. Thus down through the ages this faculty has become dimmed because of a growing involvement in materialistic activities. Mankind in general has become oblivious to things in the ethereal planes and is now conscious only of the material world or of mundane affairs.

Therefore these faculties today must be re-unfolded, as we might say, so that once more the visions and the symbols of the past can reenter the consciousness of the average man.

True, we are in evidence of some children being reborn who are immediately in possession of this sixth sense, and some individuals have quite extensive power. In others, it is there but not developed. These latter ones do, however, have many premonitions, see visions, and bring into manifestation much that is beyond their comprehension. In both cases it shows a faculty that is possessed by all, yet in most individuals it is still dormant and unused.

Agasha's light is now building up in the center of the room, and I am going to have to step aside in a few moments. However, he seems to be giving me a little more time and so perhaps we can have one more short question.

Spirituality

Question: *Dr. Navajo, could you define the word "spirituality"? I know that this is a difficult question to answer without first giving it sufficient thought, but in a few words how should a person live his life here in a materialistic world, in the twentieth century, and still be a spiritual person? What has Agasha said relative to this subject?*

Yes, I would be very happy to have a go at attempting to answer your question, and it is really not as difficult to answer as you might surmise. In the first place, *spirituality* is a word that is used far too loosely in attaching it to individuals. A person who exhibits wonderful psychic abilities could well be far from spiritual. And one who intellectually expresses beautiful thoughts, speaks learnedly of the life that is and the life that is to come, also does not necessarily indicate spirituality.

Spirituality is simply what the word must imply—something that is beyond the mundane. It deals with that which is much finer than gross material. A spiritual person is one who has brought unto himself a revelation—an exotic wonderful feeling of knowing that he is expressing good here on the earth plane.

A truly spiritual person is one who has absorbed the great light of wisdom in his growth toward unfoldment, one who stays on the path, and one who watches the behavior of his fellowman with an understanding mind, neither condemning nor condoning. A spiritual person is also one who has controlled and become the master over the physical aspects, the passions, and the gross desires of mortal living. Now I do not mean to imply that one should not enjoy the raptures that can be experienced in mortal living; no, I do not mean that. I am only stating that a spiritual person is not controlled by these passions. He is also one who meets and deals with fairly and squarely the challenging factors of everyday life that relate to his neighbors, friends, and situations. He knows that he will be controlled by no one other than his higher God-Self.

Spirituality does not abide only in the mind of the intellectual; no, not by any means. It also abides in the minds of those not so endowed intellectually but who still strive for unfoldment. Consequently one who has unfolded his spiritual aspects does not hover only in the mansion of the wealthy, but on the contrary he will find his way into the smallest home. And more often than not, it is here rather than in the more imposing mansions that he will find a gracious welcome. The meek, the uneducated, and the people in average circumstances are most certainly not to be forgotten and ignored.

Among the millions of people who attend church regularly, of course there are many who live their lives abiding by the rules of the organization as they see it. However, if it were possible to compare statistically or numerically the number of souls who really make this effort with those who live hypocritically, a large number of the members of the church group would fall into the fold of hypocrisy. We know we have evidence of this, and unfortunately this even includes a few members of the cloth.

However, if it were not for the churches of the earth plane, the world would be in a far worse state than it is in at the present time and we must salute them for their endeavors. The churches have been employed to keep men fairly straight upon the earth plane, and they are good and they have accomplished much. But even so, we are in evidence of much behavior that is wrong and we must face facts if we are to honestly appraise the situation. I might add that more wars have been fought in the interests of so-called religion than for any other cause. However, this is not necessarily the condition as it exists today.

Please understand that I have only made the foregoing statements to point out that you do not necessarily have to go to church to be spiritual. Being spiritual is being true to thine own higher God-Self. Perhaps the following affirmation given by Agasha can better express the point that I am trying to make. Agasha has told us to say, "I am the Way. I am the Light. I come here to learn and to grow, and even though I see in the behavior of my fellowman that which I cannot go along with, I am not here to make judgement for I am not the judge. The Soul judge within will make that judgement when the day comes, for I know that the day one is freed from the physical body is Judgement Day for that individual. I know that he will then gravitate to the hell or the heaven that he has earned for himself according to his actions upon earth."

Perhaps in summary we can state that the spiritual one is one who makes a genuine effort to walk in the light, stays on the path, and tries never to be discouraged by the obstacles which may block the path from time to time. He is one who not only believes but knows that as he continues through life in this manner, he will eventually attain that wonderful, indescribable feeling that is brought about through the awakening within himself of the God Presence.

There will be no need to even question whether the word *spiritual* applies to one in this category, for by his works he shall be known. Then as he brings forth light and peace, and as he excels in material affairs, he shall then accomplish that which he must accomplish in order to fulfill his mission in this particular embodiment.

No more questions, folks. Here he comes . . . .

NINTH DISCOURSE

THE SOUL PATTERN

By Agasha

MY BLESSED CHILDREN—Manzaholla and bless each and every one. The Universal God is very conscious of us, indeed. And we realize that we are striving to conquer the physical, to conquer the mental bodies, and to do everything that we possibly can to become attuned to that Universal God Consciousness or Infinite State. We have gone far and we shall continue; but in the interim, when it behooves you to take care of the many things that arise in your physical life, we realize that you must then go within the silence.

As we go within the silence and enter this beautiful kingdom, we are actually attuning ourself to the Consciousness of our homeland in Immensity. And as we go back into that consciousness, we start to study life most religiously. While you are in that state of mind, it is then that your God-Self shall speak to you; and your God-Self, in collaboration with your teacher, will see you through.

As you are now in the physical state, the imperfect state, the state often referred to as God's kindergarten, we realize that these trials can sometimes become unbearable. But you must not falter, beloved ones; you must do everything you

207

can to prepare your kingdom and to fortify it from approaching dangers that often lie so very, very near.

We know that as millions of souls are being freed from the
physical body, millions of other souls are likewise coming
into this life. Now each soul has a definite pattern to fulfill
or to follow, and this then will be the subject of my talk
tonight.

The Soul Pattern Is the Soul Chart

This "soul pattern" was created long ago at the very
beginning of our evolution upon the earth. It hovers very
near the physical body and is illuminated by the soul consciousness, or in other words, the God State. It is indeed
the chart of the life pattern of the soul; however, as you
enter this physical plane, the mortal outer consciousness is
oblivious to not only the pattern but also to what it is to
fulfill in this life. But the soul, being attuned to the God State
as well as the Consciousness of Immensity, studies this soul
pattern because the soul pattern is definitely the soul chart.
It is a chart of the three departments of your life: the mental,
the physical, and the spiritual. The soul is very capable of
reading this chart and knowing what step to take to counteract an approaching danger in your earthly existence.

This becomes a very interesting feature tonight, children,
because of the contrast between the mortal mind, which is
so incapable, and the soul that is so very capable of ascer-
taining that which it desires to know. When your body is at
rest and your outer mind becomes quiescent, then your inner
mind takes over in collaboration, we might say, with the
soul. It can then very clearly read the soul chart and in this
way understand its karmic relations and its karmic duty
unto society as well as thyself.

In this way, then, we are able to understand that the soul
is busying itself with things that concern you: your life, your
character, your earthly foundation. It is ever on the guard
so as to know which step to take to counteract whatever it
is that might befall you. So when your spirit apparently has

stepped aside, when it has projected itself into the astral realms at night while the body sleeps, then the soul takes over and observes this chart just like anyone else would read a chart on the physical plane.

Earthly historians go back into the past for 1,000 years, 2,000 years, or even 5,000 years or longer as a supposition. They chart the rise and fall of the various civilizations or dynasties. Thus they are able to observe from the chart the results arising from the actions of mankind. And so it is with the soul and thine own kingdom. Perhaps the same thing that you have failed to overcome had been your lesson innumerable times, but each time you had failed to learn it. Thus the soul goes back to study the chart, to study the condition that you did create, and to realize the lesson that you had failed to learn. It means then that the soul is striving desperately for the mortal mind to first comprehend, and then overcome that which it had failed so miserably to overcome in so many lives.

Accomplishing this enables you to become what we term in this wonderful understanding, a chief disciple. This in turn means that you are on your way to becoming an adept in time. I do not mean that this will necessarily happen on the physical plane; no, I do not mean that. But after all, striving to become an adept when you are in spirit is just as important in that out-of-the-flesh state as it is in the flesh.

We know that all of the great Intermediaries whom we have contacted recognize you people in the Western world as conquering and overcoming many things. Knowing the many temptations that you have as you live your life and the many trials that you go through, they admire you. They admire you because the average disciple on the path is greater in many ways than those that have isolated themselves from the world. This I have informed you several times in the past, and it has been so verified by the Intermediaries as well as my own teacher, Coman Coban. They recognize that you are now having the experiences that you should have in order to prepare yourself and build character for the greater tomorrow, so to speak. You live thoroughly each day so that you may enjoy the fruits of the actions that you had put forth on your own individual path.

There Are No Two Paths Alike

You must also learn that everyone has a different path of life to follow. Indeed, there are no two paths alike. They are like your fingerprints; there seem to be no two alike. True, they may be similar, but not in their entirety, and they stamp you upon the physical plane. Therefore, when I refer to your soul pattern, I am referring to that which is distinctly different from your fellows. It is yours. It is what you have created that stamps you as an individual.

It was once said by the Master, "By your works, ye shall be known." However, your works are only known by the Masters of Light, those who had preceded you in learning. It is only those who have had their ascendency who can return and recognize you by your works. You deceive not the teacher. You deceive not your soul, nor God, nor anything of a higher nature. For it is all imprinted right there upon your path of life—your soul pattern of life. There it is: everything that brings out your character, your life, your mission, your trials, your tribulations, or to sum it all up— your karma.

So there it is, right before the Master to view. It may also become visible to you in time, as you raise your vibration, and when your soul deems that you are ready. Then you may actually see this soul pattern of life, although in all probability it will not be understood.

However, it is not for me to say that I or your teacher are necessarily in a position to minutely describe that which transpired millions of years ago in your life. But we are in a position to become conscious of the soul pattern; and then through our efforts we may scrutinize it, read it, and otherwise try to more or less decipher it. We will use these terms for want of better terminologies. Then after we go through this procedure, we are better able to realize your true spir-

itual status while you are in the flesh. But we are conscious
of it only when we are desirous of seeing it; and when you
are out of the physical body, your soul pattern is not made
known unto the average astral inhabitant.

Therefore when your soul pattern shows that you are
ready, the teacher will appear. But if you are steeped in
materiality, then you are lost temporarily. This is a lesson
that I want all of you children to understand. But when you
as a true disciple say unto yourself, "I am ready," the
teacher will appear and he can then take everything into
account. He can work with you whether you be in or out
of the flesh. Isn't that a joyful thought tonight, children?
Isn't it a wonderful thing to know that you have that wonderful, loyal teacher of yours who is going to help you to
overcome that which is to be overcome in a lifetime? We
had escaped in other lives; we had failed to overcome and
it shows right there in our chart. And that which we had
failed to overcome had then brought us right back again
onto the physical plane. Isn't that something to think about
tonight, children of the earth?

Your Soul Will Put You Through the Tests

Now the Teachers of Light are descending unto you to
introduce you to your Higher Self. And once you are introduced to your Higher Self, that same Higher Self is going
to put you through the tests. I say this because someday
you are going to find yourself seemingly in that predicament.
The test will come. The test had come in the past, then it
had gone, but it shall come again. Believe me, disciples of
the earth, these tests that are given by your God-Self, the
soul, in a form seemingly as punishment, are sometimes
quite severe. Are you ready? Are you willing to face then
whatever is to come into your life and say to yourself, "I
am ready"? The many of you have affirmed this, and you
were sincere and you shall continue to affirm it. But remember, you may have a number of years left upon the physical
plane, and many events can transpire in the course of a few

years, in the course of ten years we will say. Therefore you are going to find yourself in these predicaments because your soul is going to put you there.

Now how are we going to face the issue when it confronts us? Shall we run away? Shall we be escapists? Shall we shirk our responsibilities? The answer is absolutely no! This is so because the God-Self shall show us the way and we shall know the truth. We shall learn our lesson from the experience, and it in turn will help us to build our character. It will prepare us for the greater things that are to follow as the years go by in our individual lives.

I have said unto all disciples that you are upon the physical plane to enjoy the fruits of the actions of men. You are to create your own individual kingdom, and you are not to contaminate your kingdom with evil thoughts and things of a negative nature. Then if you find yourself in a state of negation, right then and there you are to apply this philosophy. You are not going to be like the metaphysician who could talk fluently but could not act on such things in metaphysics as how to live, how to derive the most out of life, and the like. As soon as this type of metaphysician finds *himself* in a predicament, it then behooves him to know just how to apply that which he had taught for many years; but many do not know how to apply it, unfortunately. You are not going to be that type of a metaphysician; no indeed you are not. You are simply going to apply that which you have learned in this philosophy.

If we are to study the Divine Self, we do not deal only with the human body necessarily. For we can separate the spirit from the physical body in such a way that the physical body can then become only a puppet to that which we call the Divine Self—that is temporarily. This is so because when we have pure dominance of the physical kingdom through and by the powers and the dominance of the soul, then the outer expression of man does in turn become the slave, so to speak, unto the soul. Yet I do not desire to use the words "slave unto the soul," but inasmuch as many have become

the reverse, a slave to the physical, I will use that term for
want of a better name.

I would rather my soul have dominance over my flesh
than I would my flesh to have dominance over my soul. In
other words, my soul wants dominance over my physical
but my physical wants dominance over my soul. So there is
the complete battle between the two. The outer man wants
the control; the inner man wants the control. I want to give
over to my inner man because that is the Divine State; that
is the Divine Self. Once we realize that the Divine State
wants the dominance, we should then give ourself over to
that Divine State, and our Divine State from that time on
can direct our actions upon the physical plane. We are then
going to see a great deal of progress in our life.

In the earlier state of our development upon the physical
plane, we were oblivious of this dominance of the spiritual
kingdom. Therefore we began to seek in various avenues
for our religious faith, our religious affiliations, our religious
satisfaction. Ofttimes we were deceived by falsities being
brought into our consciousness, but in the beginning we
accepted them because it seemed to be the way of least
resistance.

Yet we must strive to understand that when the outer man
lets the inner man take over, the Divine Self will then lead
us to truth. It be the outer man that we be conquering. We
use the outer man; we employ the outer man; we know it
to be a vehicle of expression. Thus we will take care of and
we will mend the physical body. Yet we must be mighty
sure that the physical body will not have the dominance
over our spiritual kingdom. This is something that we must
conquer in this embodiment if we intend to arise and derive
out of this physical existence precisely that which we are
supposed to derive out of it.

We are on our way now; we have become ever so attuned
to the Divine State. God being ever present, God is desirous
of speaking through us, indeed so. Words of wisdom shall
be uttered by those who have let the soul take over, those

who have let the inner man speak, and when they are uttered they shall be sent unto the world and unto the people. These words shall then help here and there on the highways and the byways and even in the crevices, so to speak. Then many shall awaken to the great call and in turn help others to also arise.

Thus we then understand one thing: it is all up to the individual. But there is not anyone who shall be denied this privilege of realizing and knowing the purpose of life. Remember these words: "I am the way; I am the light. Follow me and I shall bring you unto the Consciousness of Immensity." But then some will say, "It is a long road, and I become very weary and torn." But I say unto those who speak in this manner that I have gone through it myself and you are going to follow. Therefore, you are going to say, "I *can* make it; I *will* stand the test today."

These are the things that behoove the average disciple to do. Therefore, you are having to face the tests that you are being put through by your soul. Remember it is your soul that puts you through these various cycles of the earth plane. It is your soul that is having you to go through these things to see how you will stand the test. Your soul is constantly doing something to you to prove unto you that it has the great force over your material kingdom. You give it the opportunity to take control when you say unto yourself, "I shall obey my God-Self."

You Have to Get in There and Dig

However, once the soul has taken control the average disciple usually says, "It is much more difficult for me to stay on the path now for I seem to have more to work out since I came unto this understanding." Why is this? It is because you are now more cautious than you were before. When you become more cautious of the steps you take on the earth plane, it seems that then you have more to work out because you become absolutely meticulous in everything that you do. Being ever so cautious then, you are able to realize that you are working out your past karma and you make mighty sure that you do not build up more karma for yourself. You want to be free, and you want to pay your karma in such a way that you will be able to ascend when the time comes for you to go into the Consciousness of Immensity.

When will this occur? Perhaps in this life, or then again perhaps in the next phase of your existence. It may take a hundred years, it may take a thousand years, it may take a million years; I don't know how long it will take, but eventually you will arise. It is the law. We have all arisen from the lower forms of expression, we have gone through all of those activities, and why should we stop now? We are what we are today because of what we had gone through in the past. Isn't this a wonderful lesson tonight, children? Indeed it is. It is the only way that you are going to understand life. You cannot just take it on the surface. You have to get in there and *dig* a little bit to find out what life is all about.

How do you suppose doctors know what they know today? How would they be able to go about their activity if they didn't study? They have dissected the human body and they have learned a great deal, of course. But have they learned all there is to know? Have they discovered the soul? The medical profession surely cannot say that it was able to see the soul as the body was being operated upon or dissected. For if the soul had left the body, it quite naturally would not be there. And even if it were there, the soul would be invisible to their sight. All they see are the remains, but at the same time they are able to work upon the remains and by so doing understand a great deal.

You Do Not Develop the Soul

After the death of the physical body the soul is lifted out of the flesh, and then it goes into its higher consciousness or wherever it is to be placed according to its just deserts. There it remains until it learns its lesson. Now I do not mean to say that the soul learns its lesson; it is the outer expression of man that learns its lesson. We know that the soul in its entirety—that is, in its pure state, in its real state, in its original state—is perfect. You do not improve the soul; you do not permit the soul to grow, in the sense of the word. The soul is just there, and in the beginning the soul is perfect.

It is you, the outer self, that unfolds outwardly in such a manner that the God-Self can then manifest and reveal that which is perfection. You follow me on that point, don't you children? Therefore, we do not say that we are going to develop the soul. We cannot develop the soul because the soul is already developed. You, the outer man, simply unfold so that the soul can reveal that which is true, that which is pure, that which is unadulterated. It can do this because, as I have said so many times before, you are infinitely intelligent.

Now that we are in a position to accept the many apparent mysteries of life, let us realize then that they no longer be a mystery. For as we study more of the Divine State which takes in the soul, the akashic consciousness, the akashic records, and their direct relationship with the Universal Consciousness of God—then all that had hitherto been a mystery becomes known.

One of the disciples not long ago said, "I cannot understand that I am God. What does Agasha mean when he says that we are all gods? How are we all gods?" Yet, that is the only way that I can explain it, children. Just remember that you are gods simply because you are divine, simply because you came from the Divine State, the Universal Consciousness God. As a member of the collective whole you sprang from that consciousness having equal amounts of power in order to motivate the respective bodies that you would find yourself in. And this makes no difference whether they be in the flesh, in the ethereal, or in Immensity. All bodies that you inhabit are motivated by the Consciousness of the Core of Life, the Consciousness of God. Therefore, I am not stating in one breath that you are God, and then turning around in the next breath and trying to contradict myself by saying something else.

I want you to become so much attuned to the Infinite State that you can actually realize your Oneness with the Infinite. Words cannot adequately describe this feeling. There are no words. This is something that you have to feel within yourself, something that you have to realize in your own Divine State. Then once you do this, that invigorating power that surges through your veins will envelop you in a most glorious way—and suddenly comes realization! Right then and there you are going to have these many things revealed unto you. But this revelation is not going to distort the mentality; the soul has no intention of doing that. It never has and it never will, simply because of the fact that it is in a state of perfection. It is only manifesting through an imperfect instrument, and this instrument is only imperfect if we make it imperfect.

When you become so still within—when you become so peaceful with the world, with humanity, and with thyself— then the Universal Spirit God takes over and the answers to your questions are given unto you, and rightfully so. But you are not confused; these answers do not tend to distort your mentality. Then you are able to be in a better position to work out your problems upon the earth and to go ahead and serve in the way that you are to serve in this embodiment. You thus find yourself becoming ever so attuned to the Consciousness of Immensity, the God State, the Christ State—whatever term you desire to use—that you are then privileged to soar out there into the apparent space and be among the exalted.

The Eye Is the Window of the Soul

It can be said that the physical eye is the window of the soul. This is a good explanation, but crudely put. For an example: we observe a tree. You say that you see that tree with your physical eye. But let me bring to your attention that in reality you are actually seeing with the soul through the organ that we refer to as the human eye. Do you follow me on that point? It is even possible for you to train yourself to close the eye (you can even be blind for that matter), and over a period of time you can actually learn to see with the soul without the aid of the physical organ.

"How is this possible?" you will ask. For an answer, let us return to the tree. Let us say that there have been several people, perhaps hundreds, or even thousands over a period of time who have come directly into the immediate vicinity of the tree. And each one thought what a beautiful tree it was. Thus the constant thinking of the various thoughts by all of those coming within the atmosphere of the tree has created a mental picture of the tree that lingers within its atmosphere.

Now let us suppose that a blind man comes within a radius of six feet of the tree. He does not know that the tree is there from a physical standpoint, but suddenly he receives the thought from the mental vibration. The soul takes over, and he not only sees the outline, but he also sees a mental picture of the tree that flashes unto him and which is just as vivid as if he were seeing the tree with the physical eye. Now that comes directly from the soul. Of course this takes training, but nevertheless it can be done.

In the same manner, it can be said that in reality we *will* by the soul, but it seems as though we are willing by the objective sense. For instance, you can go into meditation, and after considerable training learn to actually project yourself out into space. This is called "soul projection," for it is your soul that will take you, of course. Through the eye of the soul you can then tune in on an individual that you have had previous relations with, no matter where he be at the present. It could be in a little town in China, or then perhaps in a large city in Australia, for example. You may not have anything in particular to work out with that individual, but then again you may. You may tune in on him in China or Australia today, and eventually when he comes to this country you might meet him in the flesh. Your relationship may have been in a previous life before the present one. Who knows? But there is that connection.

Now your soul is capable of doing all of that, but your mortal mind is the thing that keeps it back. Therefore you must train yourself now to have one hundred percent full power and control over your will.

Your Soul Is Striving to Make Contact with You

Now blessed children, please understand that your soul is literally striving to make contact with you, the outer man. It is striving to envelop your mortal self, trying to reveal all of the things that are good for you in this life, and at the same time it is getting you to understand that it wants to take your hand and walk down your particular path of life, so to speak. This has all happened before and it will happen again.

There was a time in your existence when you were all alone; oh indeed, you felt that all had forsaken you. But then the soul had taken your hand and in the stillness of the night had said unto you, "Be still and know I am present; be still and know I am here." That was your God-Self speaking unto you. You were never alone then, and you are never alone now nor will you be alone in the future. Yes indeed, disciples, there might again come a time in all of your lives when you will feel just that way—as if all will seemingly have forsaken you upon the physical plane. But right then and there you will hear that wee small voice seemingly say unto you, "Be still and know I am with you. All will be well."

That is what I want each and every disciple to understand tonight, because if you can face every problem in this embodiment with the right attitude, then you are the victor. But unfortunately, the average mortal upon the physical plane never seems to be able to reach that point in life. He doesn't reach it because he gives over to the flesh. He gives over to the mortal, submerges his personality, and closes the door unto the Infinite State.

So remember one thing, my blessed children of the earth. The inner consciousness is that part of yourself that enables you to understand, to accept, and to believe; but the outer man fights, rebels, confuses, and says it is not true. So it is a fight. You have a war within yourself, so to speak. Your mortal self is fighting your God-Self, as I said earlier in the class. But your God-Self is not fighting in the sense that we refer to as fighting. It is merely trying to conquer the outer man, the demon-self, so as to break down those barriers and free you from bondage.

All of these things, disciples, are permitting you to realize your station in life as an individual. But basically, it is the soul pattern of life that enables you to do your work and be what you represent yourself to be today. Whether the things be good, bad, or indifferent, it is this pattern that is bringing out certain events and attracting various things unto you. These will in turn then produce other effects or results so that in the final analysis, and if you stay on the path, you will be able to carry out the plan and later become that which your soul ultimately wants you, as an outward expression of human life, to become.

Now you can see how interesting it is and how intricate it becomes. On the surface it seems so mysterious, and yet when you begin to know thy individual kingdom, it be not mysterious any more. How glorious it will be when you become so infinitely attuned! But first you must say to yourself, "What the soul wants is exactly what I want also." If we vacillate, then we are lost. If we do not stay on the path, and if we have not that stick-to-itiveness, then we are lost in that sea of confusion that seems to prevail more than ever today, and which will prevail yet for a while.

Don't you think that these talks are gradually breaking down some of these barriers, children? I think so; I am assuming that they are. I feel inclined to believe that they do a great deal for you. Rub your hands together, sound the A-U-M, and call out your teacher's name. One . . . two . . . three . . . AUM.

TENTH DISCOURSE

SOUL PROJECTION:
OUT-OF-THE-BODY EXPERIENCES

By Dr. Navajo

Good evening, friends. Let us say the affirmation, please.

> *I am master of myself.*
> *I am all powerful.*
> *And nothing can come to me*
> *Of an inferior nature.*
> *I am peace.*
> *I am power.*
> *I am all there is.*

WELL FRIENDS, here we are again to continue our activity with our blessed Agasha when he descends to control the channel. It is interesting to note the growth of the many of you disciples. It is also very interesting to hear you tell of the many thought-provoking things that have happened to you, especially since you had embraced the Agashan philosophy.

Many of these incidents fall under the general classification of soul projection, and whereas this is a very normal

221

experience for us here in the astral world, it is a very intriguing and fascinating experience for those of you who are still encased in a flesh body. Agasha touched on this subject a few classes ago, and over the years he has gone into it at great length. However, it is still not clear to many of the disciples; and in answer to their requests, I am going to repeat what Agasha has said on these out-of-the-body experiences, which many of you have been experiencing not only during meditation but also during the sleep state.

It can be said that a large percentage of the class members has had at some time or another very definite evidence of the fact of soul projection. You know it to be a fact and not a theory. Many have engaged in numerous experiences in the astral regions, and some have even brought back memory of being in the higher kingdoms of the Consciousness of Immensity while in the company of their teacher. Then too, many of you have had the experience of projecting yourself momentarily to various locations on the earth plane during meditation. Each and every one of you in time will have direct evidence of soul projection.

I can state emphatically that this proof is only one of the smaller rewards that the soul will eventually give to the true disciple who stays on the path regardless of the temptations that invariably will confront him or her prior to coming to this side of life. As you resist these temptations, and as you stand firm and strong in your convictions, you will find that this attitude will pay the highest dividends, not only in your life here on the physical plane, but also in the kingdom to come.

The Two Types of Soul Projection

Now the general subject of soul projection can be further subdivided into two basic and distinctly different categories. The first category that we shall take up tonight involves the soul's projection of the mental body to any desired location, and this is comparatively easy. You do not remain out for very long in this type of soul projection, and in just a flash you are actually there in the mental body using the psychic vibrations of the pineal gland to observe and see what is occurring. The pineal gland is also known in occult circles as "The All-Seeing Eye." It is this particular gland that enables the soul to tune in, as it were, to any point in the universe. It projects the mental body and instantly you are in two places at one and the same time, for your total consciousness does not leave the physical body.

The second type of soul projection is a little different from just projecting your consciousness to another location merely to observe or to be aware. In this more difficult type of soul projection, you actually project yourself out of the physical body and travel in your astral or spiritual body into the inner planes. This is only accomplished during the sleep state; and, of course, the astral or spiritual body is always connected to the physical body by the silver cord of life. If this cord would ever come to be severed, death of the physical body would be instantaneous and the spirit could no longer return. We will take up this second category in the latter part of the discussion.

The first and the most important thing relative to this whole subject of soul projection is a thorough knowledge, realization, and understanding by the student that you are a spirit *now*. You are not the physical body. And inasmuch as you are a spirit now, you are only limited or hampered by the flesh; you are not possessed by the flesh. You have only to learn the laws and how to utilize them in order to be able to project yourself and have these many experiences while still in the physical body.

The First Type: Mental Projection

Very well. You will find then that you can learn to eventually project your consciousness and traverse not only to New York or other parts of the physical world, but into the astral world and even into the Consciousness of Immensity

and other planets in time. There is no limit to the possibilities of soul projection. The limit depends only upon the
disciple's individual progress and spiritual growth. But then
again, it is much easier for a person to project his soul
consciousness to any particular location than it would be
for him to actually project himself out of the physical body
and thus be connected only by the silver cord of life. One
is relatively easy; the other is far more complex.

As you then extend the soul consciousness to a desired
destination, your mental body will then instantly take on
the vibrations of that location as soon as it is reached. Then
you will suddenly find yourself in the atmosphere that you
desired to be in. In other words, you have projected your
spirit and yet another part of you is still very much in the
flesh. As you do this, you are able to observe the surrounding country, observe the buildings and furnishings, and then
recognize the people you were desirous of contacting. It
would appear to you as though you could even speak to
them. But they have ears that hear not and eyes that see not
because they are not attuned to your particular rate of
vibration. Yet in a flash you see them.

We can say then that over a period of time, and as you
become more sensitive to the higher rates of vibration, you
can at a moment's notice project yourself to wherever you
so desire. But you will not remain there for any length of
time. It will occur in just a flash, but in that moment of
time you will actually be there, be able to observe, and thus
bring the vision into play. This is not limited to the physical
world. Any time that you so desire in the course of a day,
the advanced disciple will even be able to project himself
into the Consciousness of Immensity, or the Earshin Valley,
or Cocoda, or wherever it might be. If you feel that you are
not going to see, then an impression will be just as important
as the vision. But Agasha has promised many times that the
average disciple will do more than receive just the impression
of being there, that he will also actually see the vision of
the surroundings.

How to Do It

Now how does one go about doing this? Is there a pre-scribed set of rules for attaining the art of soul projection? The answer is, not exactly; this too is an individual expe-rience. However, we can point out some general exercises that will help the sincere aspirant in achieving these results. First place yourself in a very comfortable position. Perhaps you have an easy chair that you use in your meditations. Or then again you may lie there in bed. Now fix your con-sciousness on the destination that you desire to project yourself to. Create it mentally; use your imagination if necessary. But above all be relaxed and do not let your consciousness wander. Concentrate on the projection and literally will yourself to do it. Results may not be immediate, but if these procedures are repeated again and again the soul will eventually respond once it has determined that the aspirant is honestly and sincerely dedicated to achieving some useful results from these efforts. It is rare that the soul will respond merely to satisfy the individual's curiosity.

For instance, let us say that you want to project yourself back to your hometown. You have demonstrated to your soul that there is some useful purpose behind this request and that it is not just idle curiosity. Or then again, perhaps you have just singled out your hometown as a point of concentration to learn the art of soul projection. It does not really matter as long as your soul understands that your motives are sincere. You visualize a particular location in that hometown; perhaps it is the home that you used to live in. Then again it might be your old grammar school or high school or whatever. Then try to visualize the exterior of the building; now enter the portals and walk back to your classroom. Did you turn to the left or the right when the corridor came to an end? Of course, it was to the right, you remember now. And there is Miss Scott, your eighth grade teacher, and in your imagination she appears just as she did way back when.

Now suddenly, in this reverie, something is going to happen. It may be only a flash, but there you are. You suddenly find yourself in that atmosphere and this experience is completely unlike your attempts at visualization. In this school you may be finding a complete change; you see it as it is today and not as it was then because you are actually projecting yourself there. Now this experience happened all of a sudden, at the precise moment that you became ever so attuned to that location. As you remember back on it afterwards, you may think that you were there for several minutes or even an hour but in reality you were there for only a few moments. The time element is sometimes confusing.

Perhaps it is a particular person that you are desirous of contacting. You do not know where he or she is at the moment. You start by trying to project yourself to his home and it makes no difference where that home may be. Distance in miles is no obstacle; the location may only be around the corner or then again it may even be in another country. Let us say you succeed, and you suddenly find that no one is there. That person whom you are desirous of contacting is not home. Therefore you see only the atmosphere and the environment of his home. So then you want to find out where he is, and the easiest way now is to try to pick up that person's vibration.

You then ask your soul to project you and connect you with wherever he might be at the moment. Now try visualizing the individual; picture him the way you think he is dressed and try to tune in on his thoughts. You may then be able to tell what state of mind he is in. Then, instantly, there he is and for a few moments you observe his movements. Perhaps you find him walking down a street, or then again driving an automobile. You have made the connection by first picking up the animatical forces in the general atmosphere of his home, which in turn has connected you up with the animatical forces of his friends and family, and

through their thoughts you ultimately then make the connection. It seems like a mass of detective work, but it is all
accomplished quite simply and easily through the Infinite
State.

Now this becomes a very interesting feature when you
are desirous of assisting mankind at large. Let us say that
you are desirous of projecting yourself to Northern Ireland,
Cambodia, Viet Nam, or some other place where strife or
war or misery is almost a daily occurrence. You want to be
able to see what you can observe, most certainly not to satisfy your curiosity, but to be in a position to see if you can be
of help. You want to try to liberate some of the struggling
souls and try to do all that you can in that direction. This is
not in the form of prayer, mind you; this is an actual experience you desire. You want to project your mental force to
an extremely bad situation that could erupt at any moment.

Let us say that you have a momentary glimpse of some
children playing, and nearby you see a bomb that is set to
explode. You awaken from your reverie appalled and dis-
heartened at man's inhumanity to man. But do you stop
right there with just a shrug of the shoulders? Most assuredly
not! Instantly you would be calling upon your teacher for
help, calling upon the Earshin Valley, and consciously projecting as much light as you could possibly muster up to that
location, wherever it might be.

Why did your soul bring this vision to your conscious
mind? You had asked to help and there was your chance.
And in all probability the forces that you had called upon
received your message and the bomb that was set to explode
did not go off. Thus several childrens' lives were saved. And
you may not have even known the exact location, but this
is no problem as the higher forces can very easily track down
an incident of this sort through the Infinite State.

Man becomes very powerful when he is projecting his
consciousness out of the physical body as a base. In fact,
you people in the physical body become far more powerful

than the average astral entity who functions in the middle states of the astral consciousness. They are not as powerful as you because they have not a physical vehicle to project from. This is the very reason that the Ascended Masters in the Spiritual Centers still retain the physical body. The retention of this physical force then enables these Masters to be even more powerful, in some respects, than the Masters in Immensity. Agasha has pointed this out to you at some length in the past and I will not pursue it further here. But I am only bringing it up to point out the fact that when you are projecting yourself, you are definitely in a position to pick up the necessary power that can be sent to you so that you can do the most good. In the physical body, you are not so powerful; but when you project yourself from the physical body, you increase your power many times. In this way the Teachers of Light are constantly using those in the physical body who have made themselves channels for this great spiritual force.

The Second Type: Astral Flying

Projecting yourself out of the physical body and into the astral world is what the many of you do almost every night while in very deep sleep. This is the second type of soul projection that we discussed earlier. However, in this case you are not just an invisible observer to the action, but you now become an active participant. You appear in your astral body, which is a replica of your physical body, but those of us over here on this side of life know that you are still in the flesh because we can observe that silver cord of life tapering off into the distance. You also appear as a spirit to us in much the same manner as we appear as a spirit to you.

However, it is not absolutely necessary to wait until you are asleep in order to project yourself into the astral world. There is a way that you may train yourself to do this type of projection consciously; although, of course, you will actually be in the sleep state at the precise moment when it occurs. Agasha gave this exercise some time ago, and the procedure is something like this:

First place yourself in a very relaxed state of meditation. Then when you are ready, picture in your mind a tunnel. Picture a light at the end of the tunnel. Now when you can see this clearly, try, through the power of your will, to will yourself through this tunnel into the light at the opposite end. If you are able to make contact with the light, you will instantly awaken in the astral or mental kingdom at the end of that tunnel. There you may remain for a few moments, walk around a bit, test the environment; but you cannot do this for long, as the soul will eventually draw you back into the body with a force similar to that of an extended rubber band. However in this type of projection, you should awaken back in the body with full memory of the experience because it was brought about through a conscious effort on your part.

Now traveling in the astral world is by no means limited to those in the occult field of study. All individuals of the earth plane will at one time or another during their sleeping hours leave the body and project themselves into the ethereal world. You are known to us as "astral fliers" as you appear here and there during your numerous flights into the higher consciousness during the sleep state. Most people are not aware of this spiritual traveling, and if they recall a bit of it after awakening, they immediately refer to it as dreaming.

In part this could be true, as bringing back clear, concise memory of these nightly excursions and flights into the higher realms is most difficult if not impossible for the average untrained individual. In the first place, it is an out-of-the-body experience and it is not connected with the physical brain. The only knowledge the brain will have of these experiences is that which is fed into it after you have returned from your flight. But usually you slip into the subjective state and dream, and ofttimes this dream is a mixed up, irrational episode. Thus this subjective portion of the brain becomes the nemesis or challenging factor for true recall of the things that you have encountered.

This problem of recall can be partially conquered or at least alleviated through the procedure of auto-suggestion. The following affirmation will be most helpful if it is repeated positively and meaningfully at night when you are lying in bed just prior to sleep: "I *will* myself to bring back memory. I *will* myself to see that which is presented to me while I am on the threshold. I *will* my soul to awaken me objectively when I am on the brink in that twilight zone." The secret, of course, seems to be to capture that memory and seemingly photograph it onto the conscious mind at the precise moment of returning to the physical body and just prior to slipping into the subjective dream state. Perhaps this is like being an acrobat on a tightrope, but at least it offers a possible method towards overcoming the obstacles to recalling that which you had done while out of the body.

Another procedure that is practiced by many in attempting to bring the outer objective mind into conscious attunement with the inner mind is to make an effort to be aware at the brink of falling asleep, at the precise moment when the outer mind is on the threshold between being awake and falling into sleep. Then in that instant while you are on the tightrope doing your balancing act, and before you lose your balance and fall into sleep, you may be able to recall in a flash that which exists on the other side. You may see your teacher standing before you, or see a loved one, or have something presented by the soul that is all the more meaningful to you. But when you do this, be sure that you fully awaken immediately; otherwise the memory of this experience will not be retained by the conscious outer mind.

What Do You Do When You Are Out of the Body?

Thus we find that part of the time that you spend in the so-called sleep state, the state where the physical body is at rest, you are very active and very busy in the various consciousnesses of the ethereal world. Now what are you doing in these hours that you are out of the body? You could be doing many things. You could be working with your teacher or visiting with those who can be inspiring or helpful to you. You could also be spending some time meeting the folks who had preceded you to the astral world. Or you could be going on an excursion with a group of souls to offer assistance to mankind at large and perhaps be of help in assisting someone in the physical body who might not have otherwise been helped. This is perhaps one of the most important things that you do at night.

Many times in the cases of great tragedies such as earthquakes, tidal waves, floods, or whatever it might be, the Teachers of Light will gather together helpers from both the physical and the astral divisions and go on an excursion of mercy to the scene of the disaster. Otherwise the suffering might have been much greater. You people in the physical plane have simply no idea how much you are helped at times by the higher powers. And these so-called higher powers, strangely enough, are built up to a certain extent through your own assistance. This assistance most certainly does not end with just the physical world. No indeed. Many times these excursions are taken into the lower degrees of the astral to try to contact the confused individuals who are earthbound.

Thus we find that the right hand of humanity is constantly helping and assisting the left hand of humanity. But it is all one humanity! The Yin and the Yang principles are ever present; for as we assist and give forth light, so shall we receive light. Words to this effect exist in all religions known to man and express a great truth. We can advance ourselves only by helping others to advance. And conversely, if we hinder the advancement of others, we are at the same time locking the doors to our own prison. It is always refreshing to know at the close of one of these excursions that we have accomplished something that otherwise would not have been accomplished, that someone is now helped who would not have been helped had we not appeared on the scene at the time.

When an earthbound individual says, "I am ready and I accept the responsibility for my own actions," he then unlocks the doors to his own mental prison and these doors swing open. The descended messenger can then help this entity to come into the great awakening, and he appears on the scene after having heard the call. Thus one who had been imprisoned so close to the earth plane and who needed help so badly may now be liberated. This may be the same individual who had heretofore flatly refused the assistance. Perhaps he had been satisfying himself in many sensual things of a gross nature that needed to be gratified or purged before he could come into the light. Or perhaps the hatred and the revenge that he thought he was inflicting on his enemies had not yet been dissipated. Then again, he might have been entrapped in the atmosphere of a particular place or involved in someone's aura, and thus controlled by the thoughts and the vibrations that feed the physical senses. It could have been any number of things that had heretofore held him so close to the earth plane, but now through his complete capitulation and surrender to the higher he is free. Accomplishments such as this are what bring great joy to those who had assisted.

In these spiritual journeys of the sleeping hours you will meet loved ones in the various planes of consciousness of the astral world. You will begin to have an understanding of the reality and the beauty of this kingdom that will eventually be your home. You will thrill to their music and enjoy their art; you will marvel at the exquisiteness of their flowers and the loveliness of their houses. You will carry on long and very meaningful conversations and you might, under guidance, move through the different strata of the astral consciousness and visit both the higher planes as well as the lower depths that we have just described.

However, as you spend these hours out of the physical body you must remember that you are still attached to the physical vehicle and in the twinkling of an eye you can, if your body should be disturbed or distressed, return to the flesh. This presents no real problem for the entity. However, leaving so abruptly does in some cases bring about a bit of humor. You could be engrossed in a very important conversation and in the middle of a sentence disappear! It could be said to be a bit surprising to the astral entity, yet most of us here are conditioned to this and sometimes the situation becomes quite humorous. I might add, though, that in leaving so suddenly you do not lose what had been gained in the discussion up to the point of your departure to the flesh, and in the following night you may be back again picking it up where you had left off.

The Healing Shrine

Some of you have recently brought back memory of visiting the Healing Shrine, and perhaps it is in order here to say a few words about this magnificent temple that the many of you utilize in your healing efforts. Firstly, let me say that the Healing Shrine is a shrine in the ethereal world that has been visualized and created by the minds of a collective group. Secondly, it acts as a focal point for healing so that help can be sent to all of your friends and loved ones whom you mentally place within its portals. Then, as you imagine them standing there within this spacious edifice, that beautiful healing light that is brought forth by the teachers of the higher consciousness then streams down upon them. This bathes the mental body in spiritual light, and if a mental body is treated in this manner, the light most certainly must eventually reflect back to the physical body. And you may receive this benefit for yourself, as well, by placing yourself in the Healing Shrine.

For those of you who have not yet consciously remembered visiting this magnificent shrine, let me refresh your memory. The Healing Shrine is located in an extensive garden, and it stands there, in all of its beauty, as a glorious shining light in the ethereal consciousness. In this superior world the landscaping is supreme. Many stately cypress trees, correctly placed, stand erect like friendly sentinels. Flowers are in great abundance and each one is a fragile, delicate expression of great beauty. The hues are so vivid that they usually startle a newcomer from the earth plane. A winding path through luxuriant, neatly trimmed green grass leads up to the shrine.

This is a temple of Grecian architecture, a replica of the beautiful Temple of Athena. It stands out as a most perfect example of this particular period with its many majestic pillars of white marble. It is a very noble building. Broad steps lead up to its entrance and a great door opens automatically, without the slightest noise, as someone approaches and it closes just as silently as the threshold is crossed.

As you enter you are aware of being in a very spacious room. Its lofty height is dimly lit with soft, subdued lighting. A beautiful multicolored mosaic floor spreads out to the far corners of the room. In one corner, a large suspended lamp contains a flame that flickers brightly as it gives forth its light. It is a symbol of the eternal flame. In other corners and alcoves around this great hall are the masterpieces and dreams of great sculptors and painters. The feminine mystique is forever expressed in the graceful forms and exquisite faces of women, and this seems to contrast very subtly and yet forcefully alongside the sculptures showing the great strength and godlike beauty of men. But rather than give the impression of an art gallery, these art forms are artistically placed around and about so as to enhance and give warmth to the main theme of the shrine which is healing.

In the center of this great space there is a large, circular, elevated platform and three steps lead up to its level. These are symbolical of the three aspects of life which Agasha says are the mental, the physical, and the spiritual. The entire platform scintillates and glows like a great inspiring jewel as great shafts of light flash down upon it, and these shafts appear to be almost alive in their motion and brilliancy. Once you have witnessed this display of healing energy, you will never forget it. The persons to be treated usually stand on this dais but there is also, a bit to the rear, a great chair. This great chair is used on special occasions, and it is a magnificent example of the artisan's skill in the usage of gold. Above its regal splendor is a canopy which in turn is supported by slender, shining columns. A border of golden filigree completes the picture.

There is silence in this vast auditorium—absolute, beautiful, restful silence. Each of you, as disciples of truth, should become aware of this great blissful healing shrine. And language is no barrier because the shrine is under the supervision of the higher kingdom. You are calling on the Infinite State, and because of this words will be communicated in a manner that will be understood in the higher consciousness. But the great healing power lies in that inner silence.

We find then that through this source great good is manifesting itself in the lives of the many who make use of it. But just because you are a student of life does not necessarily make you exempt from the many negative conditions that seem to be almost constantly attacking the physical vehicle. And karma, if for no other reason, will sometimes prevent those who have meditated in the Healing Shrine from being cured. But in any event we find, as we make use of this very valuable tool, that we are often able to prevent many mistakes and tragedies and sometimes bring about complete healings with the assistance and awareness brought forth through the great healing light that shines upon those who meditate in this great shrine.

How to Send Forth the Light unto Others

Now is there a simple procedure to be followed in projecting yourself to the Healing Shrine or in placing someone else there in that healing environment? The answer is yes, but it does take some conscious, meditative effort on your part.

You begin by simply placing in the shrine those that you would wish to help. You do this mentally by visualizing them standing on that dais in the light. The action is the same with regards to placing yourself or others in any other temple for that matter. You then indicate the help required, as you understand it, and you let the forces of the Master Teachers take over. This will be pretty much of an automatic process, and the higher forces will then bring forth the healing power or whatever adjustment is needed.

Agasha has given this exercise before, but perhaps it is in order to repeat it again tonight for your better understanding. The first and most essential part of the operation, as far as you are concerned, is to first put yourself into the proper frame of mind. Let us say that you are preparing to go into the Silence for a moment or two. Most students of meditation do this regularly and Agasha has stressed that a particularly good time is just before you drop off into what is termed dreamland. Now there are several meditative techniques towards achieving this result. Some occult schools still the conscious mind by the use of a mantra and there are many other methods in use today. But they all lead to the same ultimate result, and that is the yielding of the mortal mind to the God Kingdom.

Agasha's method is for the disciple to give his mortal self a talking to by his God Kingdom. You may say it is auto-suggestion and perhaps it is, but in any event it works. The technique is to affirm and command that the mortal mind shall indeed obey that which is emanating from the God Kingdom. The following affirmation should be repeated to yourself, not just by rote, but meaningfully. If it is in the form of a prayer, it is perfectly all right. "I will yield unto the God Kingdom. Let me seek the God Kingdom first before I undertake that which is to be carried out mortally. Let me be wise in my undertaking and let me be sound in my thinking. Let me be ever practical for I have come to know and understand that my philosophy is a practical one. I know and realize that the God Kingdom is infinitely intelligent and that its action will be the correct action in any undertaking."

Once you have taken this attitude, you will have then placed yourself in the very lap of God. All worries should now have vanished, knowing that the Father will indeed take care of all that is needed. At this moment then, when your mind is in a beautiful state of consciousness and peace, place those who you feel need help on the platform of the Healing Shrine. Mentally see them standing there in this healing light that is sent forth from the teachers of the higher realms. Let no problems, large or small, hinder you in placing them in this consciousness. And it is not necessary for those whom you place there to know anything about it, or to even believe in it, for that matter. Yet they will be helped—mentally, physically, and spiritually.

The Primary Source of All Healing Power

The Teachers of the most high, far beyond those in the Seventh Degree or other Orders of the great Ascended Masters, are the primary source of this great healing light. And even they are not the true source, for the ultimate source is God. These great Beings send forth the power to all healers of the earth plane, and it is completely impersonal relative to either the healer or the one receiving the healing. Each individual contacted will receive the degree of healing which he had earned the right to receive—no more and no less.

However, if it were not for those who are continually sending people to shrines such as this and seeing them in the light, many would not be helped who otherwise deserve to be helped. So the possibilities of what can be accomplished are endless. You people, acting as channels of light or rather points of beginning in this assistance, need not know who has been helped or even how many you may have helped, for that matter. All that you need to know is that you are contributing and offering assistance to those in need—whoever they may be.

Therefore the glorious aspect comes when one is truly

healed and restored back to health on the earth plane. Perhaps this one who had been seriously ill had gone to many
healers or doctors, and who is to say through which source
came the healing? But it does not matter. We all know that
the ultimate source of the healing was God or the Infinite
State.

Those who have truly been healed spiritually are now in
a far greater position to help others than they were before.
For they are now walking, living, healthy demonstrations of
the great power of spiritual healing! Now as they go forth
they are able to inspire others to seek for help in the same
manner as they were helped. Thus this great healing power
is then perpetuated so that there is never an end to the healing light that is continuously being sent forth unto the world
from these magnificent Beings of the higher realms. This
light can be received by anyone, anywhere, no matter who
he is or where he is, if he would only reach out to receive it.
And if his karma is such that he can be helped, he will be
helped.

Visiting the Spiritual Temples in Immensity

Now are you not beginning to realize that your conscious,
outer experiences are only a small fraction of your total life?
It can be said that those on the earth plane are really living
two lives in one—the conscious life that you are aware of
while in the body and the unconscious life that you are not
aware of while out of the body. But occasionally memory
of these out-of-the-body experiences drifts back into the
mortal consciousness.

While you are out of the body, can you then travel on
your own volition into the higher strata of the Consciousness
of Immensity? We have said that you visit the astral planes
nightly, but the question often arises among the disciples as
to whether you are able to travel into the higher planes under
your own willpower. The answer to this question is no.
Agasha points out to us that when you go into a higher

kingdom to receive a glimpse of that which exists there in that kingdom or plane of consciousness, you are always taken there by the higher powers, and your Teacher or some other Ascended Master will always accompany you. Thus you may then receive a glimpse of the higher truths and the many things that you are working for in your efforts towards accomplishing and achieving your mission in life. Meetings are almost constantly being held in the temples by the Masters of the higher planes. If you were to attend one of these meetings, it would be through the help and power of your Teacher and according to your own state of advancement.

The members of this class have on occasion had that great privilege. Now I am not just talking of attending a meeting in the various temples of the higher ethereal consciousness. Many on the earth plane receive great inspiration and enlightenment in temples such as the Temple of El Don, the Healing Shrine, and other magnificent temples of which there are many. I am not talking about this at all. What I am talking about are temples far beyond the consciousness of this earth planet and deep within the regions of fathomless space. It is here where the great Ascended Masters—Masters not only from our own planet Earth but from many of the other planets in this great universe—assemble from all over the Consciousness of Immensity. Naturally, attending one of these meetings is not the prerogative of the average student of the occult on the earth plane. Only the disciples of an Ascended Master Teacher have that privilege, and even then, only occasionally.

Let us say then that you were to accompany your teacher to one of these meetings in that great kingdom of the Ascended Masters. Perhaps it is the Temple of Rubicon, or one of the Temples of the Seventh Degree, or any of the Temples of the Great White Way of which there are many. What would you find? You would enter into an atmosphere of indescribable beauty. Yet you would clearly see that the furnishings of these temples and great halls of learning are as normal as the great structures of the earth plane. Indeed their function is also quite similar if you were to compare it to the Parliament, the Congress, the Vatican, or the governing body of any great nation for that matter.

But you would immediately notice that there is also a very great difference, and that difference is in the very nature of the individuals themselves. Not that their physical features are necessarily different from the features of those on the earth plane, but you would find yourself in the presence of the most beautiful people whom you have ever seen in your life. Their very presence radiates great strength, love, and compassion.

You must also remember that these advanced souls have lived in this high consciousness for a great length of time. Consequently they have long since moved away from the attire of the normal individual of the planet from which they had arisen. Thus you would find them attired in robes of varied and exciting colors—hues that are far more vivid than any seen on the earth plane. And you would call the gowns worn by the women simply breathtaking. You would also notice that most of the individuals, both men and women, would be wearing around their necks a golden chain to which is linked a symbol indicating some particular Order.

Symbology: An All-Important Factor

Now symbology has played a very important part in the lives of mankind in the various periods of man's unfoldment and evolution. It also plays an important role for the Ascended Master in that the symbol itself is invariably the key to that which it represents. Some symbols express their meaning so clearly to the knowledgeable viewer that they are like a story portrayed to the reader in one glance. They can be likened to the hieroglyphic which when displayed for view can sometimes express the full reason for the assemblage of a group of people.

Symbols have long been an identifying emblem in the lives of many groups on the earth plane such as the Nazarenes, the Essenes, or any other tribe or group that you may refer to as far back as you would wish to go. This is the heritage of the symbol, and it is therefore not surprising that we find it being worn by the Ascended Master to represent his particular Order—the Purple Order, the Seventh Degree, or whatever. But the symbol that the Teacher may be wearing might only represent the work that he is involved in at the moment, and at another meeting or assemblage of a different nature he could very well be wearing the symbol of another with which he is affiliated. Who can say? But in any event the symbols are needed and play a very important part in every plane of life, whether it be the earth plane, the astral world, another planet, or any other plane of consciousness that you have come to know by name.

But this is not a matter of organization alone. Many other factors are involved. Agasha says that there must always be that which is called the focal point, something that represents a goal, in any organization that works together as a unit. Then through and by the power of the symbol, one is able to continue working in that direction and stay on that particular path until the work is completed. Therefore the purpose of the Agashan organization, and the reason for its affiliation at this time with the many teachers of the higher orders is to let you have something to hold on to, something that can be very real to you, and this is only accomplished through the use of symbology. This is the reason that Cocoda is always stressing that you meet at the fountain, the fountain being used as a focal point in order that you may actually project yourselves to that Spiritual Center during sleep.

In this striving you will never encounter anything that will tend to distort your mentality or hurt yourself in any way. Many people have been inclined to think that they should never attempt to investigate the so-called unknown. Actually, there is nothing that is truly unknown to the disciples of the higher orders, as in reality your soul knows everything that is to be known. Agasha is always stressing that he only comes to awaken you to that which you already know. Thus these out-of-the-body experiences do act as a mental stimulus in eventually bringing about the Grand Awakening. That is the goal of this organization.

In these meetings at the higher temples, these advanced souls are constantly pointing out that a major plus factor in being in the atmosphere of such groups lies in the fact that the experiences will eventually enable each disciple to bring his outer being more quickly into attunement with his inner being. Then in time you will be able to understand and know that the ethereal world is actually just as real and substantial as that which you experience in the physical world. When this knowledge is accepted into your consciousness, you will then be coming into a vibration that will enable you to bring back memory of your wonderful experiences in these other kingdoms. Along with this memory then comes the fun of sharing many psychic presentations with your friends, and I can assure you that you will most certainly be joyful as you are gradually absorbed into the grandeur of it all and most grateful for the lessons that you have learned.

The Assistance of the Teacher

All this, of course, would not be possible without the assistance of your dearest friend who comes to assist you and help you along the way. This is your teacher, and regardless of whether you know him or not, you must endeavor to understand and know that he always has your interest at heart. In your existence here upon the earth plane, many have been heard to say, "I walk alone." This is actually not so, for in reality there are many eyes gazing upon you. You have never been alone and you never shall be alone. You are only alone in the physical sense. But aside from all the others, the chief contributing factor towards bringing you into the great illumination is the particular spirit that is around you. This is your teacher, one who had previously lived upon the earth plane, but now in his present category one who can see the picture more clearly inasmuch as he had himself overcome many trials and tribulations of a similar nature. The teachers receive a great joy and are being constantly compensated by seeing you advance and helping you to find happiness upon the earth plane. But they know that that which you had accomplished was not achieved through them. They assisted, true, but advancement by any one is always through his own learning and earning every step of the way.

Thus through the assistance of the teacher, you are able to visit these great halls of learning in the higher strata of the Consciousness of Immensity. You will find the atmosphere and the environment within these magnificent temples where the teachers assemble very beautiful, harmonious, and stimulating. Indeed, those of you who in your spiritual journeys are priviliged on occasion to sit among these enlightened ones are truly blessed. You will hear discussed all aspects of life in all of its many phases, be it of the earth and this solar system, or be it of other planets and other solar systems far out and beyond. And all things are explained in these lectures to not only persons of this earth, but also to people or humans from other planets who have likewise projected themselves into this Kingdom of the Masters. Primarily, the teachers endeavor to convey unto those attending the importance of learning and understanding outwardly the things that are already known inwardly. For the ultimate purpose of these great halls of learning is to bring to the outer consciousness that which is known by the God that is within. Herein lies the secret of all life.

Well folks, the light is beginning to build up in the center of the room and in a few moments I am going to have to step aside. However, before I do let me again stress the importance of training your mind to the point where you will actually be able to recall the splendor of the consciousness that the majority of you visit during your sleeping hours. Of course, there is not anyone who does not project himself into the astral world. Everyone on the earth plane does this to a certain extent, and let us not for a moment underestimate the beauty of the astral kingdom. But I am basically referring to the halls of learning above the astral. Then, when you recall the wisdom of the words that you have heard, you may then walk along the pathway of life ever in the knowledge that there is indeed a place for you in this consciousness. This is a kingdom that is so beautiful and so breathtaking that I have no words to describe it. Once you have recalled, words will fail you also, but forever afterwards and through all of your days you will relive the splendor of it again and again.

The light that has now built up is quite different tonight. Usually I can tell when Agasha is about to manifest, but the vibrations tonight have me puzzled a bit. They are very calm, very peaceful, and they seem filled with great love and compassion. The light projects an inner peace and Agasha seems to be using a different ray. Oh, oh, you folks are in for a treat . . . .

ELEVENTH DISCOURSE

STORIES I LOVE TO TELL

By Kraio

My BLESSED ONES, this is Kraio. I have come into your presence tonight, and I feel so very elated over making the contact and being able to control the channel. I have long awaited, it seems, for this occasion to manifest and to be in your presence, and to come directly in on Agasha's ray.

Perhaps as I manifest, I am thinking of time a little more than I should because I am thinking of the past. I am thinking of that which transpired generations ago when I descended unto the earth to observe humanity, suffering humanity. I am thinking about the message that I gave, thinking of how I endeavored to instill into the minds of men the simplicity of life, that life in reality was not so complicated as men would have you to believe. And yet, through my observance down through the generations, it appears that I was unable to make the impression upon some.

During my stay I had visited a number from time to time to inspire them, and momentarily they were inspired; but unfortunately they became entangled with material conditions and lost sight of the finer things that were being sent unto them. So we had to step aside, and these same condi-

245

tions were encountered generation after generation as other teachers would go into the various lands to reach suffering humanity. We all tried to touch those who we felt were sufficiently sensitive to become teachers, to become messengers unto the people.

Nearly 2,000 years have passed, and I manifest today in various ways throughout the land. Perhaps it could be said that I manifest in the light in which men may understand me; yet, in reference to my past life, when I had appeared unto the people in the various categories of the earth, it is evident that many do not understand me. It is not that I am striving to hold back anything from humanity, no. Much that I had said has been misinterpreted. When I had earned the right to be a channel on the physical plane, it was then that I knew that I was only an individual in the Consciousness of God. I was to serve humanity like so many others who had preceded me on the physical plane.

Many teachers of the past had also given their message, and they had suffered and they had been in want for a long period of time. Yes, the tears had dropped from their cheeks many times. These were tears of compassion for humanity, tears brought forth from being among the people and seeing the horrors of men and what men were having to suffer under, from seeing the dominations of mankind and all the evil that did prevail. Perhaps it seemed to behoove the teacher himself to find out how to cope with such a condition.

I often had found it the same. I was mortal, yet I was divinely inspired to bring my message unto the people. And I knew that if I could put across my simple truths unto mankind, and if I could get it across in the way in which I received it and thought it, then there would be no question as to men misinterpreting it down through the ages. But unfortunately this was not to be so.

There was even one season in which I went forth and told mankind that they must be born again. These are the same words that I use today as I manifest unto you as Kraio. But when I spoke unto the people saying that they must be born again and again and again, that they could not possibly learn all that they had to learn in one life, even this basic fact was misinterpreted. It was right then and there that so little was understood and appreciated by the many whom I had encountered.

Then at the end of my trail and after having delivered my message, I also had to leave and go the way that I did. However, it is not for me to feel remorseful. It is not for me to feel animosity in my heart, of course not. It was I then who said unto those who were persecuting me, and those who had prosecuted me, and who later then became the instruments of wrongdoing, "All who have come unto me to cast their stone in time shall become wise and be set free upon earth." But I was not the only one. There were others near me who they said must also go the same way as I did, because they had been found associating with one who was supposed to be so wise. I said unto them that the persecutors were leading us unto the place which was seemingly to be the end of our trail. Then there were murmurs in the crowd near and around and about me. This story had never been told in the right way, incidentally. But I said unto them, "Be at peace with thyselves. You will soon be in a heavenly state. Be not faithless. Know that you shall live again, that you shall arise, and that you shall be born again. And in the other lives that you shall live, you shall have another opportunity to live the life and to have the opportunity that you are being deprived of at this present time."

Yes, there are many stories that I want to tell, and tonight, as Agasha has so generously given me the opportunity to manifest unto you disciples, seems to be the right occasion to tell you a little more about the true story of my life. But I am only an individual like you, one who came and served and then went on, never having to return or to be born again onto the physical plane. Tonight I feel very inspired, but be it known that in my last life on earth I only represented the

Masters—the Masters before my time, and the Masters who have returned generations after my expiration and my ascension. I descend then today humbly, it being all preordained, to make it known unto the Agashans that we in our simple teachings can accept this clarification of my life and know it to be true.

My Early Years

When I came into Palestine, when I came into that consciousness and entered my body, naturally it was through the same process that you children go through. Prior to this life I had lived in the great Peace Period in Austa, and I had come back during that Peace Period to bring forth light and to enjoy life. Yet I knew then that I would have to return again, that I would be sent back to finish.

In the beginning I was not aware of these previous lives and I did not understand all that had cometh upon me. Not in the beginning. I had certain things and pinnacles to reach before I could understand, very much the same as you children today. I came into life under great duress, not I perhaps, but the way that I came into life was under duress. My birth was always a mystery to some people, and it also was a mystery to me until I reached a certain period in life. Things were held back from me, things that were karmically related, but I knew that there was something going on that perhaps was concealed from me and not revealed, as the soul will not reveal anything to you until you are ready.

However, I was not born into this life in the manner they would have it today. To you children it does not matter, but I was adopted, blessed children, by those who wanted to help me. In reality, I was discarded. Yes, I was discarded. I was a discarded soul, perhaps you would say, in the eyes of man. But I was then later taken up by one who cared, and I was fostered in such a beautiful way. I was cared for and well fed, and I realized then that I was not really an orphan, but that I was merely awaiting the time when I would reach the consciousness to know who my parents actually were. Yes, it has all been confusing down through the ages. Perhaps as an individual it does not matter, but I am letting you blessed disciples of Agasha understand that my life was the same as anyone else's—only I was an instrument; I was an inspired one.

Later, after I found out that I was not with my parents, I said unto my foster parents one day, "I shall know them in time." And they replied, "Yes, you shall know in time, but let us say unto you now, that we would have cared for you and looked after you just the same. We do not know these strange powers that you possess, not altogether, but in time you will understand that we realize that you are different." I said, "No, I am no different from anyone else. It is just that I have received the call, and I want to go forth and bring my message unto mankind."

Yes, how often had I gone from one village to another, as a mere boy, and all the time that I was walking I was receiving inspirations. But it was very hot at times, and very dusty, and I can recall that sometimes I had not even sandals to wear. And yet my life seemed to be so strange, and it was as though something was being held from me. It was. But there was a reason back of everything in my life, the same as there is a reason why certain things are held from you in your life.

I also lived in poverty. I lived under great duress, yet I knew my mission. My people whom I lived with were very poor, indeed, and we had but very little bread and wine at times to partake of for health. And yet, we were always somehow provided for, because the Angels of Light saw the toil of those souls who were near me and thus watched over us. I also worked myself, doing work in the fields as well as doing carpentry, and I tried to build and bring buildings and homes into manifestation the same as any other carpenter or anyone else would do.

Now seership in those days was sought after, and prophets

and seeresses were quite well known. Many had sought the prophet for they had learned that one could foretell the future to an appreciable extent. So they sought wherever the prophet would be, and if one did not care to seek, it was his privilege. Seership was all in order and there was no harm done. There were many great prophets in my time.

Therefore when these wise men, as some would call them, men who had unfolded their latent powers, told me that here they saw a boy who had the potentials and would be the one to fulfill the mission that I had to perform, I was in awe. Heretofore it had been held from me. It was very much like what a boy today would say in his vernacular, "Who, me? You mean that I am going to do that?" So it was told but not elaborated on, and I went away and I pondered over it. I said to myself, "Could this be right? Could what they have said be true?" I had always been taught to respect my elders, but it was only mortal for me as a boy to question, "Could it be that these men have told me something that be untrue?"

Then it was revealed. Shortly thereafter I saw visions, and I saw beautiful things and I heard the voices—by direct voice, inner voice. All of that came to me, but it was not worrisome. It seemed as though when it came to me, I was expecting it; yet, mortally I had not expected it, not even after I was told that I was going to have these experiences. But suddenly it came to me. My mission was to be just what the men had said it was to be. I remember being told by the exalted ones as they descended unto me, "Now the road will be rough and there will be many, many thorns that will prick you along the way, but you must stand them. You are mortal, you are of the flesh, and there shall be many sorrowful days and you will be mortal enough to want to run away and to isolate yourself, to be far removed from society. But you must not whimper, and you must not be in despair." Thus, I realized all the more that I was getting stronger, and my mission to perform was moving closer.

Many a time I had gone into the seance room, as you call

it today, and I then witnessed the manifestations. As I unfolded, I was able to see the spirits, and ofttimes I quizzed them and then told those in the flesh the nature of the spirit that had been contacted, be it good or bad. Yes, these things did exist during that time and they are left out of the Bible, as you call it. There were many people who were mediumistic and many people were seers. It seemed to be the age when men were very psychic in that part of the world. We had schools where they could learn to unfold—not schools that I had founded, no—but there were schools and they were of different forms. Once the people had learned that they were able to communicate with spirit, there was much of this activity that did take place.

There was one particular seeress who guided my footsteps, both directly and indirectly. She, as well as the others, told me of my gifts, my power, and what I was to accomplish as the time went by. Yes, this woman whom I had contacted told me many things. She was always in the background, yet she kept her own life all unto herself. She told me about my life, not only what was to come, but also how I had come into this world. It was very difficult for me, blessed children, to understand some things she told me. Yet, these messages were sent unto me, and at times they were carried to me indirectly. Sometimes the message was that she had said this, or she had said that, and for me to be careful. Other times the message was that I had certain things to do on certain days, and these things I then did.

Yes, I was guided for a time by mortal, by a woman. Many times she told me to go see certain people, or to go to a particular location where perhaps I had never gone before, and invariably there would stand the one whom I was to meet. Ofttimes several would be seated waiting for me to come, and I can recall the voice saying, "My son, I have waited for you." Then they would tell me stories of my life; they knew that I had returned and that I had promised myself that I would return onto the physical plane.

Finally I received the call to go elsewhere, disciples of Agasha, and this I did. I returned to Egypt. There is where I met the Masters who taught me many things and told me even more of my life. They told me of the one who was to appear not very far from my village, and they told me of Mother, and they told me of the King. These men who had reached the Divine State seemed to know all about me, even before I had come to the realization of my mission to serve. Later the mysteries about my parents were explained to me; yet when I asked the teachers why these things had not been revealed to me earlier, I realized that it would not have been proper for certain things to be revealed at an earlier age. Even though I might have mortally thought it to be the right time, as I look back on it, I can see clearly why certain things were withheld.

During this period with the Masters, I learned to project myself out of the body to the Spiritual Centers, particularly to the Valley of Cocoda. Yes, I truly was a channel then, nearly 2,000 years ago, the same as I am a channel today. But it was not until I returned to Egypt, that I reached a certain pinnacle of my existence. There, I appeared among the teachers and others who had gathered for the occasion, and I learned, and I grew, and I prepared for my work.

Later, after an absence of several years, I returned to Palestine. But I knew what I would be stepping into. However, I knew that it was my mission to try to establish the kingdom upon this earth, the Universal Consciousness of God, the same as Agasha is humbly trying to do today.

The King

As I reminisce tonight, my thoughts go back to one who was very powerful in his day. This was the King. He is known in your history books as Herod Antipas. I can recall the King so clearly. He was a king that seemed as far as he was concerned to be the King of all Kings. But that was only the ego of this king that was standing out. I can see the palace so clearly in my consciousness tonight, and the sides of the palace had turned to a gray, perhaps musty color. I will use that thought tonight to describe the aura that surrounded this building. And therein was the King.

During my stay on earth I would often meditate on the hillside and then look up at the palace. And when I looked up, I would see only sadness. I felt only sadness within myself as I saw the evil that seemed to prevail—selfishness, greed, and all of the things that seem to cause man's doom upon earth.

Yet I knew the King, and I realized my connection with the King. Yes, there was a very strange attachment. My strange attachment to the King was something which was concealed from me until I had a greater awakening. But I was not told of this by the outsiders. I was told by the Teacher, by the Masters of Light, that it was through that connection on this earth that I had come to be born onto the physical plane, born in the midst of confusion the same as teachers before me. So I knew my relations with him. I knew my relationship, but I could not live, or think, or do what he had done.

For I lived in a divine state. I lived in the consciousness of God at all times. I lived by the law; I violated no laws of God, or man, or beast. I violated no laws because I knew how to live in the consciousness, because I had learned these lessons in previous lives. And I knew at the time that the King must also give forth light. But he did not know me; he had long forgotten me. In fact, he did not even know I existed.

I went to see the king on several occasions, and at first I was always turned away. But I went again, and I went again, and yet in the beginning I did not fully realize just why I was going to the palace. Later, after some thought, I realized the message that I was to deliver to the King.

It was that the people were suffering, and I wanted to save them from the torment that they were enduring. I wanted the King to change the picture so that the farmer could retain his land and be able to work his land and support his family. I wanted light for my people. I knew that as I went quietly and peacefully from village to village, from person to person, I was feeding them spiritually and philosophically, but I also knew that I needed help materially and we needed the cooperation from a mortal who had such control.

I also knew that trouble was brewing in our land, and I knew that the soldiers were in a great state of unrest. The people were suffering and they were facing a great deal of destruction. Yet the King would do but very little about it; he would only direct in the wrong direction, which was evident from the very beginning. How much I wanted to reach him as an individual, to tell him what I knew should be done for the people, for there was trouble to come upon the Jews and they would have a lot to face in life.

Eventually it came to pass that I had my audience with the King. I said unto him, "All that you possess this day is not yours to keep. And you claim everything that is within this city. You claim all that men may have out there. You claim all that men, by the sweat of their brow, have toiled for. You claim all that is within your domain, including this palace that you possess. But even as you claim all of this, know then this truth. All that you claim is only so lended because eventually it will all return to that from whence it came. The power and the lust that you have today is also only temporary. This power that you have—you have many at your beck and call—will be of no value in time. It shall eventually fade away along with everything else.

"Know then that I speak unto you this day in your behalf. I speak to you as a man, as a child of God, the same as I. Be it better unto man that you give that which is not needed unto the righteous in order to help the afflicted and those who are in want. I do not mean for you to spoil their life nor to take them out of the environment that they are accustomed to. No, I do not mean that. But if with your hand, your right hand, you extend it unto the poor, you are then going to do more good than you can possibly do by sitting here on your throne, so powerful-like, so supreme, ruling the people and ruling the villages. No, this will not give you strength because soon you are going to have to give it all up. Soon you shall perish from the physical side of life, and you will become naked in the sunlight of God when you return to the ethereal side. So let us not be naked now."

As I spoke unto him I could see his face. It became very red; yes it did, children. But I did not come to him to make him angry. No, I only spoke unto him softly and tried to be ever so convincing. I tried to let him know that while his position was important, being so ordained, he was still stepping over his bounds by taking more authority than he should in ruling his people. But he only replied, "Be it as it is. It is the fate of men; and therefore if it is the fate of men, then they shall suffer unto me."

But right then and there I answered saying, "It is not for you to determine the fate of men by decreeing that the fate of mankind be as it is. It is your and my destiny, and it is within our power, to change the picture. It is within your power upon this plane to lift the veil, to lift the pressures from man, so that he may not toil as he had toiled in the past, so that he may have and own his land, so that he may till the soil and raise his crops, and finally so that he may then raise his family and find peace and contentment and good will among men."

Yes, it was very difficult to break down that barrier. Was I successful? Perhaps to a degree. And it is the same today when you ask, "Is Agasha successful?" Not entirely at the present time, but to a degree, yes. However, I knew then, children, that Herod must live as a man and not as a power of evil if he were to bring forth light and peace. And this he was to give because he was destined to do so, for what does it profit a man to gain the whole world if by so doing he loses sight of his own soul? Once a man loses sight of the God Consciousness, he then becomes ever so empty in life.

We must know then that as we toil in the field, and as we struggle and strive to earn a livelihood and maintain bread on the table, eventually we shall succeed and that same bread will then cometh unto us. We must know that this is the right way to live, to think, and to earn our way into the heavenly consciousness.

When men had returned to have power over many—and oh, I have seen this happen so many times in so many lives— this power was given unto them, but it was given only as a test to see what they would do with it. Today we have the same; it is no different today. Yes, in the days long beyond the period of my stay, those with power are doing the same. Many of them are doing it because of greed, because of lust, because of lust for power. Others, perhaps, have different reasons. In any event, we should realize that the kings and the leaders of the past who ruled unwisely by leading their people in the wrong way have of necessity suffered the consequences of such wrong action down through the ages. Thus they have become enlightened, and through realization, they now know that the leaders of today who are on the wrong path are only building up more karma for themselves, and that they too shall suffer the consequences in lives to come.

The Little Boy

In my earlier days, it was that I wanted to bring life unto the souls who were merely moving about on earth—souls who were not conscious of God, not conscious of life itself, but merely breathing in the flesh. I came at a time when there was considerable suffering among the people. I came when there were plagues, and I came when there was much distress among the populace. I also came into life at a time when men were slaughtering one another, condemning one another, and then taking away from those that which rightfully belonged to them. Yes, one might say that it was comparable to life in a jungle where many souls were only motivated by their grossest desires. Of course, this only pertains to the few and not to the whole.

How often had I said unto the disciples, after I had heard of such, that even if a man merely speaks ill or false unto his fellows, deliberately and maliciously, he is only building up more karma for himself to pay later. And I had often said that it is much easier to apprehend a thief of the earth than it is to apprehend one who lies and speaks falsely. This is so because one can speak falsely against another's name, but then it becomes well nigh impossible to ever get to the source from which it originated after it had passed through the minds and the mouths of many. Therefore, it is difficult to get to the source that caused so much distress by speaking so arrogantly. I had also seen much thievery in my time, a time when thievery was practiced much the same as it is practiced today among the unlearned.

Once I even came upon a little child, and I spoke unto him after I had found out that this little child had taken something that did not belong to him. I went up to him and I placed my hand upon the child. Then I had a quiet talk with the child, and the child listened to what I had to say. I told him that we must not take that which does not belong to us, that in life we must earn it, and that all mankind must work and earn their way. Then, after we have earned it, that which rightfully belongs to us will come. The little boy listened to my story, and I continued on with it saying, "In time you will have what is rightfully yours, but you will earn every step of the way. Someday you are going to live again, and what you do in this life will mean the result in the next life. Eventually, by your learning, you will have good things come unto you which apparently you have not yet earned. But you have done much good in other lives, and you came back to reap your spiritual harvest." Then I told the boy, and the boy understood me it seemed, that in time he would arise and become the semblance of love and light and wisdom unto mankind, the same as all men shall eventually do, be they this or be they that as of this day.

Then the little boy put back what did not belong to him, that which he had taken thinking it was his. My little talk had made him realize that it was not his and that it belonged to another. Then all was well. That little boy then went on to grow beautifully and eventually he became a wonderful teacher. I will tell you of that boy someday because he has returned many times since my time, and it will be an interesting story to tell.

I would often walk along the village streets and observe the exchange activity that was going on. Much was sold on the street during that time including all of the various things that were to be partaken by the mortal. Bread at that time was sold—bread that would last for many days—and fruits and vegetables were also sold on the streets. We also had the jeweler, and he made his wares and he sold them or exchanged them so that he could have other things for himself and his family.

All of this exchange activity was fair, as it is today if it is done so rightfully. But I would also see in my time much thievery taking place. However, whenever I could reach these unlearned souls, I would tell them the story of the little boy who took that which did not belong to him. And always they would respond.

The Healing Power

I made the remark not long ago that mediumship in my day was a very common thing. It was common because we lived in a psychic age when there were many prophets, and there were many prophets even before my day. This seemed to have gone on for a long period before I returned into that land. Thus we find that seership, as we called it then, was practiced quite extensively. There were the lower types of mediums, seers to us, and the higher type of prophets or seers; for mediumship, as it is called today, is as old as life itself.

Now then, in my life I was what you would call today an etherealization or a materialization medium, children. By that, I mean that I possessed the power for the spirits to materialize for me. Thus in the beginning, at the height of my mediumship, I was demonstrating phenomena. Or perhaps we should better say that these phenomena were manifesting through me. We had materializations, we heard the voices, and we witnessed other phenomena. Many times, as the disciples would sit quietly, they would hear direct voice seemingly from nowhere and it would amaze them. That is why I had so many followers in the beginning; that is why I had a goodly number of disciples.

In this way then the spirits began to communicate. All this is left out of the Bible of today, incidentally. But we had communications from the next world, and there were hundreds of souls returning unto the earth plane. Thus many people came to make contact. I approved of communication with the next world for that was just what it was—communication with the next world. That is where your loved ones are today, over here in the next phase of your existence.

I even trained or helped to unfold others to do this—to be mediums in that way. In fact, there was one who was very near me who was extremely mediumistic. She lent ever so much power and was able to assist in many ways. However, others abused the privilege and the power eventually seemed to fade away because of the dissipation.

It was then that I realized that the main reason that people were following me was because I could apparently perform miracles. So I said unto them, "This which appears to be miraculous must not be referred to as a miracle. No, it can all be explained by natural law." Then I took the time to explain unto them how it was done, why it was done, and that they too could develop some of these powers, these same powers that I possessed. But I said, "This that I do is not a gift from God, but it had been earned by myself through the power of God." I told them that it was through my desire, through my wish for the betterment of mankind, that these powers had unfolded.

However, when I brought these things to the attention of the disciples, it still did not satisfy them because they had not yet developed their own power and could not repeat the demonstrations. I also saw the necessity of educating the people as too many were following me merely because they wanted to witness this demonstration, and they cared but very little about what was said. Then too, others were not really learning, because just causing someone to talk to them did not mean any more to them than if they were to visit a relative on the earth plane.

It was then and there that I decided to change the picture. I asked my teachers from the higher order not to permit these things to take place in the future. I asked them to take the phenomena away and leave only the healing power. In this way I could go forth and heal and bring my message unto the people. I wanted to give unto my disciples the beautiful things that had been given unto me; I wanted to tell them of the vastness of life and the things that I felt they could readily grasp. I wanted to tell them about the things that Agasha has told you children, but alas, they did not want to follow me in the way that I wanted them to or in the way that they had intended in the beginning.

And so after the phenomena had ceased, my disciples gradually began to fade away. They were not like you children who stay on with Agasha to receive light and wisdom; that is, the many of them were not. When I ceased to perform seeming miracles arising out of the physical form of mediumship, the many then went on their way and said that I had lost my power. Eventually it came down to where we had the number that is so very well known to you children today.

Now after I had begun to teach, the disciples who then

followed me were very faithful in the beginning. It took time for the number to dwindle away. But we had not the people to talk to. Only a few villagers would stay and listen to me. I had a very difficult time because when I spoke, I spoke softly. Yet I spoke clearly and I spoke simply, but they did not want to take it that way. The villagers had often said unto my disciples, "We do not understand, and we feel that we care not to listen." Often we had then been sent elsewhere, and sometimes we were literally thrown out of the villages.

Then we would go along the hillside, and we would partake of our bread and our elixir that we had for the day. And while the disciples were talking about the events of the day, and about how badly we had been treated in some of the villages or communities as you would call them today, we would then recline in the sunlight and I would speak to them. I would go here, and I would go there, and I would join in with the disciples saying unto them, "We are not dismayed because we were not received this day. Be it now that I speak unto you disciples, and I will now give forth a lesson." And I spoke unto them, and they listened.

I told them stories of the other world, and sometimes I would tell them about the experience that I had had just the night before. On one occasion I went on to tell them of an experience that I dearly loved, the story of my being with the Masters. And then I went on to tell them other stories that for the occasion were quite appropriate. And you know, disciples of Agasha, they really enjoyed it. In fact, one disciple sitting very near me spoke up softly and said, "Now I am rather happy that we were sent out of the village, for if we had not been, you may not have told this story that you did." And I answered saying, "Yes, it is not that we are dismayed this day."

I spoke then in the language of the time, but it means the equivalent as I speak unto you now. Yet I also said unto the disciples, "We will encounter other such experiences as we go out amongst the people."

Then one of the disciples spoke up and said very roughly like, "It would not be so if you would perform your miracles again." And I said unto him, "Yes, perhaps there is some truth in what you say, but in reality there is no such thing as a miracle. Even if I were to do what you ask, you also can do the same and there shall yet be greater things performed. It is not that we are the only ones who can perform. That which I do is from the power within me, and it is created by the Spirit because it comes from my Father's house." Then I went on to explain what was meant by the Father's house, and the many mansions, and I went on to tell of the life that is supreme.

I was proud of the disciples in the earlier days of my career. I remember one time when many of them had chosen to come with me after they had given up their work and their toil. And they followed me, but not because I had said, "Follow me, and as disciples you shall have peace and rest." On the contrary, I said, "Come with me, but if you do you will find it very rough and thorny and you will be pricked many times. But if you still have the willingness to go through this, then come with me as I bring my message unto the villagers." Yes, I was proud of many of the disciples in the beginning. But I knew I was dealing with mortal, and I also realized that I would be deceived and that many would fall by the way as I went on my way to bring forth the message.

But I also had my pleasant days; certainly all of the days were not rough, disciples of Agasha. Sometimes I was very well received, especially after I had brought forth the healing and after they had learned of the power that was at hand to be healed. Yes, there was a time when I went forth from village to village doing my healing. This was so recognized after they had seen with their own eyes that I was healing, that I was an instrument to heal. Then they told their people, and their people's people, and their children, and many came onto the side of the hill and I told them stories and then I healed.

I also brought forth light unto those who were assembled when I said, "It is not I who do the healing, but it is the "I" within me, the God-Self, working in relationship with the wonderful teachers who had arisen so long ago, that does the healing. They now descend and they help to heal and to bring forth light unto the people."

But I also said unto the people as I brought forth the healing power, "If it is a cross, my children, that you have to bear, then fear not. It may be very heavy and you may be very heavy laden, indeed, but remember that in time it shall be lighter." I helped in many ways, but there were many who could not be helped only because they had karma to pay. But many were healed because they were right with themselves and because they had finished their karma.

Then there were those who were too ill to be carried to the location. Those that were well enough would come to the village where I was demonstrating healing, but there were others who could not come. So they sent garments unto me, not that I had requested it, no, not in the beginning. But later I realized why they were sent to me, and it proved to be a very wonderful thing. I found that I could make contact in that way and that I could have a personal contact through a garment. So when they sent cloth unto me that had been worn by the afflicted one, I took the cloth within my hand and I saw the person who needed the healing in a state of perfection. Thus through just that one contact I was able to give them absent treatments and they were healed.

I endeavored to explain the phenomenon in the following way: "This that you witness—though you may not understand the laws that brought it into manifestation—has been demonstrated long before, long before I came to demonstrate the same unto you. I only be the channel through which these things come and make themselves known unto the people and those who be present. If it happens today, it happened before; it is not a miracle for it can be explained. This phenomenon, as well as the many other things of a miraculous nature that have lived down in the histories of mankind, can all be explained. Many during their lives have been accredited with having performed miracles. I come to say unto you people that all miracles can be explained and that there is no such thing as a true miracle."

Before we leave the subject, let me conclude with these few words about healing. While you are on the earth plane, disciples of Agasha, you are always subject to trials of the physical. These are things that you have to go through and perhaps crosses that you have to bear. But I want you to understand that so many of our ailments can be eliminated by our knowing that God is ever present. We must see ourself in a state of perfection. When I healed upon the earth, it was that I saw the God within, the soul, and I saw that person in a state of perfection. Then by the power and the illumination that I had, or rather that was manifesting through me, I sent forth this power, this radiation, into the body of the afflicted one. And so very often they felt relief immediately! However, without that power I could do but very little. It was only the God consciousness manifesting through me that did the work.

I also told the villagers many times that they too must not harbor any evil thought or keep things of a negative nature within their consciousness. In this way they could help heal themselves. For many an illness, many of the ailments that you have on the earth plane, be caused basically from negative thinking. You magnify the ailments, and you can sometimes even make the ailment malignant. However, in all fairness to those that be suffering from this disease, it can be said that in most cases it be a karmic condition and a cross that they must bear.

But it is not man's destiny to bear this cross forever. Indeed not. To the contrary, it be so ordained that man must eventually arise from the cross and rise above a negative karmic condition. A man is truly inspired who says, "This is not what I want; therefore, I must arise from this predicament. I am not the victim of this. It only appears that I am a victim of this because I commit myself to be

placed in this state of negation. Therefore, I shall arise."
Now when a man states this with conviction, he has truly
touched the God Consciousness and he does arise. He may
even find that he is healed, and he then goes forth and he
brings peace unto his family and peace unto mankind. And
in turn he is so very, very peaceful within for the duration
of his life.

And even though he be not healed from the physical ailment and he wakes up over here on this side of life, he still
finds that he has arisen. He finds it to be the same as when
the Masters of old had said, "I go unto my Father and I bring
light and peace unto mankind." The Father is the expression
or the interpretation of the masculine consciousness. The
male and the female principle, the positive and the negative
contact, applies through all of life. This statement means,
"I go unto my higher self, and then I am in a position to
bring peace and a better understanding unto my fellowmen."

But I always pointed out to mankind that we are now
living in eternity, and that we do not die to go unto the
Father because we are already in the consciousness of the
Father. We live only to understand the universal expression
of God. These are the words that I uttered in my language
of that day unto my disciples, unto my people, and they
are in reality the same words that Agasha is giving today.

Giving and Receiving

If I were to come upon a man, and if I found that this man
had not accomplished anything, that he had no desire to
work and earn his way and that he only desired to become
a beggar of the passersby, I would not go to him and say,
"This is a coin that I desire you to take, and this coin is going
to help you to arise." No, I would not say that. I would go
up to the man, and I would see the beauty in that man who
thought that the world was down on him. I would see the
good in that man, and I would see the same God in him to
be also the God that is within me. I would see only the good,

and then I would extend my hand unto him and I would visualize him in a state of beauty and see him in a state of perfection. Then, if I were to give an earthly coin unto him that perhaps would help to sustain him for the time, I would bless it and give it to him in the silence. It would then do him good.

But if I were to return in the tomorrows, and if I would see the same beggar there in the same location, I would not keep repeating this. I would not keep handing him the coins to sustain him for the day; no, there would be no goodness in that. Yet it is not for me to say that his actions be wrong, nor even to condemn, if I should still see him going on the way he had. But before I left him, in the first place, I would see him arising and being inspired and taking his rightful place in the world to learn his lessons. These are the things that help us to derive so much out of life, children. And when we take the attitude of always extending the hand, but never extending it to take away the responsibilities, we are then true disciples of this movement.

It is said that there are those who are born to give, and then there are those who are born to receive. Which shall I be, the giver or the receiver? Neither one, children of the earth. Here is what you are to be: You are to be a good giver, a sincere giver, but then you are also to be a good receiver. Do not say, "I shall not take this from you, as you offer it to me, because I must work it out myself." That is a wonderful attitude, but it was not given to you to take away your responsibilities. When you give something, give it from the heart. Let it go out into the world and when you receive something, receive it with the same attitude. That is the lesson that you must learn. Be a good giver, and be a good receiver.

But do not have your hands out all the time to receive, never do this. Only receive when it is right for you to receive, and then give when it is right for you to give. Then on the other hand, do not sell all that you have on the earth to give unto the poor. That is not right for you to do either.

You have a right to sustain yourself, and always remember never to limit yourself if by so doing you would then live in a cramped consciousness. Never live in that consciousness, children. Go ahead and bring forth light and live in a very prosperous consciousness, but do be practical at all times.

Let us say that I have a few coins within my hand. Yet, at the moment, I have no way of knowing whether or not in the future these coins shall be multiplied into others. But I have implicit faith that as I send forth, so shall I receive. I do not clench my fist with the coins and say, "I dare not give or release these coins, because if I do I will get no more." Then you violate the law right there. When you have the coins in your hand, then let them flow and bless them and have implicit faith that other coins shall come to replace them. This system of exchange on the earth was so devised for you to survive. Thus other coins will come.

Perhaps I might have a loaf of bread before me. I partake of that bread and I share my bread with others. Now I don't say, "I do not dare to partake of this bread because tomorrow I shall not have bread. I cannot break bread with my fellows because if I give him my bread, or part of my bread, I shall not have sustenance for the tomorrow." Then that is a violation; we must not do that. Rather we should say, "I shall partake of the bread that is put before me this day, and I shall share it with the passerby. I shall give him his share, and then when tomorrow comes I will have another loaf. It shall be so multiplied." I taught this principle unto the disciples, that if they would live that way there would then be plenty for all. And it was so done. By having the right attitude, it seemed as though we could feed the multitude in that way.

On one occasion, I called my disciples together and I said unto them, "Never allow yourself to become attached to material. Yet bless the material as you would bless your fellows, once the material had served its purpose. When things become of no value, no intrinsic value, we are not to say, 'This is of no value to me because it is worn and torn.' Rather we should say, 'This that I discard today has served its purpose for me. Now may it go forth to serve others.' With this thought we then give it power; we then give it something that will also enable others to make use of it."

Then I said unto the disciples, "Return to your abode and take all that you have hoarded, all that you have accumulated and have not seen for a long time, and bring it out into the sunlight. Look it over and think, 'Is this of value to me now, or should I go and give it unto those who need it?' Be it an old garment, be it jewels, or be it anything material, go now and fetch it." And so they did. They went through all of their belongings, all of their belongings which included things that they had not seen for many a year, and perhaps there was a great sentiment attached to each thing that they brought into the sunlight. But they did not hold on to the sentimentality; they simply took the garment that they had discarded, but yet hoarded, and they gave it unto the poor.

But I also said unto my disciples, "If you come upon a garment that you had forgotten about and you find that you need the object at the time, then wear it and use it, whatever it be. Do not say, 'Now I must give all that I have unto the poor because it is so ordained by God.' It is not wise that we give all unto the poor, for then we in turn will become naked ourselves. We are first to replenish, and as we replenish and after we know that our needs are supplied, then when the right time arises, we can extend a helping hand and give forth the garment or whatever it is unto our fellows. Then it is rightfully done. But if you become so endowed and believe that it is right to give all that you have unto the poor, and if by so doing you deny yourself to the state that you become a pitiful sight unto society, then you injure yourself and that you have no right to do. This, as I have told you in previous talks, then becomes a sin. It is right for us to give, but we must know how to give, when to give, and to whom to give. It is always right to live in that light."

Perhaps these are not the exact words that I used then,

but they express the general thought. I gave them this lesson because I had often stepped into the abode of some of my disciples, and I had seen that they had accumulated, hoarded, and stored away many things that I knew were of no value to them. Then too, many of my disciples in the earlier part of my career on earth became enamored with possessing gold and jewels, feeling that by so doing and by accumulating much wealth it would give them power and domain over their fellows. I wanted none of that, and I tried to discourage it as much as possible among my disciples.

What I really wanted them to see and understand was that actual power is sent by material things when they are given sincerely and unselfishly. Once we bring things out into the sunlight of God, and we bring them out unto man and to be among men, they will then do their work until they be of absolutely no value whatsoever. Then when a thing has not any more power within it to send, it shall then go back into the elements of the earth from whence it came, only to serve again in a future time in some other capacity.

Tilling the Soil

Yes, if I had the time to spend, I would like to tell you many stories of the past. I would like that very much as I like to tell you stories that help you to understand not only your life today but the real life that is to come. Many things are said in my name, but as I manifest unto you I would have you to understand that I as an individual matter but very little. When we refer to an individual, we must understand that all are equally important unto God.

I had always pointed out unto my disciples that they should first listen to the message from the one who is desirous of bringing the message unto them, and then either accept it or reject it for whatever it is worth. But we must not accept the outer personality, disciples of the earth; it is the *One* of the inner consciousness that brings out the truth. This inner man is far more beautiful, and we can very easily understand once we have become attuned to Him. Yet we

cannot discard the fact that the outer man is also very important. This is so because what a man is within is likewise
reflected on the outside, whether he be cheerful, or sad, or
forlorn. Many times I have come upon men and women who
immediately showed me their sorrows. They did not need
to utter them unto me, and sometimes the outer man would
attempt to cover them up. But the inner man would always
reveal what they were suffering under, and I could see so
clearly what they were having to bear.

When I would see a man who was toiling in the fields, or
who was struggling in some way, I would always lift my
hand to assist. As this assistance was not usually physical, it
was said at one time among my enemies that I would not
work, that I would not toil. Naturally, when I heard this
I smiled. It was all I could do to go from village to village
to speak of things that they could not understand. Yet I
tried to give them the understanding that we are all working
in the consciousness of God, that we are all doing the work
that is set before us, and that we are not to criticize whatever
that work be, or whatever it is that man must do to earn his
way and to fulfill his mission.

I remember one occasion when I came upon a man who
was working in the field and toiling laboriously. He had to
get out his crops and he had to do his work. I watched him
for a while as he would till the soil so laboriously, and then
he would sit down and rest for a moment. It was very warm
that day and he would wipe his brow many times. After a
time I walked over to him and I talked with him saying,
"This has been a very difficult day for you as I can see that
you are striving to receive as much power as you can because
you are fearful that you are not going to get in your crops."

Then I told him a story. It was just a little story, but it
helped him and it showed him how to go about his work. He
listened very intently and then he spoke unto me apologizing
for being so very dirty and soiled. I answered him saying,
"No, you are a part of Nature and you are not soiled. You
are merely toiling in the field and tilling the soil. This gar-

ment that I wear as I appear before you may appear to be very beautiful and shiny, but remember this: Your garment and my garment are made of the same materials, and there within we can have the same consciousness."

Then I showed him how to go about his work and how to make his work easier for him. I told him that he was putting too much fear in his work and that he was afraid that he would not be able to get it out. Then I told him to take his time and that all would come out right in the end. And it did. I also helped him in the field for the rest of the day, and I showed him every step of the way. After a while he said unto me, "It appears that you know very much about this. Have you tilled the soil before?" I answered, "Yes, I have. I have done much of what I am about to show you as well as what I have shown you already, but I have done it earlier in this life as well as in many lives before this one." Then I told him about reincarnation, how he too had lived many lives, and that in this life his mission was to till the soil, whereas my mission was to go out and show men how to live and how to derive the most out of their lives.

These are the things, children, that I enjoyed in life. Just little things—showing this one and that one what to do and how to conquer fear, showing each one how to conquer so many things that become so very difficult to overcome. So this little lesson tonight is to show you that when you are laboring, when you are toiling, or when you are doing whatever it is that has become so burdensome to you, just stop and think that this work that is put before you must be done. And the sooner that you accomplish it, the better.

Just say to yourself, "This work was put before me, but I know that as I accomplish it and drink from the fountain of life, my cup shall runneth over. Then I shall pour forth from my cup, and I know that I will be able to fill it up again." However, if you do not pour forth from your cup, then you can never replace any more within. Therefore pour forth, and as you pour forth so shall you have your cup filled, and the supply will always be there awaiting you.

The Stranger on the Path

Basic truths are very simple. Yet I have often heard the Teachers, as they descend unto the earth to bring forth their many truths, express the thought that they must always strive so diligently to bring them forth. It is that they want to help and assist the mortal, the outer man, as he walks his path in life ever seeking understanding and the answers to life's many problems.

We have all walked on that very dusty path, children of the earth. And as the dust would reach our nostrils, perhaps we had but very little elixir or water to quench our thirst. We would sit down and we would wipe our brow. Then we would arise, being ever so thirsty, and we would walk on to the next village because we had our affairs to take care of or we had a relative or friends to meet. As we did, we would find ourselves wondering about life, perhaps. We would be thinking, "Why is life as it is? Why am I as I am today? How soon shall I be freed from the body; and when I am, where shall I go? Who can tell? Who can prove to me that I shall live again?" These would be the thoughts that would enter the minds of so many.

I recall one occasion when I saw the illumination on a passerby as he came near me. I saw him in the light that I wanted to see him in. He had the illumination. Yes, he had sack and cloth as well as the vessel that he had just drunk from, the gourd. But as he quenched his thirst, I could see his radiation, his light. Of course, he did not see it, and as I neared him he spoke unto me in a friendly manner.

I too spoke unto him, and then he looked at me rather oddly, perhaps. But I knew why. He had noticed that I did not have a vessel. Ordinarily we always carried the vessel from which we could partake and quench our thirst because of the dusty path and the hot sun that beat down upon us. But there, as he gazed unto me, he noticed that I had not vessel nor bread to break, although he had bread and he had vessel. As I say, he then looked at me rather oddly, and after speaking to me in such a friendly manner and with a very wonderful smile, he then said, "Would you care to partake and break bread with me and drink from the vessel?"

This pleased me, of course. Then I obliged myself and reverently gave forth light unto him as I broke bread. I partook of this bread and it gave me strength, bodily strength, and I quenched my thirst from the vessel. After I had done so, we sat down along the dusty road and he began to talk.

We had a long conversation, and during that conversation he said, "I don't think I have ever talked so much for a long time, and why I am speaking to you in the vein that I do, I do not know." But I said unto him, "It does us well to speak of self, and of conditions, and of people, and of life, and to be ever so philosophical when we express our attitude toward such things."

Then as I spoke to him, he asked me a question in more of a mortal vein as to where I was going and whether I had business to attend to in a neighboring village. I answered his question, and he told me that he likewise was going to a neighboring village. He called out the village by name and said that he had walked for perhaps many miles but now had but a few more miles to go. I answered him saying, "Yes, I have just come from that village."

Then he asked me, "Do you know of a little girl there?" And he spoke of a little girl, calling the little girl by name whom he understood lived in this particular village and whom many villagers had been talking about for some time. He asked me if I could give him the correct location where she resided, and that I did. I told him of the little girl and the stories that I had learned about her from her parents. Then he said to me, "I am going to this village because I was told that I could be helped if I went to see this little girl. I understand that she is very strange and has visions; yet many people think that she is possessed of the devil. But I am told that if I go there I may be able to help her, and in turn she may see visions for me."

At this point, I must interrupt my story about meeting the stranger on the path and explain that during my time there were many children who could see visions. Many people of my day saw visions, heard voices, and this became a very interesting subject among the villagers. This child that I am referring to was apparently, from a physical standpoint, suffering. That I understood. But I also knew why the child seemed to be suffering in this manner.

However, the man whom I had just met on the dusty road, and with whom I had partaken bread, did not know the true reasons. He believed he understood the mind and how it produces and brings forth the creative powers, but he did not have the correct interpretation. He had studied the body, according to the understanding of his time, and because he had trained himself in this direction he believed that he could go and perhaps physically help the child and thus be permitted to ask questions as to what she could see psychically. This interested him very much because the child was supposed to be wonderful in many ways; she could describe her visions and tell many interesting things.

I said I had just left the child, and then I told him the story about the child and why she could see visions. I said, "Many can see visions upon this earth, but a great number do not tell others of their visions for fear that the many would not understand and think them strange." Then I proceeded to tell him that this child was not afflicted biologically, but that she would take on conditions belonging to those from a plane of consciousness in the astral world. This would be especially true when a person would be in the child's presence to receive a message from an individual in the astral world. Then the condition that had freed that person from the physical body would temporarily take over the child so that the one who had come back could be identified.

After I had explained to him about the child, he was thus

satisfied and he bade me farewell and went on his way. I learned later that this man had gone to the little girl and was able to make contact with a very blessed one whom he loved very, very much, a very wonderful loved one, and this pleased the man so greatly.

The rest of my journey was uneventful. I did not pass anyone other than the one that I refer to, and I soon arrived at my destination where I then joined with the many who had been awaiting my arrival. Since I had broken bread and I had partaken from the stranger's vessel to quench my thirst, I was not too depleted, but I was still greeted with the same when I arrived and soon I was replenished quite satisfactorily.

I then told the group about the man I had met and broken bread with. I described the illumination that I had seen as he gazed unto me rather oddly, and it was reasonable to understand that he too had blended his force with mine. There was first the friendly attitude, the breaking of bread, and then there was his intention to help the little girl whom he thought in his own mind he could help.

Now then, this story may help you to understand that everything in life is in order. You come to serve humanity. You come to suffer, it seems, but as you suffer upon this earth you are all the more compassionate, and you have love for those near, and you have love for the world. Somehow, you have the correct understanding of love universally. Yes, you hear people say today that God is love; and God is truly love, but love is also understanding. Love is something that you do not turn on and off at a moment's notice, no indeed.

And I say unto each and every one that you too may meet many as you tread your rough path of life, and you may invite them in to break bread with you, and you may help them to quench their thirst. This, which is symbolical in character, may come to pass. And as you do, you must remember that as you give forth light, so shall there be light shed upon you. You shall know the way because the "You", the "I" within, is the God-Self. And when you go within to understand the purpose of life, the "why" that you are here and the "where" that you are going, then you shall truly know the peace that passeth understanding.

The Shepherds

Now I would like to tell you the story of the shepherds. We would often see the flock on the hillside, and then not very far away would be the shepherd. Perhaps he would be resting under a tree, and sometimes he would remain there for a long time because the flock would stay in the same location for many hours and sometimes seemingly for days. Yet, as I look back and see the shepherd on the hillside watching over his flock, I can see that very often he is in a state of meditation, and as he sits there he is looking out into space. Perhaps everything is very still within him. Yes, it has become so. It seems that he has become, as it has often been said even in your life today, as quiet as a little lamb.

Now this, of course, is merely a statement that is made today, but as we drift back to the earlier stages of our lives on earth, this became a very important feature among men. It was always said of the shepherd, as he had gone out with his flock, that he was able to meditate. It was the shepherd then who later became very much attuned to the Infinite State because his occupation gave him time to think, to meditate, and to attune himself to the universe. And by so doing, he communicated. Yes, how well do I know that. But the shepherd was able to communicate with his higher self because he communicated with Nature. And by communicating with Nature, he was communicating with God. The shepherds of the past were truly infinitely attuned to the Divine State for they were Godly men, learned men in their day, and I might add, in every sense of the word. They carried out their activity merely to be, as I say, close to Nature.

When I was just a mere boy, I can recall meeting the shepherd. And the shepherd told me many things. He told me things that would come to pass, and he told me of the sorrows of men. He told me that the land would be confiscated along with other things which would also be taken away from mankind. Yes, the shepherds were very wise men in those days.

They were men who returned for a special purpose; perhaps we will call them men of destiny, if you wish. They knew the laws that govern men and they became ever so attuned to the Infinite State. They knew of their mission in life and special missions to be performed from time to time. It has often been said that while the flock was busying itself with the grazing, the shepherds were known to go into the nearby village and sometimes do wonderful things for humanity. And then they would say, "It is not I as an individual who doeth the work, but it is the Godly consciousness within that doeth the work." But this was true with all men who had become Godly—divinely attuned to the Infinite State. And so it was that they went forth and they did much.

I recall the time when one of the shepherds had come into the village. Nearby was his flock. He asked to take a drink of water from the well, and then he was granted the privilege, of course. But to the shepherds little things were always a privilege, not because they were so denied, but because they were grateful for everything. They were very, very humble indeed. After his thirst had been quenched, on this particular occasion, the shepherd then spoke unto one whom I knew very well. I can recall that as he spoke unto this wonderful lady, he then told her many things. And as he looked at her he said, "I believe I know you. I believe our paths have crossed before." She smiled and answered, "Yes, I believe so." Then the shepherd went on to say many things unto this blessed woman, and he told her of the trying days, and he told her of the future. He then thanked her again for the water from the well, and then with gladdened eyes and with a smile on his face he turned aside, after blessing her, and then returned to his flock.

Things of this nature, disciples of Agasha, were very commonplace, you would say, in our day. But then at the same time there were men and women who did not appreciate what had been given by the many who had become attuned with the Universal State, God. Men were fighting through greed and selfishness in much the same way that they do today. These things, along with animosity and jealousy, have held men very close to the earthly garment. But now that earthly garment has become ever so soiled, and now you must cleanse that garment so that you will be able to lift up thine own eyes and say, "I am the way and I am the light."

You and I then, in much the same manner as the shepherd whom we refer to tonight, shall then become good shepherds in our everyday life. You are going to have the opportunity to be good shepherds of the earth; so then go into meditation at night when you retire. Attune yourself to the Infinite State and call upon your blessed Teacher, as I did in my day. Then there will come in the stillness of the night that wonderful peace which shall prevail.

When you make an effort in this direction, you can truly lift up thine eyes and say unto the Heavenly State, the Godly State, "I am ready; I am going back home. I am learning every step of the way for I love life and I shall enjoy it. I shall give all that I can unto suffering humanity which includes my love, my thoughts, and my cooperation. I shall then live, not by the material rod, but by the spiritual rod and the spiritual staff. Then, as I gaze unto the shepherd, I will be the same. I am the true shepherd of life because I watch over my flock, and I am giving all of mankind, be it nation or be it individual, my love. I know that they have ears, but they hear not. I know that they have eyes, but they see not. They have not the understanding that I have; therefore I am patient. I know that they only punish themselves as they go through the hells of the earth until such time as they come unto the understanding. But I also know that in time they too shall reach the same divine state that I am reaching at this time. May the time come soon when the nations of the earth will blend harmoniously and work together to bring forth light and peace unto suffering humanity. It is forthcoming and I am grateful for that."

Once the disciples of the earth of all religions, and of all races, and of all nations make this affirmation, there will once more be peace on earth and good will toward men.

The Symbol of the Cross

Yes, how often had I said unto the disciples, "The time is coming when men shall be free," but I told them that it was going to take a long time before men would come to the understanding. I also said unto them, "Men shall never be free until they have tapped that great consciousness that is within. Know then that ye must seek first the Kingdom of God that dwells within, and then all things shall be added unto you." This was, of course, given in the language of the time, and then I said that it must be that we have the key within our soul. I told them that we do not go out there in space to receive the answer, but that it is all within thyself. I said, "We look at the great universe and we see what we may, but in reality there is a universe within that body of yours, and there is where you have everything hidden. That is why when ye seek the Kingdom of God that is within, understanding shall then be added unto you."

Many came unto this understanding in my day, but then again many did not. Many also had much taken away from them, things that they had earned, and much of a negative nature did befall them. On the surface this seemed unfair, and many thought that perhaps God had failed to enlighten these souls. However, the truth was given unto me and I spoke unto the disciples saying, "This day you are having to face this problem. The cross that you are having to bear at this time is very difficult, and it is that you are heavy laden. And I will also tell you that in time our crosses shall become very heavy. My cross that I am carrying at this time is weighing me down, but I know that the cross in time will be the symbol that will be carried down through the ages. The cross will come to symbolize the burden to mankind. It will show that men have a debt to pay to society and to the Universal Consciousness, God. Men will suffer for many generations, and then when the suffering subsides, men will realize that all can be understood. A day shall also come when I shall return in various ways to bring my message again unto the people, but I shall then be misunderstood the same as I am this day."

You see, disciples of Agasha, I want to bring unto you that I was told, and I actually saw many times, the future of my life. I also knew that I would be coming back, while still remaining on the spiritual side of life, in the generation that would mark the end of a cycle and which would be vital unto mankind. Then at the conclusion of this cycle, heaven would be established on earth. But there were very few who believed me then, and I could see that there would be many, many people who would not even believe me when I would come back in the twentieth century. But I said unto them at the time, "I shall return, and I shall return many times although not in a physical body."

Then I placed certain things upon a scroll, upon a tablet of time, and as I placed them thereupon, I said, "In time man shall realize that he is a divine entity and that he is infinitely intelligent. Then he shall know that that which I give unto mankind this day is within him. He has only to knock and the door shall be opened unto him. Then he shall know the truth and he shall be on his way."

Yes, all these things had been handed unto the disciples, and unto others, and I realize today that there must be a clarification whereby mankind will come to know the truth. Therefore I have returned. However it was believed then, when the writings were placed therein upon the tablet of time, that there would be many who would ask, "Did such a person actually exist?"

But I only represent humanity. I am a symbol for all mankind who has had to face the same. Yes, men have been crucified down through the ages, and today someone else was crucified. And tomorrow another one is going to be crucified, and in the tomorrows to come still others shall be crucified. There is no difference in the crucifixion, children. However, there are many ways to crucify. The cross is only a symbol.

This then brings my thoughts back to the last of my days on the earth, and just before I was to bid farewell to the material world never again to return unto the flesh. Then as I was just about to take my last breath, I glanced down and there stood before me one whom I immediately recognized. She was my mother, disciples of Agasha, the one who enabled me to come into this life to serve as I did. She was also one whom I knew very well in a past life. You have heard me speak of her before when I referred to the seeress who was living in the palace in such great distress. Yes, she was my true mother.

So then today I have returned from the spiritual side of life to let you know that you children who remain in the flesh are to go on and learn your lessons. Never let a day pass by when you cannot truly say, "I have served this day in a humble way. I have learned and I also have enjoyed my life this day." But remember one thing. It is, that as I manifest occasionally telling you stories in my humble way, please endeavor to understand them. For the average man will not believe me today any more than he did during my time.

You then, as a divine entity, must realize that your days are few. And soon you are to come over to this side of life. So then prepare yourself now so that you can receive the blessings when we meet on this beautiful shore. Then you will have revealed unto you your life that shall be greater than all of the lives that you have ever had. These are the finishing-up periods. These are the latter days. This is the age when Agasha, as well as other earthly teachers, are to bring forth the light once again. Then it will be proven unto mankind that the change is forthcoming. It is now at hand, disciples of Agasha. There is no other way out of it and you must try to understand.

So then, do as Agasha says by having laughter in your heart, and by always being mentally alert. Do as Agasha says in all things and remember that you cannot then go wrong. You and I are in the higher occult field of expression, and you and I have the understanding that it is through Agasha's message, through his simple teachings which he brings forth to clarify the way, that you will be set free in the Consciousness of God.

Bless you. This is Kraio, and good night.

TWELFTH DISCOURSE

CYCLES, NUMBER, AND VIBRATION

By Agasha

MY BLESSED DISCIPLES—Manzaholla and bless each and every one. Again we have the opportunity of reassembling so that you may absorb the power brought into this room. Disciples, in regards to my manifesting, no doubt you have often thought about how difficult it would be for me to select any one single subject, so that if I were to talk only on it in the course of an evening, it would do the most good insofar as reaching the different types of consciousness is concerned. Therefore I usually cover a variety of subjects in order to hit your individual keynote, as it were, sometime during the course of the class.

However, it is not necessary for us to manifest and to be apologetic because we realize that we are going to reach those who are ready to receive the message and thus understand this beautiful truth. You and I know that our sole purpose in life is to learn, grow, and expand. Therefore let us absorb what we can and try to receive that particular measure of help which will enable us to enjoy the niceties of life.

Occasionally you hear people say that a certain individual is beyond his time. Now what do we mean by the term "beyond his time"? It would appear that many men have been beyond their time, because the things that they had talked about and believed in actually came into manifestation some fifty years later. Why is this so? The answer is that their individual life cycle was out of phase with the life cycle of humanity in general.

In their various lives, all men go through the cycles that they do because everything in life is a cycle. But while everything in life goes through a cycle, the cycles do not necessarily harmonize—the high point of one individual being at variance with the high point of another. Therefore in the forepart of this class tonight, let us try to harmonize our thoughts on this subject, bring them into phase with each other, so that we may have a better understanding of cycles, of the true meaning of number, and of that much overused word *vibration* as well.

The Study of Cycles

You are told that when you first come into this life, laying aside the subject of astrology for the moment, your soul has a cycle. There are certain cycles that karmically you must go through. Are there those who are capable of knowing these cycles? Some people believe, numerically speaking, that they can calculate precisely when certain cycles are going to transpire and the length of their duration. They will say that during that period of time you will have good luck, or bad luck, or whatever it is that is supposed to transpire. Can they do this? Are they able to read these cycles from the Akashic contact? Perhaps they can, but you see we cannot take too much stock in that at the moment because we have no way of proving it. However, I might add that your teacher, through his findings in the higher planes, is very capable of giving you the soul's cycles and the various material cycles that you will have to go through.

Human life goes through cycles and the earth does also. For instance, every 7,000 years cataclysms, violent upheavals of either a physical or a social nature, usually take place on the earth. It has always been that way, and as far as we can see, it will be that way in the future. There is the shifting of the earth which causes earthquakes to occur in different parts of the world, islands to sink and others to arise, and sometimes even the complete submergence of an entire continent such as the submergence of Atlantis 172,000 years ago. Nature, indeed, goes on a rampage.

Disease can break out, pestilence can take place, plagues can come into manifestation. Mankind can also be karmically affected through wars, crime, and political upheavals such as that which you are in evidence of at the present time. All hell seems to come over the face of the earth at the end of every 7,000-year cycle, and your present cycle is no different. It is as I always say, "The pot is boiling over; the boil is coming to a head."

As I have said innumerable times in the past, the year 1965 marked the end of the previous cycle and the beginning of the new age—the Psychic Age, the Space Age. Of course, all this does not happen overnight. Nature does not listen for the clock to strike twelve, so to speak, and then instantly bring all into manifestation. The ages overlap, and it takes a span of many years for the old to give forth to the new.

The forces of vegetation must go through a cycle. The cells in your body go through a cycle. Everything that comes into manifestation goes through a cycle. You are now functioning in a cycle. Therefore, inasmuch as everything goes through cycles, everything can also be said to be circular. If anything were to become semicircular, then there is not the completion and we would have to consult the records to find out why that circle or cycle was not completed.

The circle as a symbol is vital. During the time of Atlantis, and then again in Austa, Egypt, the symbol of the pyramid surrounded by the circle, the perfect circle so to speak, was very important to us. This symbol, and especially the illumination on the outer cusp of the great circle, indicated the power and the completion of a particular civilization. In other words, this meant the completion of life, the comple-

tion of the cycle, the completion of the activity of the civilization, and so on. It was symbolical in character, indeed,
but at the same time it meant that we understood that everything goes through cycles. Now it is up to you, and also up
to me as an entity of the Divine State, to ascertain numerically just how long a particular cycle will last.

Subtly, we can determine when a particular cycle began
by a study of its vacillations or fluctuations. Numerically
speaking then, we can deduce when it was first brought into
manifestation. A cycle also means a rate of vibration. Let us
say that there is an action brought into play at a certain
given point. Then its rate of vibration will determine the
result at another point over here. This in turn will bring
about a new action at the second point, and a new result will
manifest at still another point, a third point over there. Thus
we have what we might term an endless chain of reactions
taking place as the direct result of the action originally
created. Do you follow me on that point? It is really not as
confusing as it sounds.

All Things Are in Circular Motion

Let us now leave this thought for the moment, and return
to the fact that everything in your life is circular. Or perhaps
we should say it is in circular motion. Let us take a germ. We
realize that when we observe the outer casing of any germ
force we may not find it circular in shape, but we would
know most assuredly that the life force within that germ
would definitely be in circular motion.

It even has been said that the soul or the God Consciousness that today rests within man is circular in form. But on
the other hand, we have often chosen to describe it by saying
that it is egg-shaped in form. However, it is still more or less
circular although most people would say that it be oblong.
This way or that way, it does not make any substantial
difference. We can still say that the soul is circular. We find
then that in life everything seems to congeal more or less in
circular form. This is applicable to plant life, mineral life,

and all life, although the true form is perhaps not as we observe it to be. But when we take into consideration the aura or the life force surrounding the outer casing, it seems to always form in circles.

Even the results of the majority of men's actions upon the earth plane are found to be circular. By that I mean that the results of the effort put forth will usually return to the one initiating the action—either for good or for bad. We call this by the term *karma*. Therefore if you were to chart it, you would have to chart it in the form of a circle.

All of nature follows the same pattern. Drop a speck of water; it will fall in the form of a raindrop which is circular. Spill some ink on the table; it will smear in a curved or circular fashion. Drop a pebble into the pond; the ripples will move out in circles. You may say that there is nothing out of the ordinary in all of this, but let me bring to your attention that the reason that everything is circular is because it is in harmony with the relationship of the vibratorial rays of the God Consciousness. Do you follow me on that point, disciples?

Take a drop of blood. If you were to scrutinize it technically and scientifically, you would find that the red and white corpuscles would be in circular motion. Cell life is in circular motion; everything is in circular motion. That is why many of the symbols of the past contain clusters of minute circles, embedded together, and always in circular form.

Therefore, in our circular motion upon this earth one might say that we have a tendency to go in circles. We have often heard someone use the expression, "I am going in circles." This means in your vernacular that you are confused, that you do not know whether you are coming or going. Isn't that correct, disciples? Well that is just an expression; it has nothing to do with the circles that I am referring to. When I say that everything is in circular motion, I mean that everything that is out there in space, everything that is around and about you, even every force that is not even detected at this time—all of these things are revolving and moving in circles, or spirals, or some other form of curved motion.

We have the atom; we have the anim; we have the animatical forces in between. There they are, and they are all in circular motion. There within a circle comes another circle, and another circle, and another circle. There within a tiny drop of water we find billions and billions of atoms and molecules—all in circular motion. And within these atoms, which in reality are only the outer rim of the anim, is the anim with its corresponding animatical forces—all of these things are in circular motion. Each is playing its part; they are all part of one and the same. Everything is in harmony with the universe, and being in harmony with the universe, it must out of necessity always be brought into manifestation in a circular fashion.

Your aura is around you. It is not around you in a square manner; it is around you in a circular manner forming the contour of the physical body. And this same aura, which is invisible to your physical sight, is in circular motion. The colors that are seen occasionally are the result of the circular vibration of the anims. Even the blood which is circulating through your body is in circular motion. Your blessed thoughts, if they are potent, can mentally build a light around yourself. But you do not say that you are going to put a *square* of light around you; you never think of that. You would not think of doing that and you don't do that. You are going to mentally *surround* yourself with light. Therefore a light immediately surrounds you.

The Wheel of Life: An Atlantean Symbol

Let us turn our thoughts now to the study of a very ancient symbol. It is called the Wheel of Life. Let us begin by picturing in our mind's eye the symbol of a perfect circle right here before us. We are going to study it. The next thing for us to do is to divide the circumference of this circle, sectioning it off rather, into a certain number of parts. Let us say, as a supposition, that we use the number 150. We divide the circle into 150 different parts, and each mark that we place on that circle represents a life. We should put some of the marks very close together at first because our embodiments would be more frequent in the earlier part of our evolution. Then we should place the others gradually further apart.

We realize then that as we go around the complete circle, we find there in the center what is termed the hub. Let us call it the Core of Life. In the Core of Life we find this great force; it is coming out from the hub, and each force of light seems to come out in the form of a spoke. Do you follow me there? Each spoke then is reaching one of the little marks that you have made which represents a particular embodiment. Now I am referring to you as an individual. There you have a chart, crudely made, and yet it represents the lives in a circle that you have lived on this particular earth plane.

The Atlanteans were well aware of this symbol: in fact, the City of Atlantis was carried out architecturally in the same manner. It was built as a circle with all the avenues leading out from or returning into the hub. Within the hub was a circular building where they carried out their scientific experiments or discussed whatever it was that they desired to discuss, be it political or be it this or that. Therefore, the avenues always led you into that building, a great building that was esteemed to be so very, very important to that city and to that civilization. There we have the general lay-out of the City of Atlantis, but we will leave Atlantis for the subject of another class.

The hub of the wheel then represents the Universal Consciousness God—the Core of Life. There we have the radiation from the hub, and this radiation is reaching you today as a single entity in your respective circle. So you see, disciples, the Core of Life is sustaining you at all times. It has sustained you through the many lives that you have lived on this earth plane, as represented by the marks on the rim of the wheel. Now then, we multiply that, and the multiplication is seemingly endless. The wheel can be made to represent the seemingly countless lives that we had lived, not only on this earth, but on the various other planets that are too numerous to mention.

This symbol can also show you that the combination of all of this, the sum total of all of your lives as it were, would be in that Divine Spark of Divinity. This spark, originally coming from the hub, had also been in every body that you had ever inhabited on any planet whatsoever. This is the Wheel of Life. You are now going through the Wheel of Life, and as you go through it, keep in your mind that wheels, like everything else, always turn in circles.

Therefore, this mental picture that we have now put before you is the same symbol that was used in Atlantis. It was also used in various other stages of our growth, such as 7,000 years ago during my stay in Austa, Egypt. This, of course, extended into the 2,000-year Peace Period where it remained to be very significant unto the people. The hub would sometimes appear in different forms such as the sacred bird, or the sacred animal, or the pyramid, or the All-Seeing Eye, or perhaps the All-Seeing Eye encased in a circle. Naturally the symbol was very important to us. It was important because we felt that this symbol of the great Wheel of Life was in harmony with the Universe.

The Cabalah and the Higher Calculus

You have to understand the higher calculus in order to properly appreciate the vibratorial rates of the Universe. Once you are able to do this, you can then from your higher learning actually know the approximate time this earth is to be disintegrated. You can also find out how long the sun will be in manifestation and when it too will burn out and then play no important part for a time. Eventually every planet and gaseous body will revert back to its original etheric state. The vibratorial rates of these higher forces are determined numerically, but they are recognized only through a study of the higher calculus and the numerical forces that are brought into play.

In our day back in Austa we sought for mathematical answers, and thus eventually we too came to understand the laws of the higher calculus and what effect numerical activity has upon mankind. These laws were well understood during the time of Atlantis, and we became aware of them through contacting the Atlantean teachers directly. Thus we became very conscious of numerals. Of course, the way that you draw numerals today would have had no significance during our period then. We drew them differently, but they meant the same and amounted to the same as your numerals of today.

Therefore in the beginning of our great Peace Period, the various disciples were taught in their lessons that which was known as "numerical activity and its influences unto men." We worked with numerals; they were very vital to us, very important. We knew that in working with numerals the information was absolutely correct in every sense of the word. We knew that numerals do not lie, that they relate to facts. And then through them we perceived much pertaining to human behavior and the cycles that men must go through from life to life.

We knew that a great deal could be derived from knowledge of the date of birth, the date the individual drew in his first breath. Then we would progress the cycles, starting with the heartbeat, into the equivalent in minutes and then in hours. Thus we came to know the cycles of the days, the weeks, the months, the years. Finally we reached the higher calculus where we could then realize the vastness of life itself and its relationship to the numerical forces which always are the basic motivating factor behind any revolving object.

Then several thousand years later, the ancient Hebrews were able to pick up and revive once more much of what we had learned back there in Austa. Thus they taught what is known today as the "Hebrew numerology" or the *Cabalah*.

These teachings played a very important part in the lives of the scholars during that period; yet the teachings are all one and the same. They were simply an offshoot from what we had taught in Austa and which had been originally given in Atlantis. Therefore the Hebrew numerical activity of that period was most accurate in determining various things relative to the stars and planets and the effect of same upon the human body. They also combined the numerical forces with the astronomical forces through a mild form of astrology.

Now the system of Numerology that is employed today has deviated considerably from the true course that was given during our period, and much has even been lost from the original Cabalistic teachings of the Hebrews. Therefore, today you have a compilation of many subjects in that which is loosely termed *Numerology*, and much of it is not accurate. There has been only a smattering of correct information given unto those who would seek in this direction. Now I am not necessarily saying that Numerology as taught today is inaccurate; I am merely saying that it has deviated considerably from the original teachings.

But even though they be not fully understood, the numerical influences on the lives of men are just as powerful today as they were then. We are all controlled by that force. Although this is not generally accepted scientifically, nor is it usually accepted by all people who study the occult, we know that numerically speaking you are controlled by numerals. It follows then that numerals play a very important part in your life, more than what you might readily surmise on the surface.

The Digits

Before we can fully understand these numerical forces, we must first have an understanding of the numerical influences of the digits themselves. Since all of the natural numbers are built up of digits, the force exerted by each individual digit becomes a very important part of the number itself. Then too, any natural whole number can be reduced to a single digit by successive addition. Therefore, basically you are controlled by the digits from 1 to 9. It may be a 9, 7, 6, or 4 that is controlling your present circumstances. It may be any one of the digits from 1 to 9. The 10, being a two-digit number, becomes silent and naturally reverts back to zero. These digits, from 1 to 9, are influencing every action that you make, and it is in order that we now briefly review them individually.

The number *one* always denotes a new beginning and will usually bring forth *activity.* It also represents the principle of unity and the Oneness from which all things sprang forth. If multiplied by itself forever, it will always remain that which it always was—one.

The number *two* means *uncertainty.* It is the symbol of duality and always represents pairs of opposites such as male and female, positive and negative, good and evil, and so forth.

The number *three* means *abundance,* and it always represents the triad or the trinity. What is the trinity? You have a misinterpretation of the trinity on the earth plane because the trinity can mean many things. But it is always the three. Everything that exists in life always comes into manifestation in threes. The trinity then is one of the highest vibrational rates of any force that you may employ because it means all things. It is the God force, the positive force, and the negative force. It is the Universal Consciousness God, the creator of all things, bringing into manifestation the positive and negative forces, the masculine and feminine aspects of Being. All three then are brought into one harmonious relationship called the Trinity. And viewing it in this context, you may capitalize it.

And now we come to the greatest enigma of them all—the number *four.* It is a very negative number and it spells *trouble.* Indeed, it is a number to labor under if you have that digit in your vibration. It can be symbolically represented by a square of four sides in the same manner that the number three can be represented by a triangle of three sides. And like the trinity, the square can also mean many things. But it is always the four; a square always has four sides.

The study of astrology can reveal much in this direction. Put the triangle in the circle and we have harmonious aspects; the forces are in harmony with each other. Put the square in the circle and we have either opposition or we have forces that are perpendicular to each other; thus we have tension, stress, strain, and so forth. If a force is *squaring* another force, it means there is a blockage, there is an obstruction.

So the number four may be said to be an obstacle in your path. It is something to be overcome, something to be conquered so that you may become a stronger individual. Therefore it is a mixed blessing, for without the number four throwing obstacles in your path, so to speak, you could not grow, you could not overcome. However, some individuals fall victim to the number four and here is the tragedy in life. They did not show the strength necessary to overcome that which they were supposed to overcome, and therefore they failed in that particular incarnation.

Number *five* is a *physical* number. It is frequently symbolized as a five-pointed star or a pentagram, with the body of Man placed therein with his arms and legs outstretched. Being at the midpoint of the digits from one to nine, it is also the bearer of the *unexpected.* Many unexpected things may arise in the lives of people who be influenced by the five.

The number *six* is a *material* number. It is definitely material. In fact, it is so material that if one is truly functioning on the material plane of the number six, disciples, he can become extremely materialistic to a fault, although it need not be so. It is usually denoted by two interlaced triangles, one pointing up and the other pointing down, showing the complete balance in Nature.

The number *seven* is *spiritual*: indeed, it has always been known to be a spiritual number in the scheme of things. Down through the ages, those who were advanced in the field of the occult have known that there are seven ways in which man may attain, seven ways in which he may reach the Divine State. Indeed, the seven is within you. But these seven paths pertaining to your life may all vary. Your soul may take any one of seven ways to carry out a plan or bring about a result.

The seven is also a *universal* number. By that I mean that every seven years your body changes, every seven years you change spiritually, every seven years your mental kingdom changes. Everyone is affected by the universal seven. Even the cataclysms and the things that cause destruction on the earth are usually within a seven cycle.

The number *eight*, like the number six, is also a *material* number. It has to do with material affairs and life on the earth plane. One under the influence of the eight is usually interested in the material, and the number eight can be quite beneficial in this direction. It is good for business, and it can be utilized for the benefit of a person who has come to the realization of the eight.

Now we come to the number *nine*, and it can be said to be *profound*. It is the most profound number, numerically speaking, over all of the numbers from one to nine. But it also can be a disturbing factor if it is not utilized properly. The number nine is therefore called an occult number in many occult circles, and rightfully so. This you can well understand. Being the last of the digits, it can also be said that it is the number of initiation.

The number *ten* denotes *completion*, and as we just pointed out, it becomes silent and reverts back to zero, the point where we started. The digit one, which stands beside the zero, is now ready to begin a new cycle of manifestations in a higher phase of the evolution of the numbers.

Therefore, as we go up and down the scale we find that we will come right back to the same answer: everything is in circular form. Absolutely everything that comes unto you comes as a circular force. This means then that you are now going through a cycle. But each cycle that you as an individual are going through has a number attached to it. All of the digits are good numbers, helpful numbers, with the possible exception of our square friend, the four. And even this number in reality is not bad, because it enables us to grow. After all, disciples, life would not be interesting if it were not for a villain or two lurking in the shadows, so to speak, to prod us on to higher and greater achievements. So therefore these digits are vital to each and every one when you ascertain precisely the digit or the numeral that is now affecting your life.

The Larger Numbers

Perhaps we should now take a brief look at the larger numbers. Is a 12 different from a 21, or a 39, or even a 165? Of course it is. But all of these numbers are still only higher octaves of the number three, since any natural whole number can be reduced to a single digit by successive addition. The single digit then strikes the keynote for the entire number no matter how large it be. But this is certainly not to imply that there cannot be a vast difference in the characteristics of each of the numbers in the higher frequencies. I hesitate to use the word *octave* here as this implies a system of eight.

We must remember that everything in life has a number attached to it. Absolutely everything is vibrating on its own particular frequency, and that frequency can be expressed numerically. No matter how great or small that frequency be, it can still be expressed numerically. It is even true that every word is the equivalent of a number, and every number can be said to be a word.

But in your classes I have refrained from going into these larger and more complex numbers. Indeed, it becomes an entire study in itself, as a thorough understanding would not only have to embrace the Cabalah, but also that which I have termed the "higher calculus" as well. Therefore, for the present, let us be content with our understanding of the single-digit numbers from one to nine.

Your Physical Vibration Point

Before we leave the larger numbers completely, however, let us look into the physical force that governs you biologically. Every individual has a definite vibratorial point that is established for any given life. This vibratorial point is purely a biological force. It is a physical rate of vibration, and it can be the same as it was in a previous life or it can fluctuate from life to life. However, once it has been established it will remain constant during your entire life. It may be an 82 or a 96 or whatever. Your teacher is in a position to give these rates to you.

But I would like to bring to your attention that if your vibratorial point is below 30, then you are too weak physically; likewise if it is above 97, then it is too high and that is dangerous. Of course, the higher the rate of vibration the more sensitive you are, and the easier it is to bring in information from the ethereal world. Those in the 70's, the 80's, and the 90's are very sensitive, with the genius-type mind manifesting in the higher 90's. But these high rates of vibration can offer problems, and having too high a rate of vibration can be just as bad as having too low a rate of vibration. On the whole though, if your vibratorial point lies anywhere between 30 and 97, it can be said that you have a healthy and normal physical force.

But this rate of vibration is no criterion for judging your *spiritual* growth. It is purely a physical or a biological force, and if yours be an 82 and your neighbor's only a 63, this certainly does not mean that you are any higher spiritually. It means only that your physical frequency is different in the same manner that a base tone is different from a shrill tone. Again I say that if your rate is above 97, then it is too high and you are at the danger point. It would be just like you were ready to explode, and you would become hypersensitive to a fault.

Your Key Number: The Date of Your Birth

Another number that will remain constant throughout
your life is that which we call your *key number.* It relates
to your date of birth. To ascertain your key number: the
month, the day, and the year of your birth must all be taken
into consideration. Then these numbers are added together
by successive addition and reduced to a single digit. The
result be your key number or digit.

Let us say hypothetically that a person was born on September 14, 1925. The numeral for September is 9, since
September is the 9th month. The 14th day reduces to a 5.
The numerals in the year 1925 add to 17 which reduces to an
an 8. Now add the digits: 9 + 5 + 8, and the answer in this
example is 22, which would mean that your key number
would be a 4.

Then as you add the vibratorial rate of the current year,
whatever it be, to your key digit, you may find what the
year holds in store for you, generally speaking. If your key
digit is 4, as in this example, then 1974, a 3 year, when added
to your key digit would make it a 7 year as far as you
individually are concerned. The year may also be broken
down into months. Then you can pretty will understand
what is going to take place month after month as far as the
numerical influences arising from your key number will
affect it. For instance: January will be a 7 + 1 or an 8 month
for you; February, a 7 + 2 or a 9 month; March, a 7 + 3 or
a 1 month, and so on down the scale.

Thus you can see that numerals play a very important
part in your life. You cannot do anything until a certain time
has expired. Isn't that true? No matter how much you fuss
and carry on, it will not be brought about until the proper
time comes. This means then that an action dating back
generations ago set in motion a force that enables you to be
controlled or influenced by the vibratorial rate of, let us say,
the number nine. Do you follow me there? Or it may be a
seven, or a four, or a two, or whatever. Numerically speak-

ing, we observe its reactions upon man, the earth, the country, or any number of things that are affected by it. Therefore it could be said that past actions affect future events through their numerical influences.

You might ask, "Do the stars or planets have anything to do with it?" Perhaps they do. The influences of the planets have been known by the astrologer for a long, long time. But isn't an astrological force also a numerical force? Everything, when we get right down to it, is really number. Therefore, we know that cycles must be completed before a certain something is consummated. This is the law.

Your Path of Life and Soul Cycle Numbers

Before we close this little talk tonight, we should at least touch upon two other major cycles that affect your life. These are the path of life cycle and the soul cycle. Everyone on the earth plane is functioning within both of these cycles. The former tends to control your life as you lead it on the earth plane; the latter governs your spiritual growth. These numbers are always a single digit and may vary between one and nine, and your life cycle number is not necessarily the same as your soul cycle number. In fact, they are usually different.

How does one determine his life or soul cycle number? You cannot on the surface do this; they have to be given you by your teacher or one who is knowledgeable along these lines. You see, everything is in relationship to the karmic vibrations, and these life and soul cycle numbers were determined prior to your birth on the physical plane and will remain with you for the duration of your physical life.

They begin with your time of birth, the first moment that you drew your first breath, and continue on, on a yearly basis, throughout your life. This means then that if your life cycle is nine, as a supposition, then every nine years from your date of birth you are entering a new cycle. Now let us leave astrology out of it for a moment; let us think numerically if we may. Then you are going to change every nine years either for good or for bad. If you had nine years of good fortune, as you say on earth, and if you have grown mentally, physically, and spiritually, then when your birthday comes around again you are going to enter another cycle for another nine years. But the conditions of the new cycle will be the direct result of your actions, thoughts, and deeds during the previous cycle.

We can see then that we ourselves are responsible for the things that come into our lives. The only thing that could change this pattern would be a previous karmic debt, one that was being carried over from a prior life. This karmic debt then would be lying in wait to either challenge us or reward us at a certain point in our life. If this were the condition, then the karmic debt would also have to be taken into consideration, as it could change the picture considerably.

Your soul cycle number will affect your life in much the same manner as your life cycle number; but it will basically pertain only to your spiritual growth. It is not so much concerned with your material affairs. Your soul cycle number also relates back to the germ itself, to the beginning of its spiral evolution upon this earth. So then if you live your life in harmony with this number—if it is a seven, we will say, and you do everything in a seven consciousness—then you are in harmony with the Universe.

Thoughts, Vibration, and the Germinal Kingdom

Let us now study the practical application of the term *vibration*. Vibration is created from what? Thoughts, or any form of action. Every thought you think sets up a vibration. And this vibration will then affect the environment either for good or for bad.

To illustrate this, let us take a single germ. The germ is standing there before us. Now what do we find within this germ? We find the God force. It is a God germ because everything in the Universe belongs to God. Therefore if the germ be negative, you cannot say that it is the devil force because the germ is evil, because it destroys. So then you cannot call it a devil germ, can you? No, you cannot. You understand that in your philosophy there is no such thing as a separate entity coming unto the earth who be called the devil. That is without taking yourself into consideration, of course. It is the mortal mind that is the devil, as I have said innumerable times in the past.

Therefore, this germ that we have standing before us belongs basically to the God Consciousness. It is a part of it. In its pure and uncontaminated state, the germ is manifesting in its true light. There within this germ is the trinity: the God force, the positive force, and the negative force. Each force is revolving in a circular form and all is in harmony with God. Very well. We can say that in the original state of the germ, the God Consciousness is definitely within it.

Now let us say that man comes along within the vicinity of this germ. His mortal mind, through negative thinking and actions, then sets up certain vibrations that are inharmonious and naturally opposite to God. Through certain laws of polarity the germ is attracted to these vibrations, and it intermingles with these negative forces. You and I then as mortals color this germ with our character, with our thoughts, and it then becomes other than the godlike expression it had in the beginning. It becomes negative itself and it takes on completely different characteristics. It then multiplies and multiplies, and as it multiplies it does its destruction because we had invited such destruction unknowingly through our actions. Do you follow me on that point?

Let us now go back to the origin of the cycles that we go through and the reactions that we have. You and I as mortals had set in motion the forces that caused these cycles to occur. Our negative thinking had simply set up certain vibrations that be inharmonious and naturally opposite to God, that is, presuming that it is a negative cycle that we are in. If it is a germ that be our problem, we must remember that the germ that we have contacted is only following orders. It will do its destruction wherever we had so directed it and with whatever force or character we had given it. It will react much the same as our negative thoughts react by going out, hurting, destroying, and holding us back.

Therefore we are going to have to pay the penalty, and there is going to be trouble for us in our life. We had fallen out of step or out of harmony with God; or more simply, we were not in rhythm with the Universal Consciousness God. Thus this god-like germ that has now become demon-like will attack mankind for a long period of time or until such time that the cycle will have expended itself. Then with harmony once more restored, the germ that destroys mankind today will no longer destroy mankind because there will be no reason or cause for such destruction. The cycle or circle will then be complete.

We are now reverting back to the point from which we came. But we do not make a straight line back to the beginning; we spiral with the great Wheel of Life in a circular motion back to the beginning. This action is all a part of your training; it is all in harmony with God. You and I in our unfoldment are striving ever to be in harmony with the Universe, with our own kingdom, and with our fellowman. Then as we do this, we definitely will have many things revealed to us that heretofore have not been able to come because the door was not ajar.

Always remember, disciples, that everything manifests in cycles to become whatever it is supposed to be, and that all of this comes about through the numerical influences which are vital to every form of life. Rub your hands together, sound the A-U-M, and call out your teacher's name. One . . . two . . . three . . . AUM.

THIRTEENTH DISCOURSE

OUR JOURNEY THROUGH THE COSMOS

By Agasha

MY BLESSED CHILDREN—greetings. Another evening in which we can come together, blessed children, and have the joy of becoming reacquainted with the many things that we at one time had learned, but had become oblivious to, down through the ages. In reality we are not oblivious to them; we need only to awaken the soul so that the information may come to the surface.

In descending tonight, I was conscious in a flash of the earth as it loomed before me. In that split second, I became attuned to the universe, it would seem. I recalled the creation of this great planet that you live on, and I saw again the history of man as he evolved from the lower form of life, returning innumerable times unto the physical plane. My soul also revealed unto me that this was brought so vividly to my consciousness tonight for a very special reason.

It seems that it has been difficult for some of the disciples to comprehend the many things that I have endeavored to give during these past years; so I will take you on a mental journey tonight into the vast Consciousness of Immensity, back through seemingly endless space and time, and review the major events that have transpired since the moment when you first sprang forth from that Divine Consciousness, the Core of Life. As well as being a comprehensive review for your mortal consciousness, it will also act as a stimulus towards reawakening impressions from the soul.

As One Planet Disintegrates Another Is Born

However, before we go back these billions and billions and billions of years to the origin of life, let us begin with the present. Let us gaze out into space and observe the seemingly countless stars, moons, planets, suns. In our mind's eye let us observe a planet that is now being formed. As it hurtles through space at a terrific rate of speed, it begins to form and to collect all the particles it needs in order to be brought into manifestation to become an earth, a planet, or whatever you might call it. I simply want to indicate to you that out there in the vastness of space planets are actually being formed every 24 hours, and every 24 hours others are going through a state of disintegration. I use the term "24 hours" because it is the amount of time considered a day upon the physical plane. I use the expression simply to indicate that within the course of a day, a planet comes and a planet goes. And this is applicable only within your own region of the universe!

Now let your imagination stretch out into the seemingly endless reaches of space. Try to think of what is going on out there in the apparent nothingness: what is disappearing in the respective solar systems, and what is coming into being. Think of the millions or the countless solar systems— let me emphasize that—countless solar systems with no beginning and no ending—that are spread out before our eyes. This becomes a tremendous thought, and one so vast in scope that it is very difficult for the average disciple even to visualize it, let alone comprehend it, and of course there is momentarily no way to prove it.

In My Father's House Are Many Mansions

So then as we gaze out there into space, we are filled with great awe and wonderment as we marvel at the majesty of it all. But our *wondering* or questioning gradually turns into *wonder* as we begin to realize one basic truth. It is the same truth that was so beautifully expressed by Kraio when he made the statement, "In my Father's house are many mansions." Now what did he really mean by this? The answer, disciples, is that the term *mansions*, in its true interpretation, relates to planets—spiritual planets, degrees of consciousness. *Father* then means universe, the collective whole, everything that is. Call it by whatever name you choose. The Father's *house* is the great Consciousness of Immensity which embraces all things—absolutely everything of a material or a spiritual nature that exists out there in fathomless space. Therefore in the Father's house, the universe as a whole, are many spiritual planets, or mansions as it was expressed by Kraio. This is the true meaning of what is meant by the phrase, "In my Father's house are many mansions."

Mansions then are the blessed states of consciousness where we can reach wonderful states of ecstasy and live therein. They are the great spiritual planets where the many have their own individual kingdoms. But if we were to take one spiritual planet individually, and call it the Father's house, then the many mansions contained within this one planet would relate to buildings, great temples, or halls of learning. It is in this context that the term *mansion* is usually used when expressing the thought that through our actions and deeds upon the earth plane, we create the mansion or the house that we shall live in. Each of us then has his work to do.

All teachers have what is known as their individual temples. These temples are like homes to you people upon earth. They are truly magnificent structures, and they are

also called "halls of learning" for it is here where the teachers
carry out various activities, where they teach many wonderful things unto their disciples. For instance, when you
visit them while out of the body during the sleep state, they
bring out certain points in your life; and in the interim
period they are teaching and bringing valuable information
to other souls who have lived over on this side of life for
two to three hundred years.

The Seven Solar Systems

Let us now mentally try to visualize ourself in one of these
temples receiving instruction from the teachers. Let us say
that the subject is the universe itself, and we are in the
Temple of the All-Seeing Eye for here we can observe, from
the standpoint of symbology, a model or a chart of that
which is termed the universal "seven solar systems." Yes,
disciples, the countless solar systems (we use the word *countless* because they are so numerous) are actually grouped
together into systems of seven.

This principle has yet to be discovered by the scientific
mind, for it is a spiritual relationship and not necessarily one
of a material nature. But one supports the other; the systems
are interlocked and interwoven into a pattern. Each group
of seven solar systems is interrelated and closely associated;
each planet therein draws power from the various other
planets to sustain itself. We also observe that some of the
planets sustain life; but in each instance we find that the
physical plane life seems to be influenced, unduly sometimes, by the frictional forces that are created or set up
vibratorially from one planet to another. We realize then
that there is much to be derived from this model or chart
of the universal seven solar systems.

Now let us step over to another chart in the Spiritual
Temple (these things are not necessarily taught only in the
Temple of the All-Seeing Eye), and what do we observe? In
this new chart we have what represents our own cluster of
seven solar systems. We see it perhaps as a map. Over here

is a planet that has been in existence for a period of time, and the life on this planet is advanced. On some of the planets over there life is not so advanced. The teachers point out everything in these seven solar systems and link them together; they show you their interrelation. Then they might bring forth some of the Masters of Light who had arisen from these various planets, and perhaps one of them will speak. He will go into even further detail regarding the items on this great chart, things that can very easily be depicted, as he stands there to show them to you. Your spiritual consciousness can very readily grasp all of this, for when you are out of the body you are attuned to the Infinite State. You see clearly; you better understand because mortal is not now in the picture. Therefore, all of the important things on this chart or grand map of our group of seven solar systems are pointed out unto the disciple.

We make an impression here, and as we do we tell you that this impression represents a planet that was in that location but has since disintegrated. We then go to other parts of this group of seven solar systems and show you what has happened. Then we point out that certain other planets are yet to come into manifestation, perhaps even in this present period of time. You are able to see very clearly how new planets are being formed at all times—coming in as well as going out of manifestation.

You learn then that human expression first came upon your earth 25 million years ago—a comparatively short time. Then perhaps 50 million years ago we were living on this planet over here, and before that time on a planet over there that has long since disintegrated. How long ago was that? The time element is not for me to say at the moment, but remember, disciples, we have reembodied ourselves respectively in the various categories of our cluster of seven solar systems for a very long time.

Then the teacher, whoever he be, will point out and convey information to you according to what he had learned of the many things that will concern not only your life in *this* material cycle of lives, but also your life in the final stages of the growth of mankind, in the great Consciousness of Immensity. This means then that every form of life is eventually to become a part of that great Consciousness.

The Importance of the Sun

Let us now take a look at the sun force, that great force that emanates from the sun and nourishes the planets within each system. When your planet was first slushed off from the other etheric planets in the beginning, it was the sun that was basically responsible in helping to bring the earth into manifestation—the same as it helped the moon, the same as it helped the other planets within your respective solar system. We realize then that it is the sun that supplies the nourishment. It is the sun that feeds the planets; it is the sun that gives forth the light and the radiation which is so very vital. Without sun, you could not survive upon the earth plane. You learned that as a child in school, but nevertheless, it is so very, very true. Now there are other suns whose energies never reach this earth, naturally. You not only have your own sun whose rays reach this earth and the other planets within your respective solar system, but beyond in the countless other solar systems, there are countless other suns that are doing likewise, you understand. It is a part that must be played within each planetary system. Otherwise there is no growth, no life, and no form of habitant whatsoever could continue upon any earth plane. Every planet that is inhabitable must have the sun ray, this great energy, in order to sustain life.

Let us say that for days the sun cannot come out; and when the sun finally does come out, it is said that certain plants have not grown during the interim period. This is true. But let us also understand that you can survive for days and days and days without having the sun. The reason for this is that you have absorbed so much of the sun's rays, atoms, anims, energy—call it what you like—

within your body that you can survive for, oh, a long period of time without the sun coming out. But if the sun would not appear and shine upon the earth plane for months and months and years, you could go along for a time, but eventually you would become ill. Every plant would die and everything would perish from the earth. Therefore, we find how vital the sun actually is to the planetary force in your solar system.

In past civilizations, it was believed by various sects of the earth that the sun played a very important part in man's life. While realizing that the sun itself did not support life on its surface, these ancient sects supposed the sun to be the positive creator of all things that ever came upon the earth. They believed this to be true because they observed the sun to give growth unto flowers, to give growth unto all plant life, and to aid in the growth of mankind. Consequently, it was believed by various sects of the earth that after physical death, the spirit would reach the sun and dwell therein in a heavenly state. Of course, that was a false belief.

Today we realize that eventually even the sun itself is going to burn out. But it will take many, many, many millions and millions and even billions of years before it is actually burned out. The more the animatical or life-giving force of the sun recreates this intense heat and radiation, you understand, the more it also is feeding itself by the great light, the great atomic explosion. Yet it cannot be said that its rays are going to set off the explosion of the atomic force within the planets; no indeed, the controlled atomic explosion is within the sun itself. If it were not so, this earth, or any other earth for that matter, could never have been brought into manifestation.

Earth: A Planet of Destiny

Thus we come to our little "pea" planet Earth, and here is one thing I want you to bear in mind. This earth is comparatively new; it is a newly created planet and relatively small in comparison with some of the others. But it is a very important planet. It is a planet that I would term to be a planet of destiny. Isn't that an interesting point tonight? Now why do I say that it is a planet of destiny? Is it because you or I, as an individual attuned to the Infinite State, knew that this earth would be brought into manifestation? No, not necessarily. We have to go a little deeper than that.

The fact remains, disciples, that after we had arisen from another planet, and from other planets even before that, after we had grown, after we had reached a certain state of consciousness, then this planet that you call Earth was actually chosen and selected by the great Masters of Light. Now follow me carefully please. The Masters of Light, in conjunction with the Intermediaries, and who in turn were acting in conjunction with those we term the great "Pillars of Light," selected this particular planet as being the planet most capable of giving us the experiences that we needed, and still need at this present state of our evolution. Thus we can truly say that it is a planet of destiny.

Now prior to the time that we were brought onto this planet, millions and millions of years were required for the earth to go through its cooling process. This applies to all planets, for they must out of necessity go through these same cooling stages. There were earthquakes, there were volcanoes, and there were many gases that hovered within the earth's immediate atmosphere. Therefore, until these volatile conditions had subsided, there was no way for the different forms of life to come onto the physical plane.

Then, gradually, life was brought into manifestation. First there was the germinal life, and this in turn was then followed by plant life. But we must remember, disciples, the importance that water played in this process. That is why I always say that all life originally came from the sea. Perhaps it was only a lake, or a pond; it makes no difference, it is still water. Then we have the smaller forms of animal expression, then the mammoth animals, and finally, when the environment was ready—human expression, which as you have learned in your classes, appeared approximately 25 million years ago.

Now all the time that this was going on, you and I, being active entities in some other environment, were quite unaware of this planet Earth. We had lived on other planets, particularly in our own solar system; and I can say unto you that you have lived outside your solar system, perhaps many solar systems away as far as distance is concerned. You existed there, you moved and had your being there as a respective entity, and you are the same entity today that you were then.

The Seven Manifestations of the Universe

Let us now study your present group of planets, this relatively new group of planets that is in existence today. This group has been in manifestation for a certain number of billions of years. But there will come a time when everything that is out there in the countless solar systems, everything in the form of planets, moons, stars, suns—absolutely everything of a material nature in the universe—will disintegrate. The universe goes through that process at all times. It always has and it always will. Every physical body will revert back to its more sensitive body, its sublimated body, its spiritual body. Everything in the imperfect state will revert back to its original perfect state, and all will definitely be spirit. True, it may be many billions of years before this occurs—I have no way of telling nor even of knowing the exact time—but when the time comes, all will once again be part of that great Oneness. All will have returned into that greater life.

You must remember, there were several groups of planets that were brought into manifestation and that disintegrated over a period of billions and billions of years, long before this present group of planets was brought into manifestation. Now when I say "group of planets," I mean everything that is out there in the vastness of space—absolutely everything of a physical nature. This includes all of the countless solar systems and galaxies.

The average disciple will then ask, "How long has this process been going on? How many groups of planets have come into manifestation and then gone out of manifestation since we first sprang forth from the great Core of Life?" These are good questions and deserve good answers. It has been claimed by the Intermediary, this great Master of Light whom I have consulted innumerable times here of late, that our present group of planets is the seventh, and consequently the last, group of planets to be brought into manifestation in this particular round—that is, since we sprang forth from the Core of Life as a Divine entity.

Then what preceded all of this? There would be no way of knowing the answer to that question. I am only telling you, or quoting rather, what I have been told by this Intermediary. This is the last group of planets in the countless solar systems to be brought into manifestation; and I personally, as an individual, could not possibly know even a fraction of what is in those solar systems, let alone know what preceded them. But I have been informed that there were six other earlier manifestations before this seventh and last one. You might say that this is the grand finale.

In the beginning of the seven cycles, the first group was brought forth. This is the original group of planets. We study it. We observe that it has been in manifestation, we will say, for a period of 50 billion years. Now this is just a supposition, you understand; it is not accurate. This is only an expression to give you a clearer picture. Then we find that it disintegrates. Everything in the countless solar systems, everything in the vastness of space, absolutely everything of a material or atom nature disintegrates and goes back into its sublimated state.

Then we have a lapse of time when nothing is in physical manifestation. How long is this lapse of time? I cannot say. Perhaps it might be comparable to the length of time that the group of planets was in manifestation. Who can say?

But we are only speaking of equivalent time, mind you, because in reality time would have been nonexistent. So let us just say that during this period the outer Consciousness of God sleeps.

Now the second group of planets comes into manifestation. We study this one too. Then comes the lapse of time again. This then is followed by the third group, the fourth group, the fifth group—each one, of course, being separated by a lapse of time. Then after the sixth group we come to your present group, the seventh group, the last group. It is significant that here again we find the seven, the numeral seven that is so prevalent within the Universal Consciousness of God.

Now if there were seven different periods in which the physical planets were brought into manifestation, we are getting back to what? We are getting back to the point where we can see there just might possibly be a beginning somewhere. Yes indeed, we are approaching the great Core of Life. But before we embark upon that subject, we will first have to attempt to answer the question as to what we were doing during the great lapses of time between manifestations or materializations of planets. Now what were we doing? Were we reembodying ourselves on planets? No, there was the lapse of time. It took many billions of years for the planets to be brought back into manifestation. But we *were.* Therefore, if we were, we must try to understand what we were doing and our state of consciousness at that time.

You Are but a Teardrop of Your Greater Self

Yet before we can properly understand what we were doing during this lapse of time, we must review again the subject of our own Being. Man is a triune being operating in three basic states of consciousness: the objective or outer state, the subjective or inner state, and the soul or God state. We might refer to the God state as being the inner core of the subjective state. Now when we give up the mortal or the objective state of consciousness, we become more or less oblivious to the objective outer world, and we are conscious of it only subjectively. This is understandable. It is the reverse of operating in the outer state, being a mortal in the physical world, and being conscious of the inner world of the soul only subjectively. While being conscious in one state, we seem to be oblivious to a certain extent to the other, that is, in comparing the objective state with the subjective state. Are we in want of cohesion? Not necessarily.

You see disciples, the soul or God state is never oblivious to its own inner kingdom. All the time that we be on the outside, oblivious to that great inner consciousness, or that great Infinite State, the soul is very definitely not oblivious to it and is very much awake. The soul only becomes oblivious temporarily to its outer state and needs to be awakened by the mortal. But the soul itself never goes into a state of oblivion because it is constantly attuned to the inner consciousness and to the Core of Life. Thus we become acquainted with the three different and distinct states of consciousness of our own Being—one entity only, but with three levels of consciousness.

The person that you are today is only one teardrop in your sea of consciousness. The person that you were in a previous life is but another teardrop in that vast sea of consciousness. The outer being that you represent yourself to be is the individual drop; the inner divine state is the vast sea of all of your previous beings. You are oblivious now to certain things that you did long ago because you are employing the outer expression, but the things that you are oblivious of today, in reality, are far greater than you are able to express in any one life. But they are not lost. All of your previous actions in all states of consciousness dating back to the time you first sprang forth from the great Core of Life—absolutely all of them—are recorded and retained within the soul. A tremendous concept, isn't it disciples!

When I come to you and in your earthly terms say, "You are now chipping away the corrosion from the soul," this is only an expression to let you know that you are giving your soul an opportunity to manifest and reveal valuable information unto you. In other words, you are endeavoring to make it possible for you, the outer mind, to be conscious of that which the soul, the Infinite State, is conscious and never oblivious of. Therefore, you realize that as you become more sensitive, as you become more attuned, as your body responds to your thoughts, as your nervic center then responds, as your sight centers become attuned, it is then that your soul can reveal and transmit this information unto the outer world, your mortal consciousness. But you have to first tap this great reservoir of wisdom; then it can come to the surface.

What We Were Doing In Between Manifestations

Now we are in a better position to understand what we were doing, or rather the state of our consciousness, during the great lapses of time between the physical manifestations of the planets. Naturally, as no physical planets were in existence, we had no physical body or outer garment, we will say, to clothe our outer mind. Thus it became necessary, as a natural course of events, for our outer, objective consciousness to be in a state of oblivion for these many millions or billions of years during the interim period. But disciples, this certainly does not mean that *we*, as active individualized Sparks of Divinity from the Divine Godhead were oblivious. It does not mean that at all.

We were an individualized soul in between the manifestations of the planets, and we are an individualized soul today. But in that state between manifestations we had no outer, physical vehicle of expression; we had simply reverted back to the State of Divinity. We had reached that Consciousness, we were functioning in that Consciousness, and we were conscious of everything that was in that Divine State.

Now the mortal will ask, "But if there were no planets in manifestation, and if we still were in existence, then where and how did we live, move, and have our being?" The answer to this question is quite simple, disciples of the earth. Remember, children, just because the physical planets had disintegrated certainly does not mean to imply that the entire spiritual universe was no more. Nothing could be further from the truth! As I said earlier this evening, the physical planetary bodies, having gone through a process of disintegration, simply reverted back to their more sensitive bodies, their spiritual bodies, their ethereal bodies. The solid, dense forms, which had originally slushed off from their spiritual counterparts, simply reverted back to their perfected state.

A Universe of Spiritual Planets

This then leads us up to the point where we have to consider an entire universe of spiritual planets—planets that were created long before the first group of physical planets was ever brought into manifestation. And this spiritual universe has remained in manifestation ever since.

These spiritual planets do not depend upon a sun's rays or other planetary influences from any planet of a physical nature for their sustenance. They depend upon an entirely new set of laws that you are not in evidence of at this time. Of course, all laws do intermingle and there are certain basic laws that we have to take into consideration. However, the spiritual planets are revolving in their own orbit and by their own right. They are operating under a "pure law," and when I use this term, I mean a law that definitely could not bring forth friction.

Therefore everything is perfection within their orbits. Friction is nonexistent because there are no disturbances in the ether that could cause it. There are no negative planetary influences or other types of static. There is nothing that would cause the bowels of the planet to erupt, as it were, or that would cause these great tornadoes, storms, earthquakes, or other types of cataclysms to take place. There is none of that in spirit because everything there is working in harmony; everything has always worked in harmony on the spiritual planets since the very beginning.

After the first group of spiritual planets had been brought forth, and after they had multiplied as it were, we lived in that environment in a spiritual body. This answers the question put forth earlier as to how we lived before the physical planets were brought into manifestation. We were living then in the higher spiritual consciousness and motivating a spiritual body in a form that was very ethereal. We have to take the etheric relations into consideration when we refer to our outer garment at that time.

Now the average disciple will usually ask, "Well how did we appear?" It is said that we lived in a body that was created "in the perfect image and likeness of God," and that is true. But does that answer the question in its entirety? No. The term "perfect image and likeness of God" is not meant in the sense that it refers to its physiognomy. It refers only to the God Consciousness. It is the Spark of Divinity that is in the image of God. The image of God that dwelleth within is the Spark of Divinity; and it is not as you represent yourself to be, in reference to your individual personality, or in reference to your physiognomy.

The Fall of Man into a Physical Body

So then we moved about in the higher spiritual consciousness in accordance with the God plan. Undoubtedly, however, we either had not learned or were not learning our lessons in that perfect "image" that we were representing ourselves to be. We evidently needed more experience, and who am I to say why the Universal Spirit God deemed it necessary for us to have physical experience? It is not for me to say at the moment. Perhaps eventually I shall, but at the moment I am not in a position to say it. I can only tell you that in the spiritual bodies that we were living in, we were not having the experiences that we were supposed to have. Thus it was the divine plan that we would have it— as you people so often say in your vernacular—"rugged". In other words, we were cast out of the Garden of Eden, which represents the paradise of the etheric worlds, and down into the gross vibrations of the physical plane to become veritable "fallen angels". There is much truth in mythology if we take it symbolically and not literally.

But before we could take on the flesh, and by that I mean have bodies of flesh, bone, blood, et cetera, the great physical planets had to be brought into manifestation. They were created out of the etheric force by bringing many, many billions of atoms together into the great fusion, which in turn produced the solidity, or the solid force. It was the result of this solid force being brought into manifestation that enabled a physical planet to be born. Then, while all of this was going on, you and I were hovering in the atmosphere of the chemical relations of these planets; and it was through this procedure, carried on over a period of many millions of years, that we were able to finally become attuned to the physical plane. Or perhaps it could be said that we became a part of the physical or material plane because in reality we be a part of everything that is.

Now it was time to take on the animatical or the life-giving forces. It is the animatical force that enables life to come into manifestation. Thus we came into the power of the cell force and the cell life. This enabled innumerable bodies of many different forms to be produced for our earthly manifestations, and soon we were not only of the world but we were also in it as well. Of course, we first appeared in forms far different from that which we represent ourself to be today as human expression. This is the reason why I have so often tried to tell you that though we have lived in bodies that might appear to be animalistic bodies, I will not necessarily put us in that classification.

On second thought, I don't know why I shouldn't; but I won't do that. I will say though that we have lived in many and varying bodies while manifesting in the physical earth plane before we reached the body that we have today, the body that we represent ourself to be as human expression. And this takes in many billions and billions and billions of years since the time that we first descended from the higher spiritual consciousness.

And before we descended we were in this higher spiritual consciousness, and before that we were in the great Core of Life, a subject so vast in scope that it must be left for another evening. However, the reason for these words tonight was simply an effort on my part, as I stated earlier in the class, to provide a stimulus towards arousing impressions from the soul. If you are able to receive these impressions, your soul can then add considerably to what was discussed tonight. It is simply humanly impossible to adequately cover a subject embracing billions and "illions" of years in less than an hour's time.

But you might try standing back some clear night, and then gaze upward toward the evening's far distant pinpoints of light. See them, study them, meditate on them, and try to understand the beauty and the vastness of life. And then try to realize that from out there somewhere the great Core of Life spewed you forth to begin the journey that is eternity.

Rub your hands together, sound the A-U-M, and call out your teacher's name and your disciple number. One . . . two . . . three . . . AUM.

FOURTEENTH DISCOURSE

THE CORE OF LIFE

By Agasha

MY BLESSED DISCIPLES—Manzaholla and bless each and every one. I shall begin the class tonight by saying, "In the beginning. . . ." Now this phrase should send your inquiring occult mind racing back through eons of time, flashing out through seemingly unending, uncomprehendible space, darkness, light, eternity. But there is no way for the human mind to conceive how the beginning really was, or when it was, or even if there were a beginning, and we certainly don't know from a mortal standpoint if there will ever be an end. However, as students of the occult we *know* that there will never be an end. How do we know it? We know it intuitively and not necessarily from our reasoning faculties. It is a godly instinct that tells us that there shall never be an end, and as far as we are concerned, there was never a beginning—that is, a true beginning.

The only way to say that there would be a beginning would be to say that on this particular planet, for instance, there was a beginning. You have learned in your classes that some 25 million years ago you, as human expression, first came onto this planet Earth. There was also a beginning on other planets, and a beginning on still others that were in existence even before this present group of planets was born; and it goes on and on back to the time when you, as a Spark of Divinity, were first spewed forth from the great Core of Life, the Divine Consciousness, God itself. But even this was not the true beginning because before the beginning, we were.

We Were Back in the Core of Life

We were back in the great Core of Life—that great Oneness. We were an integral part of the collective whole, the God-Self, the Universal Consciousness God. I am incapable at the moment of saying how we first became a part of the God-Self, or how we first came into manifestation. I can only use the terms "beginning" and "ending" when I am in reference to leaving the Core of Life or returning back to the Core of Life.

Thus you are not to ask questions such as: "When were we first brought into the Core of Life? How were we brought into the Core of Life? Who created the Core of Life?" There has never been a teacher whom we can refer to—that is, a teacher who has used the language of the earth plane—who has explained that. The only thing that we can say regarding it is that we are now living in eternity, we have always lived in eternity, and we always shall live in eternity. We have lived forever and we shall live forever. We have always been and we shall always be. This is a tremendous thought, indeed!

Therefore the ultimate must now be studied, that is, if we can possibly employ a language to express it or describe it. I can only say this: Long before the countless solar systems were brought into manifestation—in reference to the many planets, stars, gaseous bodies, and so forth—space was null and void of all that is now in existence. The theater of infinite space was empty. The actors had not yet made their appearance. Everything, every solitary atom, was back in that great Core of Life, the Divine State, the Oneness. We might say that infinite space, that vast outer consciousness of God, slept.

However, the inner consciousness of God, the focal point of Infinite Intelligence, the Godhead, if you wish to use the term, was very much awake. That is where we were. That is where you and I had our Spark of Divinity, but in the beginning we were fused together in such a manner so as to become an integral part of the collective whole. Therefore collectively, we represented the God consciousness. We were the God then and we are the God today, only today we are individualized expressions of that Oneness.

But let us strive to understand that we are now visualizing our state in the beginning, if we can. There were no solar systems in the sense of the word, planets had yet to be brought into manifestation. We were all living within the etheric consciousness, but we were fused together. We had our spiritual body, but it was so minute that it cannot be adequately described in the language of today. We will not say that it had no description, but it is more accurate to place ourselves in the category of being just a part of the collective whole. So there we were—a part of the great consciousness called the Core of Life, the source of all. Now you can only imagine it the best way you can; I can't help you on that. In fact, it is very difficult even for me to imagine it.

The Core of Life Is Like a Great Sun

Some of you disciples try to picture the Core of Life as a consciousness composed of wonderful temples, buildings, structures, and very beautiful places. However, this is not the way that I want to describe it. The Core of Life is the life force itself. It is the universal God-Self that feeds the individualized God-Self within your soul, and the God-Self within your soul is *You.* When you actually become attuned to the Core of Life, you become conscious of pulsating with it. You then realize that you are receiving that great force which enables you to move about in your physical body—

or in any body that you will ever function in, as a matter
of fact—and which comes directly from this great God-Self.

This God-Self is the controller of all that is brought into
manifestation. It is constantly nourishing every atom that
is out there in space, every atom that is within the earth,
and every atom within your own physical body. Thus it can
be said that the Core of Life may be pictured as a great sun;
and yet this would not amply describe it, for it is larger than
any sun could ever possibly be. And if we were to try to
measure it—and there would be no way to do this, indeed
there would not—we would find that it would encircle not
only one entire solar system, but many other solar systems
beyond it.

Now where is the great Core of Life? Just where is this
great ovalness of light, power, and creation? If we are able
to see the planets, the stars, and the various other bodies in
the great Consciousness of Immensity, can we as divine entities, as advanced souls, also see the Core of Life? Can we
go there in our spiritual body in the same manner as we are
privileged to visit the various divisions in Immensity? Is it
our privilege to observe it in our spiritual body? These are
the questions that the average disciple is likely to ask, and
so let me answer them in the following manner:

It cannot be said we can select a special location in the
vast Consciousness of Immensity, and then state that is
where the great Core of Life is located. We cannot do this
because the Core of Life is *within* all of that, and no matter
how far you would travel in the Consciousness of Immensity, you would never find it. For the Consciousness of
Immensity could be likened to the rim of a wheel or the
surface of a sphere, and the Core of Life to the hub or the
central point. However the soul, being a part of that great
core, is pulsating in perfect rhythm with the Core of Life;
and thus you are permitted, after you have reached a certain
level in your initiation, to go immediately to the Core of Life
and become conscious of that core of great illumination.

Then you may say to yourself as an individual entity unto the Consciousness of God, "This is from whence I came; this is where I return; this is where I receive my supply."

God Can Be Likened to a Principle

Your consciousness while in that state is then a far cry from the mortal state of consciousness of a small, inquiring child who asks his parents who God might be. Perhaps you did this as a child and then, not receiving a proper answer, you began to think about how God created the earth in so many days, and how God first created Adam and then Eve. These explanations would suffice for a while, but then a child's curiosity would usually cause you to ask, "Well if God created you and me, then who created God?" And this same question has been asked by mortal man for a time too long to remember. But this process of thinking can now definitely be eliminated, once and for all, because we are now at the origin of everything, and in a state of consciousness where life is no longer a mystery.

How then can we answer the child's question? The simple fact of life, disciples, is that you and I, as divine entities, have always been, and it is not for me nor you to question the Universal Spirit God regarding this premise. We will accept it if you please, because if we do not accept it, we are going to be confused individuals falling back into the same line of thinking as the child. But rather than just take this statement on its face value, we can substantiate it with a bit of symbolic logic.

We start with the premise that God is a principle—a universal principle. Let us say that it be similar to the principle of mathematics. Now you know as well as I know that no one ever created the principle of mathematics. True, these principles may be forgotten at times, but the principles of mathematics have always been and they always will be. For instance: the sum of the squares of the two sides of a right triangle in any flat plane has always equaled the square of the hypotenuse and it always will. Neither you nor I nor God created this principle. It just is. Therefore, we can say that you and I and God just are.

The Fatherhood and Motherhood of God

In addition to all of this, we can further state that God is both male and female. You are male and female; you are positive and negative. And we can put God in that same light as being positive and negative, male as well as female. The great rays of energy which radiate out from the Core of Life and activate the outer consciousness of space relate to the fatherhood of God. The fatherhood of God is the active, positive, masculine force of God. The motherhood of God could then be said to be the actual Core of Life itself—the source of all life from which the radial, active forces are projected. It is the passive, negative, feminine principle of God.

The positive principle of God then makes the connecting link and brings forth that which we term the counterpart of itself into manifestation within the etheric consciousness, the same as it was there in the original source, the Core of Life. Therefore, we see that God is both male and female; yet it is all God. We cannot say that the positive state is either greater or lesser than the negative state. It is all the God Consciousness, that consciousness that is far supreme, the Universal Consciousness called God.

Now you are told in this class that you are a part of this Universal Consciousness, and you certainly are. You are told to not embrace a personalized God, but to embrace a *consciousness* of which we are all a part—a supremacy of all that exists. However, the ultimate nature of this God Consciousness cannot be known until one has become as a Pillar of Light, and in the meantime you will have to be content with your own individual concept, whatever that may be.

Yet a simple analogy exists which perhaps may provide a hint towards understanding the God Consciousness. That analogy is *you* when you put yourself in the same light. You as an individual are either positive or negative; you are either male or female. Yet you have another part of yourself that makes you into a complete whole. This is termed the counterpart, or the soul mate, if you wish to use the term. But there is still a third part, and that third part is the *active* principle of God which makes the connecting link between the two *passive* parts of itself, the male and the female counterparts. Therefore, we have a trinity in unity. We may carry the analogy all up and down the scale, but this will have to suffice for the moment.

We Plan the Forthcoming Universe

Let us say now that we find ourself in the Core of Life. But not only that; let us go back to the beginning, to the point in time before even the very first group of planets was brought into manifestation. Here, we recognize ourself to be an individual spark of the great Divinity, God. We find that we are individual sparks of the great Core of Life which encompasses everything that is, everything that was, or everything that will be. We must remember that absolutely everything, even particles as small as the germinal kingdom itself, has now reverted back into the great Oneness. This is where we come to the origin of life, disciples, so let us try to understand that in this state that we now find ourselves in, we are truly a part of everything that is.

Now when we go back this far in time, into the very depths of our own Being, we find that you and I had just as much a part to play in bringing the planets into manifestation as any other man who had ever moved or who had had his existence upon any earth. The same thing could be said for setting up the laws for the evolution of mankind, or in fact, the bringing forth of all that is. For instance: if I were to stand here and look out and see a star, I would say, "God created that," and it would be true. The Consciousness of God did indeed create that star, but when I say that God created it, I would also have to refer to myself because I helped to create that star. This is true because my Spark of

Divinity has gone through all of the processes of creation over and over and over again.

Long before any planets were brought into manifestation I was a part of that star. I am now a part of that star. I pick up a grain of sand; I place it in my hand and I say, "I am part of that grain of sand and that grain of sand is a part of me." We can then multiply this with everything that is, and it would still be true because I am all there is. Now certainly I don't mean that I, being a Teacher of Light, or you, being a mortal upon the earth plane, are all there is. Certainly not. It is the "I" within that is all there is. And that "I" within me is the same "I" that is within you. Thus we find that we have to get to the origin before we can receive a better explanation of what we mean when we say, "I am all there is." This is not just an expression. It is not just a phrase. We must try to understand that you and I actually are a part of all that is, and then we should try to visualize it.

So let us then go back once more to the beginning before even the very first group of planets was brought into manifestation. You and I are now in the Core of Life as part of the *total* consciousness of God. In reality, we cannot even refer to that which we term the "Pillars of Light" because there would be no Pillars of Light at this stage of creation. The previous cycle of manifestations has now come to a close. The Universal Spirit God has called all of its children back home to the source, home to their original state. We might call it a universal conclave.

Here the total God Consciousness can assess the accomplishments or lack of accomplishments of the previous cycle of manifestations. We will assume that the collective groups of Divine Sparks can discuss the matter to their full satisfaction, being individual parts of the whole. Here we have sparks within sparks within sparks, worlds of intelligence within worlds of intelligence within worlds of intelligence— all brought together within one gigantic whole! And this collective whole, mind you, has not yet decided what it is going to create or bring into manifestation in the forthcoming round. That is, at this particular point in time it has not.

Very well. Now let us move forward to the point where this vast inner consciousness of God has just planned out the forthcoming universe in all of its entirety. Every last detail has now been worked out. In the particular case of the last round, the collective whole had so chosen to become individualized in that same Consciousness of God. There is only one consciousness, remember, and there always will be only one consciousness. And in the round before the last one it might have been something else. Who can say? But in any event, let us presume that the mathematical principles to be used in the new cycle of planets, or whatever, have now been agreed upon by the collective whole. All that remains to be accomplished is for the outer consciousness of God to now awaken, and to bring into manifestation these principles.

The Etheric Universe Awakens from Its Slumber

Gradually a faint ripple of vibrations stirs in the outer consciousness of infinite space. The positive, radial forces of the God Consciousness shoot forth from the Core of Life causing the spiritual planets to awaken from their slumber. They multiply. Yes indeed, the dawn of a new day again comes upon the face of the great abyss. Now remember, this is long before the first group of physical planets were brought into manifestation. These are the etheric worlds only, mind you, that now return into consciousness. . . .

And so they remain today. These etheric worlds or spiritual planets are now in a state of perfection, and they have always been in a state of perfection. It is only the physical worlds with their frictionized forces that are imperfect. Therefore, it is well to remember that everything of an etheric nature was in a state of perfection long before the slush-off of the great solid forms began.

The Core of Life may also be compared to the yolk of an egg, and the Consciousness of Immensity to the white. Yet they are both part of the same egg. Now let us say, as an illustration, that we break the egg. We break the yolk of the egg and it begins to spread throughout the ovule. In a like manner the great Core of Life spewed forth in the beginning the many billions and billions and "illions" of entities with the first grand explosion. Now all of these entities, Sparks of Divinity who had originally been a part of the Consciousness of the Great Core of Life, then found themselves individualized as separate entities within the vast Consciousness of Immensity.

Therefore, it was the mission of all of these entities to then live for millions of years in the etheric state, in the etheric consciousness, and evolve. Yet they continued to receive their power from the great Core inasmuch as there was no other way for them to receive their power other than from the Core of Life. Thus each Spark of Divinity, having clothed itself in an outer casing called the etheric body, then motivated this etheric body and expressed itself as it lived, moved, and had its being.

We find then that these minute, divine sparks from the Godhead had once again become independent entities. That is, they had been individualized in a way that they could be pointed out. But as they were moving about in their etheric bodies, we must realize that they were also awaiting embodiments in the great physical worlds which were not yet created. It would be many millions of years before the physical or dense worlds would be brought into manifestation.

The First Physical Universe Is Born

Then either gradually or suddenly (it depends upon your viewpoint in the great consciousness of time) the animatical forces of God caused the great solid forms to be slushed off, and this in turn eventually brought the first physical universe into being. This is indeed a very interesting process, disciples. You see, the slush-off from the etheric states of matter caused friction, and this in turn caused gross material to begin to form, or to begin to solidify. And when it did, the planets began to form. First one began to form over here, and then another one began to form over there, and these in turn were followed by still others until gradually, within the great power that is concentrated at the point where the planets were revolving, a great solar system came into manifestation. Then after their birth, the planets were dormant for many millions of years while they were going through the cooling process.

Now then, in our supposition tonight this was the first group of solar systems ever to be brought into manifestation. This was the first. Now through all of this activity, where were you and I? Can it be said that we were in the etheric consciousness awaiting embodiments upon the physical planets? No, not necessarily. Why do I say this? You see, disciples, inasmuch as we represented that which was to become human expression, we would probably have been still within the Core of Life at this point in time. We had not yet sprung forth as a Spark of Divinity of the human expression.

First the planets had to be brought into manifestation through the animatical forces. Then gradually, over a period of millions of years, the Universal Spirit God—which means you and I—brought forth the germinal kingdom upon the planets through the etheric relations. This means then that it was the germinal kingdom that first brought the different forms of matter, bacteria, et cetera, into manifestation. These in turn then brought forth the various bodies, the animalistic kingdom, and the other forms of life that would be needed to help build and prepare the way and become an assisting force in eventually bringing forth the human expression. But you and I, representing that which was to become human expression, were still in the Core of Life.

The Various Species Are Sent Forth

Let us not be confused. We must remember that in the beginning the various forms of life sprang from the great Core of Life in wave after wave after wave. Then later, out of that in the germinal kingdom which had earlier sprung forth, other germinal forces were produced, other bacteria as it were. These in turn brought new forms of life into manifestation after the original species had left the Core of Life.

In this way, then, we can strive to understand one important point. That which was to become human expression was only waiting there in the Core of Life for the right time to come when it could take on an outer body, an outer etheric body, and then live for a long period of time in the higher spiritual realms of the etheric consciousness. Then millions of years later this same human expression, you and I, would be destined to become "fallen angels" as it were, and descend into the physical realms where we would have to evolve through the lower forms of life so that we could eventually return once more into the higher spiritual consciousness of God.

Were we chosen children of God? Were we chosen to evolve out of the animalistic state so that we could later become human expression? The answer to these questions is definitely no. There is no such thing as a chosen child of God. If there were there would be partiality, and God shows no partiality. Remember disciples, we have all had an equal start if we revert back to the true beginning, the beginning before the beginning so to speak.

Now here is how we explain that; we explain it in this way: Somewhere within the infinite manifestations of the Universal Consciousness of God, your and my group of Sparks of Divinity, our species if that explains it better, somehow earned the right to represent human expression and be the directors, as it were, in this present cycle of manifestation. And even then, we have had to earn every step of the way, evolving up through the lower forms of life to what we represent ourselves to be today.

Each species or class of entities then left the Core of Life at the right and proper time in order to have the opportunity to learn its particular lesson or serve in the way it was supposed to serve in the overall picture of life. Consequently it would then become greater in the Universal Consciousness of God than it was in the beginning, or during its previous cycle of manifestation. Everything is all in order. Your and my group simply put forth a little more effort than some of the other groups in order to be where we are today. And even today, we have a long, long way to go.

Finally Our Own Moment of Truth Arrives

Therefore, for the reasons just set forth, we find ourselves remaining in the Core of Life for a considerable time after the other species were spewed forth. But finally our own moment of truth arrived. Having helped to write the Book of Life, it was now our turn to experience the result of our creation. Thus "illions" of years ago, so many years ago that there is no way of knowing the time at the moment, our particular group sprang forth from the great Core of Life. You and I and all who represent themselves to be human expression today were in this group. Yes, indeed so. And this includes all of the other souls who have long since arisen into the higher consciousness.

Yet the average disciple is still a little confused on this subject, and he will usually ask, "If we all broke away from the Core of Life in the beginning, then is it possible that some newly created spirits or souls are now for the first time visiting the earth plane?" And the answer to this question is no. There is no such thing as a freshly (we will use that term, freshly) created entity coming to this earth plane. All entities appearing on this earth in the flesh have had innumerable contacts with this particular planet for many millions of years. And these same entities also lived on the very first group of planets to be brought into manifestation. That was seven groups back, mind you. We are living on the seventh group of planets.

Therefore, there are no new souls being born; all human expression left the Core of Life at one and the same time. But remember, disciples, the male and the female principle was of course in manifestation; each Spark of Divinity clothed itself in either a male or a female type of expression. Thus once again you and I, as individual entities, ventured forth to begin the long journey that is eternity.

Epilogue

Now the time will come, as you have learned in your previous classes, when there will be no occasion for any physical planets to come into manifestation. They all will be in spirit. In other words, we are all reverting back to our original state. This has to come eventually. How long? I don't know. I can only tell you what I as an individual am studying, and I then pass it on to you from my higher learning. I learn from the higher Intermediaries. I also go into my soul when the opportunity arises, and I contact the Universal Spirit God, the Infinite State, directly. This you also can do in time. But in the meantime, you will just have to bear with me and accept that which I bring to you from class to class. So then eventually we will go back to our original state. We know that life is eternal, and as I have said so many times in the past, we know that we are living in eternity now, we always have, and we always shall.

Where shall we find ourself when the time comes that there will be no more physical planets? Eventually everything of a material nature seems to fade into the nothingness. But we shall be very much alive in spirit because where there is life there will always be life. And you can rest assured that you shall be someplace. This includes not only you as human expression, but it also includes absolutely every form of physical life in the various stages of its advancement. It includes every form of the germinal kingdom, every form of the plant kingdom, and every form of the animal kingdom. All life forms will have become greater than they originally were. And in this state of consciousness all will be spirit, and there will be no need for any physical expression whatsoever. There will be no form of birth—now follow me carefully on this point—there will be no form of physical birth at all. And all life forms will be freely expressing themselves in their spiritual bodies.

Now you as a mortal might think that life would become rather monotonous without trials, tribulations, or anything of that nature. But there will never come a time when life will become monotonous to us because there will always be interesting things. No teacher can say that there will ever come a time when we cease to learn. Although the physical planets be out of the way, life will still be expressed in the great Consciousness of Immensity and life there will always be extremely interesting. That is not a hope; it is a fact. We know this intuitively, and we can always receive confirmation of it from the God Consciousness.

And then eventually, in the far distant tomorrows, all life will return once again to the Core of Life. But having lived so many times on so many planets, we will most certainly be individualized for we shall not lose that individuality. We shall never become so collectively merged in a consciousness that we lose our individuality. We are individualized at all times because we have our individual Spark of Divinity, the God-Self. There is also the counterpart to be considered, that part of the male and female principle that belongs to us.

If then we become so merged in that divine consciousness where there be no form of physical expression, then what shall we be? Can I, as a Teacher of Light, inform you as to what we shall be? Can I see the events and show you the picture? I may not be able to see clearly, but I can give you what I have learned from the great Intermediaries that have brought the message unto me through their instrumentality. And what is their message? Their message is simply that we shall then have what they term "the greater life". No other words can adequately express it. When there is no physical expression or physical life, when all is in spirit in sublimated form, and when all is ultimately back into that great stage of Divinity—well, the only thing I can add to that is that our life will be supreme.

Thus one day far away, we shall become again a part of that great Oneness—the Universal Spirit God. The words "universal spirit God" explain the Universal Spirit God. It is just that. It is you and I and all that is. Then we shall be back in that greater life, and having certainly learned our lessons by that time, we shall truly live in a heavenly state. From that point on, we won't question as to what we shall then do or how we go on. We just know that we will have apparently reached the ultimate, and yet I never want to use that expression. We will just use that term for the time being. Let us now sound the A-U-M, if you please. One . . . two . . . three . . . AUM.

FIFTEENTH DISCOURSE

THE SOUL ATOM: THE SPARK OF DIVINITY

By Agasha

MY BLESSED DISCIPLES—Manzaholla and bless each and every one. On many occasions in the past, the most recent being just a few weeks ago, I had endeavored to speak unto you disciples relative to the great Core of Life. Now let us return once again tonight to that blessed consciousness where all was created in the beginning. But tonight I am going to dwell more upon (1), the overall picture of the soul itself, and (2), that part of the Core of Life that broke away from the Godhood as a minute spark, as a separate entity of light. This is the Spark of Divinity.

Yet before we can understand the soul, and especially this "Spark of Divinity," we must first understand the Core of Life of which it is a part. They are one and the same. A spark of light, or a spark of life if you wish to use the term, is the consciousness within that life or light. It is the energy within the fire. Sometimes we refer to it as the soul atom.

Let us try then to understand that in that consciousness where all was created in the beginning is a world that is so vast that we might say it is measureless. Moreover, we must also realize that the Core of Life in its original state, before the universe was brought into manifestation, was a world that was as real as any world could possibly be. And there, in that Divine Consciousness, is where we were.

You Are Infinitely Intelligent

In the Core of Life, we were attuned to the Infinite State. We were an integral part of the Infinite Consciousness. That is why we make the statement that in reality we are all knowing and all powerful. Therefore, if we are all knowing and all powerful, we have to go back to our original state to express it, as it can never be fully expressed in any one lifetime.

Now you might ask, "Inasmuch as we are infinitely intelligent, have we become infinitely intelligent because we have lived many, many lives upon the planets, or is it that we were endowed with that power in the beginning?" The answer to that question is that we were endowed with that power because we *are* the Gods of the earth plane. We are an integral part of the Universal Consciousness God. Therefore, we cannot say, "I am infinitely intelligent today but tomorrow I shall not be infinitely intelligent because I shall be oblivious." If a man becomes oblivious, he is not oblivious in reality insofar as being infinitely intelligent is concerned.

For indeed, we are a part of God and we are infinitely intelligent. It is only that the mortal self is not conscious of that fact at this time. Yet our soul is conscious of everything that is on this earth plane and everything that had been brought into manifestation ever since our original departure from that great consciousness called the Core of Life.

However, we do not necessarily refer to this original departure from the Core of Life as creation in the strict sense of the word. The word *creation* is generally used only in reference to the beginning of life upon the earth plane. When we speak of ourselves in relationship with the Core of Life, we realize that we have always existed. But we were not individualized then in the same manner that we are individualized today. Not at all. Many occult students state that at that time we were bodyless. Yet I do not refer to the body particularly; I refer only to the Divine Light.

Now this Divine Light, called the Spark of Divinity, was as minute as an atom itself. This then is the reason that we call it the soul atom, or the atom of the soul. In reality, of course, it be pure light or energy; as every atom was in its energy or etheric state originally. Nevertheless, the Spark of Divinity is generally referred to as the soul atom.

That Which Was One Now Becomes Two

In speaking of the Spark of Divinity, we must also refer to what we term "the double." The double relates to the twin sparks, the male and female aspects of the atom soul, that left the original source, the Core of Life. Therefore, we find that that which had been *One* within the Core of Life now became *two* minute sparks of Divine Light, one male and one female, one positive and one negative.

Then after breaking forth from the Core of Life, these minute Sparks of Divinity hovered out in space for a long period of time. Each clothed itself with the etheric substances of the consciousness that it had found itself in, and this Spark of Divinity taken together with its outer garment is what is termed *the soul*. It is like an egg. It is an egg-shaped form and basically it is white. This soul egg varies in size according to the entity's spiritual growth and development. Sometimes it might appear as large as a small to medium sized egg. At other times it is quite small. However, as we said before, the Spark of Divinity itself is as minute as a tiny atom.

Therefore your individual Spark of Divinity is there right now within the soul, and it is located in the very center of the human anatomy, the solar plexus. There within the core of life of the physical anatomy, if I may use the term in this manner, is the seed. There it is: that Spark of Divinity, the

God kingdom, the soul atom, that which is you throughout eternity. But the *soul atom* itself is so minute that the physical eye could never possibly detect it. Of course you could not dissect the body and then pick out the soul either. No one has ever been able to do that, for the soul is something that is on a different frequency from the physical body. Yet the soul is there.

In summary then, the Spark of Divinity, as we have so chosen to call it, is the very same spark that originally broke away from the Core of Life. It was an integral part of the Oneness. Then it burst forth, and as it burst forth it displayed both its positive and negative aspects. In your waking state you are not in evidence of it, but everything that you know is right there in that portion of the anatomy—the solar plexus.

The Silver Cord of Life

Occult students often refer to what is termed "the silver cord of life." This is an expression used in the occult field, and it is a very good expression too, for it is used to denote the connecting link between the Core of Life and the frequency you find yourself functioning in. When you project yourself out of the body during the sleep state, this silver cord always remains attached to the physical body, the physical frequency that you are in at this time, and it becomes the lifeline connecting your astral or spiritual body with the physical body.

If the physical frequency becomes too low, then the silver cord of life is severed from the physical body and the spirit could no longer reenter the body. This silver cord is seen only with the sixth sense or the clairvoyant eye as some people call it. The clairvoyant eye is the All-Seeing Eye, and it is this All-Seeing Eye that enables you to tune in on the frequency of the silver cord of life. If you are able to do this, you see what appears to be a spider web. It is as if the sun were shining on it and it seems to be endless. It varies in thickness. Sometimes it appears to be the size of a little finger and at other times it is much thicker. And then it might taper out and become thinner or, reversing the process, it becomes thicker. It appears in many different forms, disciples.

How the Soul Leaves and Enters the Body

It is interesting to know that when you leave one degree of consciousness of the ethereal world permanently to be in a consciousness of the most high, or to be in a division that is higher than the division that you had previously lived in, the process is the same as that which occurs at the death of the physical body. The body which you had previously employed—the outer casing of the soul—then disintegrates. It goes through the process of disintegration just the same as when your physical body is cremated on the earth plane. So you literally die, if I may use that term, from one division of consciousness to another.

This then leads us up to the question of how the soul leaves the physical body. Many people think that when they are freed from the physical body it is always a set law that you leave from the top of the head. Others will say that you go out just the opposite way. Well all that is just theory. The truth is that it depends entirely upon the circumstances. In the case of an accident, the soul or spirit may leave from any portion of the physical body. Ordinarily however, the circulation gradually cools from the lower extremities to the upper extremities so that when you take your last breath, the spirit or outer consciousness will seem to leave from the top of the head. But the soul will almost always actually leave from the front part of the body, just in front of the solar plexus to which the silver cord of life is connected.

What causes the soul to leave the physical body? We all know the answer to that. The reason that you have to get out of that garment, the house that is the soul's dwelling place, is simply because the heart stops beating and the organs stop functioning. This in turn causes a multitude or a series of events in the human body, and it is just like your automobile when it has run out of gasoline. You don't have any fuel and the motor slowly dies. Or it might be the case where the body would explode into the apparent nothingness and you could not find one particle of that physical body of yours. You could fall into a vat of molten steel and your body would be in a few seconds only a puff of smoke. What happened to the soul? Was the soul injured? No, the soul was not injured; you cannot injure the soul. It would not make any difference to the soul whatsoever whether the spirit left one way or the other.

What enables the soul to enter the physical body? First, the powers of conception set in. We realize that one single cell can produce life when it is set in motion. Then it starts to multiply and soon the cell life is multiplied tens and thousands and billions of times. From one single cell many cells begin to form, and through that process they gradually begin to build the body. It is the life force within these billions and billions of cells recreating and reproducing, over and over again, that enables the tiny body within the womb of the mother to come into manifestation. Eventually the soul is able to take over the tiny body, and then it also helps to produce the physical body as you represent yourself to be today.

This is a very mysterious and a very intricate subject to understand, disciples; however, today it is largely understood by the average individual. Today almost everyone is privileged to learn a great deal from books and from what the scientists have found to be true. Yet there is still much more to learn, but the important thing to bear in mind is that life began when a single cell was set in motion. Once the life force within the seed is set in motion, and the multiplication process begins, then it will continue unabated until that which is contained within the seed is reproduced again into the physical world.

Now the physical size of the mother allowing the new life

to come into manifestation is not a limiting factor. How interesting it be that a little mother, one who is very, very tiny indeed, can make it possible for a soul to come into this life who is almost a giant, we might say, in comparison with the average height. He is a giant only in comparison with the mother, of course. He could be three or four times the weight of the little mother who had originally brought that soul into life.

Every Form of Life Has a Soul

Now this doesn't apply only to human life, no indeed it does not. This principle applies to all of nature. A single grain of wheat will bring into being that which it represents itself to be—no more and no less. It will not represent itself to be anything other than wheat. But the wheat that is finally brought forth from only a single grain of wheat in the beginning will eventually produce enough material to sustain human life. It will so multiply itself that it can be said that one grain of wheat can produce in time as much wheat as would ever be needed to sustain the people of your country for many a year to come—all this from one grain of wheat! Of course, this process is assisted by the proper use of chemicals that are drawn from the earth plane; but out of only one grain of wheat comes the wheat field. Out of one watermelon seed, we can have many, many watermelons. We know that this principle is applicable to all forms of plant life and eatable foods.

But at the same time we know, from the standpoint of the flesh, all will eventually die. All forms of life will pass out of their outer casings, so to speak, and will revert back into the etheric realm or the astral world. It makes no difference whether it be flower, insect, or human expression—all must revert back. I take a seed. I plant it and I cultivate it. In time it bursts forth producing whatever it is supposed to produce. It has life; it pulsates. Using the power from the sun and the chemicals from the earth, the seed is able to produce plants, fruits, vegetables, and the like to bring forth other life of the same species. But soon it too shall die. It will wither away and revert back into the essence of the ether, so to speak. And from there within that great consciousness, it will eventually return again unto the physical plane. Everything, absolutely everything, goes through the same process of reembodying itself.

We must strive to understand that every form of life has the essence of life right there within itself. It has a soul. Everything that is brought into manifestation which has life also has a soul. Be it a rose, be it a fruit, be it a flower, or be it this or that—it still has a soul. It has a consciousness, and perhaps neither you nor I can divinely attune ourselves to its particular rate of vibration; but through our love, our thoughts, or whatever it be, it can respond because it too is pulsating with the Universal Consciousness God. If you and I are pulsating with the Universal Consciousness God, then all other species must also be pulsating with that same consciousness, because everything has life.

When a rose dies on the earth plane, it begins to live where? It begins to live in the spiritual life. If you have flowers on the earth plane, that means that we have flowers over here on this side. A spiritual rose, or an etheric rose, is just as beautiful to us on this side of life, and it is far more brilliant in color indeed than the flower that comes upon the earth. Yet eventually it must take on the physical garment. We would say that the physical rose is the imperfect rose. Over here, it is the perfect rose because it has depth. It has brilliance. It seemingly pulsates more readily with the Universal Consciousness God. Yet it returns onto the earth only to revert back again into spirit. Then it returns once more onto the earth, and even after you pluck it, it will live as long as it can on the earth plane until the essence of that rose begins to fade away again and to revert once more back to the place from whence it came.

A rose that was born on the Pacific Coast perhaps ten or fifteen years ago, or even less time than that, may now be in manifestation in other parts of the nation or country. There it is multiplying and allowing other roses to manifest on the earth plane. Then when it eventually disappears and seemingly disintegrates from the sight of men, it only goes back into the ether from whence it came. It is constantly being reabsorbed and reproduced. The element that will be reproduced ten or fifteen years later may not be the same, no, but the essence is always the same. The soul is the same.

Yet even the same element of that rose will eventually be reproduced given enough time. It may take a million years or more for the larger cycle to complete itself, but eventually —and it makes no difference whether it be on the physical plane, the astral plane, or in the various other regions and divisions of the world over here—that same element of the very same rose will be reproduced once again. Everything eventually claims its own; everything seeks its own level in time.

Therefore we find that each form of life has the essence of life right there within itself. Each has a soul, and all souls do have life. All souls will always be, and all souls have always been. But when I make this statement, I am referring to the original state, the divine force, the atom spark. It is the Spark of Divinity that you cannot destroy, that you never will destroy, and it is that that we must always take into consideration.

The Spark of Divinity Embraces a Universe

In speaking of the Spark of Divinity, I would like to again stress its minuteness. It is the atom of the soul; yet it becomes a world that is as powerful as the universe itself. Now follow me carefully; I am going to repeat this. Your soul atom, the atom of your soul, is as powerful and as mighty as the universe is itself. It is a world within a world, and a world within a world, and a world within a world. Now that may not mean anything to you at the moment, but nevertheless it is true. It is such a tremendous thought, indeed it is!

Today the scientific mind has discovered many things

about the atomic power. We realize that within a tiny drop of water there are millions and millions of what? Atoms. Isn't that true, children? According to your understanding, it is true. There within the atom we find the electronic force. Then we find many, many other forces and forces, mind you, that have not yet been discovered by the scientific minds. But eventually they shall discover them.

Now as we study the hydrogen atom and the oxygen atom, we realize that billions of these atoms will go on to make up the element of water. Other atoms will combine into something else. In fact, everything is made up of these mighty atoms. Your body, the air you breathe, everything that you are, everything that is around and about you—absolutely everything consists of these great and mighty atoms. Yet an atom itself is as mighty as the entire universe. Now that may sound rather strange, but nevertheless it is true. And you may include your own individual soul atom here also. Your Spark of Divinity, that is so minute, is a world as powerful as the universe itself.

One of the ways that we can arrive at a partial understanding of this universal truth is through the use of the higher calculus. But the only way that we can completely understand it is by going within the soul. Human deduction and observation can give you but very little. It is only through the soul consciousness that you can arrive at the point of knowing.

The Soul Itself Is Its Outer Casing

Now then, what is the soul? The soul itself may be said to be the outer casing of the soul atom, the Spark of Divinity, the God part that originally broke away from the great Core of Life. But what is also important is that the illumination from the soul is constantly enveloping the human body. This is what constitutes your aura. Now this illumination from the soul can sometimes be seen. You can see it occasionally while you are lying in bed and when you become ever so still. Then gradually, as you become at peace with thine own kingdom, it is possible for you to become conscious of being enshrouded or enveloped by this great illumination. So then try to understand that this great soul illumination can come to us when we are making way for it. It can come when we have full control over the body itself, over every nerve of the body, and when there are no outer disturbances and we are perfectly still within.

Thus we find that even the outer physical body is contained within the illumination from the soul. But the core of the soul, the atom of the soul, is the part that seems to control everything in your life. It records everything not only from the time that you first came upon this earth, or upon the other planets, but it also records every experience that you have had since you originally left the Core of Life before any of the worlds were born.

Therefore, in the final analysis, the soul consciousness itself is found to be within the soul atom. The soul consciousness is within the soul atom. I repeat this for emphasis, children of the earth, because this means then that the soul atom is housing everything that ever was, everything that is, and everything that ever shall be—past, present, and future. It contains all of its actions of the past, the results of today, and the results of tomorrow. The soul atom then is the sum total—now follow me carefully—of everything that is and everything that you have done. This is you! It is a world that is equally as important as the universe is itself, as I have just said a few moments ago. And when you use the word *universe*, you embrace everything that is. This means all of the countless solar systems, everything that you could ever possibly be. Now that is really something to take into consideration!

In Time You Can Attain the Same as the Masters

I want to take you now into the higher Consciousness of Immensity; I want to accompany you there, and I know that your teacher does too. Your teacher is in an excellent position to do this because in all probability he had given up his physical body long ago and is far more privileged than the average teacher who might be in a lesser degree. Therefore, these trips and excursions into Immensity are so arranged so that you may have experiences out of the body and observe the many happenings to give you a greater understanding of life. The only unfortunate feature is that the many of you do not usually bring back the memory to your waking state. But on the other hand, some of it is retained at times in the form of a very vivid dream.

Your soul will always see to it that you remember what you are supposed to remember, disciples; so then let us not complain that we never bring back any memory. In time, your soul is going to let you have every imaginable experience that is necessary for your proper unfoldment; for it is your soul, in reality, that allows you to have these experiences. If your soul deems that a particular experience is to be had, or a certain thing is to be observed, then no one else will have any control over it whatsoever. It will definitely be your soul that allows you to enter into a particular consciousness and observe whatever it is to be seen. And, I might add, some of these things to be seen might appear to be rather fantastic, and you will not be readily able to ascertain or understand them on the surface.

Therefore, you as an individual, in time can attain the same as the Masters. The majority of you are striving diligently to attain that which they have attained, and it is not a tremendous task, in reality. It does not become so confusing to you that you cannot understand. This is what I have been working up to all these many months and years. All this time I have been trying to break down the barriers, build you up, and take you away from the physical. I have been trying to take you away from the earth plane by first taking you to the Consciousness of Immensity, and then gradually easing you into still another consciousness that would be very difficult for the average student of the occult ever to enter.

This is the Consciousness of the Soul. In other words, I

am not trying to do the impossible, but I am doing every-thing that I possibly can to gradually introduce you to your Higher Self. Then after this has once been accomplished, the soul takes over and you are well on the way to returning to the origin of life from which you sprang and where you shall find yourself for millions or billions of years hence.

The Most Climactic Experience of Them All

Now we come to the most climactic experience of them all. That is the experience of going within the soul atom. Knowing that every one of you will eventually have that experience, I am naturally cautious as to how I bring it to your attention. But it is going to be a glorious experience, indeed it is. But remember, disciples of the earth, you are going to be in a far better position to have that experience when you are over here on this side of life and out of the physical body. This is not to say, however, that it cannot be attained while still in the flesh.

Of course, limited experiences usually filter down to the outer consciousness of the average disciple while he is still in the physical body. I realize that about 50 percent of those in the class tonight have had such things as the grand ex-plosion and various other reactions. Sometimes very strange happenings seem to occur, and very strange pictures and scenes can come unto your mortal attention. They usually are given to you lightly, indeed they are, but at the same time we realize that what you had thus received is very valuable, very helpful, and most inspiring. But on the other hand, they also can be quite confusing at times.

However, I am not in reference to those particular things tonight. What I am in reference to is that grand and climactic experience that occurs when you are in a certain high spir-itual consciousness, and you are thus able to contact the very core of the soul—that mighty atom, the soul atom, the atom that houses every emotion, every thought, every deed, absolutely everything that you had ever done. When you go into that consciousness, you are in direct relationship with the Core of Life. In other words, during this experience you are conscious of pulsating with the Core of Life. You can actually see the power that is being sent forth. This power is the great motivating force; it is *your* motivating force that is being sent forth from the Universal Consciousness God, the Core of Life.

Now that is an Adept's privilege to do, and in order to have that experience he will take advantage of it every time that he possibly can. He may be in the flesh or he may be out of the flesh, but he still has that same privilege. I also have done it. I have not done it as much as some of the teachers I have met, no, but I have done so and I found it to be extremely interesting. Please recognize that when I go into that state of consciousness, I am just as conscious of my life in that state as I am talking to you children here tonight. There is no way to describe it in your vernacular, I appreciate that; but remember, disciples, a time will come when you will be so much attuned to the soul consciousness whereby you can then experience it for yourself. As I expand, so shall you expand; therefore in time you shall have the same privilege.

However, this ultimate experience of going within the soul atom cannot be achieved until a disciple of the earth plane has passed the initiation and has thus become a full-fledged member of the greatest order ever established in the universe. This particular order is called the Purple Order. When this transpires, it will mean that your true light, your true self, can then be revealed.

You will then be able to enter that great chamber of wisdom, and that great chamber of wisdom is your soul. Yes, disciples, there within that soul of yours you will be able to take any thought, any problem, any question, and there it will be solved. The soul will be working in perfect accord with your teacher. There within that chamber of wisdom you will have it all brought to the surface and explained, and it shall be explained to your full satisfaction in every sense of the word. This be the privilege of all disciples who pass that final initiation and who, as I have just said, then become a full-fledged member of that wonderful order called the Purple Order. Indeed, this is the greatest order ever to be established in the universe.

A Journey into the Soul Atom

When you take your initiation, you will be in a great massive auditorium in a consciousness above the rim of Immensity. This is on a particular spiritual planet that I have talked to you about in previous classes. You will find yourself among the exalted teachers who had arisen from their respective planets. It is a huge temple indeed where many of the Masters have assembled, where they have become attuned to the Infinite State and to the Core of Life. It is truly magnificent and the atmosphere is very beautiful. You are privileged to enter this temple, and it is a privilege indeed. You must not take this too lightly; take it very seriously as it is a most solemn occasion.

Under the guidance of the assembled teachers, you will then go into a deep state of meditation and become oblivious to the universe. You will become oblivious to your lives while you ascend and are gone for a few hours of earthly time. You will go into a world as vast, and as great, and as tremendous as the entire universe itself. You will ascend into the soul atom, which is a universe within a universe and a universe within a universe, and there you will contact the very core of your soul. You will literally become that atom, that soul atom which is the Spark of Divinity.

There you will take inventory of all of your actions which will date back for millions of years as a soul. You may go back and not only see the past, but also see the results of your actions which be the present, and then even see yourself henceforth for many millions of years to come. You will thus have extended vision by being in the position to actually see yourself a million years hence, or even as it has been said by some of the Adepts, to see yourself perhaps billions of years hence. You may also go back and explore the past; you not only just see it, but you may also relive it. Right then and there, while you are in that state of consciousness and only while you are in that state of consciousness, you may relive events dating back in your existence many billions of years in the past. Therefore you will be able to realize from your actions of the past what your path really is, what your future path will look like which will date for many millions of years to come.

You may even see yourself attuned to the great Pillars of Light, because your spiritual body will enable you to traverse there while in that state of consciousness. You will observe their kingdom. You will be in a position then to actually observe those individuals, the great Arisen Ones, the Ones who have been in their kingdom for many hundreds of thousands and even billions of years to the time long before these worlds were brought into manifestation. This will be your privilege because you will have so earned it. But as to how much you will actually retain and bring back unto your outer consciousness, I cannot say. This will be entirely up to the soul.

Then you will awaken. After being gone for only a few hours of earthly time, you will return to your outer being. You will realize that your true self is the inner, conscious being of which the outer self is only the shadow. But you will not have to take my word for it, or any other teacher's word for it, for you will simply *know* it to be true. It is this particular initiation into the Purple Order that enables man, the outer man, that is, to awaken and to become conscious of his true conscious Being. It is then and only then that we are able to understand the intricacies of life, of the universe, of humanity, and of all forms of life in every phase that we refer to from time to time.

This becomes a tremendous subject. It becomes a very interesting and a very intricate subject, indeed it does. It goes far beyond the average man's concept of life for it takes one to that great powerhouse, the source of all, the Core of Life. Therefore, tonight we have reverted back in our class to the "Sun Core of Life," if that explains anything to you; for it is by visualizing the sun that brings forth a mental picture of the Core of Life, as I always say. And the soul atom, which is the Spark of Divinity, then sprang forth from that Core of Life.

We sprang forth as a Spark of Divinity, as an atom of energy in its most minute and most powerful state. That represents you. That is you forever; that is you throughout eternity. That will always be you; that will always be the atom that represents you.

Rub your hands together, sound the A-U-M, and call out your disciple number. One . . . two . . . three . . . AUM.

SIXTEENTH DISCOURSE

PILLARS OF LIGHT

By Agasha

M<small>Y</small> BLESSED DISCIPLES—greetings and bless each and every one. It is very gratifying to me as the many of you assemble here to receive whatever it is to be received vibratorially. This becomes your training that you will later oh so very much appreciate. If a statement is made by me, or by your teacher, that the more you learn and the more you conquer the more humble you be, let that be one of the most important things ever to be recognized in a lifetime. For to be humble is to come into the *knowing*. Therefore the more advanced you are, the more humble you be. Remember these words.

When we study the earth and the history of man and all that moveth upon the earth, we become very interested in the great depth of life itself. But there is also much for us to understand about a consciousness that is far supreme. I touched upon this consciousness a few classes ago, and I am in reference now to the great Pillars of Light.

It is said that we are a part of the Universal Consciousness God, and we most certainly are. We are told that we do not embrace a personalized God but that we embrace a *consciousness*, a supremacy of all that exists, of which we are a part. In reference then to the Godhood and the Core of

Life from which we sprang, we now have the opportunity
in our higher occult studies to return unto that consciousness
and become conscious of the great directors of the universe.
These directors are called "Pillars of Light," and that is my
subject in the forepart of your wonderful class.

Who Are the Great Pillars of Light?

Now just who are these great Pillars of Light who took
such an active part in preparing our little planet Earth for
our forthcoming embodiments? Yes, disciples of the earth,
the Pillars of Light are basically responsible for your living
on this particular planet that you are living on today. "But
who are they, and where did they come from?" you will
ask. "Did they evolve from a physical planet similar to ours,
and where is that planet now?"

We can answer these questions in the following manner:
The Pillars of Light, those great Beings who are so far
removed from your and my consciousness, are human expression the same as you and I. And they did at one time
roam the physical planets. This is the law. They have had
to go through the same process that you and I have had to
go through in their evolutionary spiral from the great Core
of Life. However, any planet that they had roamed upon has
long since disintegrated, for the group of planets that formed
the basis for their evolution is no longer in existence.

Again I repeat: The Pillars of Light are souls who are
advanced far beyond the consciousness of all here in this
present group of planets. They are Beings that have never
been directly contacted by anyone of the earth plane or
anyone of the other physical planets. They have not even
been directly contacted by the Masters you are aware of in
the higher consciousness. Yet the Pillars of Light are humans
—even as you and I. However, they have not been on any
of the planets that are now in existence. Their worlds—the
worlds where they evolved and had their experiences in
order to learn, grow, and expand—have long since moved

back into the anim world through the inevitable process of change and disintegration. Our present group of solar systems—which includes our own system as well as all of the other systems, some of which are so far out in space that they seem mythical in character to the lay mind—is to these Beings, the Pillars of Light, just a new group of planets.

You have learned in your previous classes that before these present worlds and gaseous bodies were brought into manifestation, there was a lull—a period of time when there was not one thing that could be identified as a gaseous body or a planet. This was for a period of time that extended into millions and millions of years. And you have also learned that prior to this lull between the physical manifestations of the planets, there were six other cycles of planetary manifestation. Our present group is the seventh group of planets, or seventh physical universe, if I may use the term.

Now the Pillars of Light of today arose from planets in the very first group—the first manifestation or materialization of the planets over this long period of time. We also lived on that first group of planets. Therefore, the only difference between the Pillars of Light and us is that they were the ones who arose and made contact with the Infinite State. As they did, they reached the Godhood. We did not.

These Pillars of Light are individualized in the Consciousness of God with the male and the female principle, the divine force, ever present. They have also become a part of the great Oneness that we often refer to, and they definitely have gone far beyond the consciousness of the average teacher who, we will say, is in the earlier stages of Immensity. Indeed so! But at the same time we know that these great souls who had arisen from their "earth" planet such a long time ago are still receiving the same power, from the same source, as we are today. I am in reference to the Core of Life. We believe this and know it to be true. It is as true as the fact is that I am speaking unto you tonight, children.

Where Is Their Consciousness?

The question often arises as to the relative location of these great Pillars of Light within the Universal Consciousness. "Are they beyond the Core of Life?" you might ask. "Are they independent from the Core of Life?" Never could it be said that they be independent from the Core of Life. Nothing could be independent of the God-giving force, that God-giving fluid that is invisible to man and which enables him to have life throughout eternity. Therefore, we cannot say that the Pillars of Light are beyond the Core of Life.

But we can say that they are separated from the Core of Life insofar as we would refer to a location. It might be said that the consciousness of the Pillars of Light radiates outwards from the Core of Life reinforcing and directing the active, positive principle of the God force. Only this is just a supposition for your mortal consciousness tonight. Let me tell you what the Intermediary, that teacher from the Spiritual planet whom I have been conversing with of late, told me regarding this same question. He is so nearly attuned to the Pillars of Light that he is able to receive information from their consciousness, and this is what he said:

"It is that they have the most beautiful consciousness. They have a very beautiful location and it seems to be beyond all planets. It seems to be beyond all solar systems; it seems to be independent from every connection with any solar system. It is in a solar system all by itself. It is the only consciousness within this system and yet it is dual—the male and the female principle. It is not like having many planets within a solar system, and it is a solar system that seems to be independent from other systems. It stands off alone. It is there that we have the Pillars of Light."

This, children, is what this Intermediary of Intermediaries related unto me. Therefore through the great powers of God, the Pillars of Light are helping to create because they have attuned themselves to the Core of Life. They are directly attuned to the Core of Life—you and I are too, but we are not working in that consciousness at this time. We are not working independently, you understand, as we are not as near and not as concerned with the Core of Life as they are. They are working directly out of the Core of Life; and that is where all of us had come from, and that is where we are all going to return in time.

The Function of the Pillars of Light

Let us take a look now at the general function or purpose of the Pillars of Light. First of all, they are the directors of the universe. They direct all that be in the great Cosmic Consciousness, all that be in the various planes of consciousness in the great Consciousness of Immensity. Oh think then of the vastness of Immensity, disciples, and think of how far it be if we may pinpoint a planet or star far beyond your solar system. And referring then to all that be out there in fathomless space, what tremendous thoughts can come into your mind when you think of the vastness of Immensity, the vastness indeed. And the Pillars of Light are the directors of all of this!

For instance: when the time comes for a planet to disintegrate, the Pillars of Light are just as conscious of that disintegration as you are conscious at this time of being in this room. Furthermore, I am told by the Intermediaries of Intermediaries that the Pillars of Light then take measures to make mighty sure that not too much destruction takes place, so that all of the souls may then revert back to their rightful level and reembody themselves on another suitable planet for their further physical expression.

Did the Pillars of Light cause the planet to disintegrate? The answer to this is no. Then was it simply that the planet was due to disintegrate at that time? And the answer is yes; it was the right time for that particular planet to disintegrate. When you look out there in space and you see the countless stars, blessed disciples, you must always remember that the countless stars that you gaze upon will all eventually disintegrate. The disintegration of the planet was part of the same process. When the time comes for a star or a planet to explode and disintegrate, then it will explode all on its own, and not by the direction of any Pillar of Light or any other group of souls.

We find then that the Pillars of Light are conscious of all life; not of individual life, no, but they are conscious of life the same as you would look down upon the ground and see millions of ants. You would not necessarily be conscious of any one ant, as all you would be conscious of would be the millions that are moving about.

Therefore, if the ants were being destructive and were destroying that which is around you, getting rid of only one ant would not solve the problem. You would have to get rid of all of the ants in order to solve the problem, and it would take time to destroy them all. You would not pick out any one group of ants in particular; you would have to destroy the whole colony if you were to rid yourself of the pestilence.

Now are the Pillars of Light in a position to destroy all forms of life upon the millions of planets that are inhabitable? It is not for me to answer this directly, but the answer to the question is that there is no need for such destruction. Nor do they ever direct the power to destroy because of evil actions upon physical planets. Indeed not! They don't do this because they are conscious of the fact that each entity must evolve into a higher form, the same as they themselves had evolved such a long time ago. They realize that it is the overcoming of the evil actions of others that builds the strength, the wisdom, and the compassion within each entity which is so necessary in becoming attuned to the Infinite State.

Thus the Pillars of Light are constantly sending forth light not only unto the arisen, but they are also sending light unto all evolving human expression. They send light unto all planes of consciousness and unto all planets wherever they be, for this light is sent to be utilized for the gradual awakening of the God kingdom within.

Then lastly, the Pillars of Light bring into manifestation, when the proper time comes in the evolution of the human, completely new ideas and concepts. The knowledge of certain things in the Cosmos can then be revealed that had heretofore been withheld; for those upon the earth plane had not been ready in their evolution for the revelations to be revealed unto them. You can see clearly the many, many things that have been brought into manifestation scientifically just in the past half century. The average person will say, "Well, isn't it a pity that these things were not given to mankind a thousand or two thousand years ago." But mankind was not ready for those things to be revealed. So they had to utilize whatever they had—things ever so crude when compared with what you have today.

Therefore, man has to reach certain pinnacles of unfoldment before he can be given enlightenment. Today you are coming into the light when certain things can be revealed by the Pillars of Light once again; and these things can then be brought into manifestation on the earth plane. But remember, disciples, they will always be given in the direction for the betterment of humanity.

The Teachers of the Seventh Degree

Strive now to understand one thing. All teachers and intermediaries—even the Pillars of Light—had to go through their trials and tribulations in their evolving. They had to go through the same things that you children are now going through on your own particular group of planets today. Thus by striving and overcoming the trying conditions that arise in our lives from time to time, we grow and eventually reach the consciousness of the most high. And the more we go into this subject and the more we strive to understand it, the more we realize from a mortal standpoint how tremendous life really is.

Now life becomes just as tremendous, even more so it would seem, when we are in the Seventh Degree, employing our spiritual faculties, and listening to the teachers as they descend unto us. But you are privileged to make contact with these Seventh Degree Teachers, the same as I had done in the past, only because you have striven in that direction. It is said that all children of the earth plane are privileged to do the same as we have done. All the Masters of the past have said unto their disciples, "That which I attain you shall attain, and even greater things shall you do." If this be true, and we accept it to be true, then we know that as these Seventh Degree Teachers come unto you, they will bring the knowledge to you in a way that you can grasp it. This is through the great consciousness of the Universal Language.

The Seventh Degree of the Consciousness of Immensity is of the most high. It has to do with the planetary force. It has to do with the great solar systems—especially the seven solar systems that you are directly connected with. If I were to come and say unto you, "You are connected with all planes of consciousness in reality because you are all there is," that answers one thing. But to give you the answer to many things, we must draw the line somewhere so that we can have what could be termed a resting place. The resting place then would be the Seventh Degree or the seven solar systems.

That is why I stay within the range of the seven. I stay there because the seven is significant unto each particular division. But it is certainly not the ultimate. We are going to understand that we can go beyond the Seventh Degree; I say unto you that we can go into degrees far beyond the Seventh.

The Intermediaries of Intermediaries

If we were to rise above the Seventh Degree, we would first have to contact one who is termed an "Intermediary." What is an Intermediary? An Intermediary is simply a teacher who is a spiritual medium or channel. I use the term "medium" because it explains it better.

You understand that the degrees of consciousness on this

side are so constituted that the souls who dwell in a particular consciousness cannot readily contact souls who are far beyond their range. This is not a range of vision; it is a range of consciousness. Therefore they would have to depend on a channel, and on this side we call the channels "Intermediaries."

When I contact an Intermediary, I find that Intermediary to be a very highly developed soul—an exalted person indeed. To me, that person becomes my channel whereby I am then privileged to contact souls beyond the scope of my consciousness, the same as I am contacting you disciples tonight. No doubt this is generally understood by the average disciple, but nevertheless I think it is an important feature to bring to your attention.

How far then has the average Intermediary, one who had arisen from the earth plane many thousands of years ago, gone in studying the Pillars of Light? Has he actually seen them? The answer is no. It is always said that we have our superiors, those who are beyond us; but all we can do is talk about those who be beyond us. Out of necessity then we have to have those whom we would term the "Intermediaries of Intermediaries." These exalted teachers are just what the name implies—intermediaries, channels or mediums, for the Intermediaries themselves. Thus they are called the Intermediaries of Intermediaries because they relay the message that is sent forth from the great Pillars of Light.

We realize then what the Intermediaries of Intermediaries are doing for this wonderful movement. We also realize what we have accomplished by making contact with them in recent months. This contact, of course, has been the direct result of our having passed our initiation. Therefore it has indeed been a pleasure to contact these personages from that level of consciousness, and I know that as we continue in our studies, we will be well on our way to contacting still other Intermediaries whom even I or your teacher have not yet been able to contact.

A Visit with an Intermediary

Let us leave this physical plane for the moment and travel mentally to a very beautiful consciousness—one that is on a very high spiritual planet. Let us go afar once again and make contact with the Intermediaries of Intermediaries. We will find ourselves shortly in a particular temple, and as we do we will become attuned to a very wonderful teacher.

This teacher is the Intermediary whom I have conversed with several times of late. If he were to appear before you, you would find him dressed in a very beautiful purple and gold robe. He is a wonderfully appearing person, indeed. He has a slight smile; and yet when he speaks, he speaks emphatically. He has a definite personality; indeed he does.

He is also conscious of my growth. He is conscious of me as an individual. He is conscious of my life and my experiences insofar as he is in a position to read my akashic (the record of the soul). He has given me much information pertaining to not only *my* future growth, but also information that will enable me to pull you children right along with me so that as I expand, so shall you expand. Then as you follow me, as I beckon unto you, you will be able to eventually be in the same consciousness that I am striving to attain at this time. That is a consciousness that is far beyond the Seventh Degree of the Consciousness of Immensity.

This intermediary has not lived upon this earth, nor will he ever come upon this earth to live. He has become attuned to the universe. He is even attuned—or I should say very near to becoming so attuned—to the Pillars of Light. He is truly on his way, and it is often said by the Intermediaries with whom I have been conversing that he will ascend. They say that he would have ascended unto the Pillars of Light a long time ago, but he had a special work to do before this ascension could take place.

Why is this particular teacher so far advanced over many of the other teachers in the Consciousness of Immensity?

The answer is that he arose so many, many millions of years ago that he had never lived on any physical planet, at any time, during the present cycle of this new group of planets that is now in manifestation or had come into manifestation during these past many millions of years. And if you were to converse with this particular teacher, you would find that he had lived on the earth plane of a planet that dates back the third—now follow me carefully—the third group of planets ago. This means then going back three periods of manifestations of the planets. Consequently his original earth planet is so far removed from everything you now see in the universe, that there is no way for me to give you the time element.

Can We Contact Any One Pillar of Light?

Another question that arises in the mind of the average disciple is, "Do you embrace the Pillars of Light as a whole, or do you embrace them individually?" The answer is that we embrace them as a whole because they are individualized within the consciousness of God Itself. By that I mean that they are in that consciousness in which you and I as individuals cannot reach. I cannot contact any one Pillar of Light because that is beyond my range—beyond my consciousness as an entity, as a Spark of Divinity. Therefore I can only refer to them and embrace them as a group, as a whole.

That privilege is also not even extended unto the Intermediaries we are in reference to at the moment. They too, until they have their ascension and become as a Pillar of Light, must out of necessity receive their communications from the group consciousness of the Pillars of Light as a whole. Therefore, no one in this class can claim that either he or his teacher has contacted directly any one Pillar of Light.

Now this is not to say that they do not want us. They simply don't for the most part know us as individuals. Yet they are a part of us. They are from the original Core of

Life and the Core of Life of today, even as you and I. But they have become individualized in that consciousness whereas you and I are still going through the process of becoming.

Man Must Once Again Regain His Lost Estate

We have gone through this process over a period of billions and billions of years, and we find then that we had faltered. We are the "fallen angels" insofar as we would use the term *angel* as representing an exalted one. Therefore, as we revert back to that great exalted state of consciousness, the original state, we consider ourselves to be fallen angels. We can do this because we know that in going through this process so many times, over and over again, we had failed. They, whom we term Pillars of Light, had learned and consequently ascended from the lower state into the higher. Yet they too are from the same original state of consciousness as we are.

The Pillars of Light are *in* that consciousness. Now they are able to direct. They be ever conscious of the whole universe, the whole of the Consciousness of Immensity, at one and the same time. They are living in that consciousness continually. They are in that state of consciousness in which they are conscious of everything that is, whatever it be. But when I say this, I am not singling out every grain of sand because you and I and all that is, and all the peoples of the land, and all the planets, would be merely grains of sand. You would not take the time to count the grains of sand upon the seashore, nor would the Pillars of Light in their state of consciousness do the same thing—or even want to, necessarily. But they do understand and are conscious of the collective whole of that which we represent ourself to be today. Therefore they understand our particular spiritual growth, our state of consciousness. This is not to say though that they cannot become aware, at times, of certain individuals who have become a part of the Great White Way.

The Pillars of Light are of the Godhood. You also are of

the Godhood, basically; and we are all coming into the Godhood and recognizing it as we study our higher lessons. Now strive to understand that in your philosophy, as you become so attuned to the Infinite State, you recognize your completeness with God and your oneness with God. Although you may appear to be extremely insignificant unto mankind, you must recognize your position and your mission to be fulfilled upon the physical plane. You are a physical entity unto the consciousness of God; therefore, you are just as significant as a Pillar of Light.

If this be true, and we know it to be true, you must realize then that what they had attained you are also going to attain. It is not said when you will, but it is believed and known by your soul that eventually you shall. "All that I have done, you will do too; all that I have attained, you will attain too." Remember these words. Therefore, we are gradually reaching that level where all things can be understood.

Godhood: The Ultimate Destiny of Man

Whereas the different forms of life upon the earth become greater than what they are today, man becomes the exalted soul, the exalted individual, the Teacher of Light. He then goes on to become attuned to the greater powers and becomes the great Initiate. The next step is to become an Intermediary, then an Intermediary of Intermediaries, and then finally, after reaching the Core of Life, the last step is to ascend into this blessed consciousness of the Pillars of Light. This means then, blessed disciples, that you and I, each as an entity receiving the very same power from the very same source that is sent unto the Pillars of Light, will eventually reach the Godhood and become as they.

"How long will this take?" you ask. I cannot answer that directly; it might not be for many millions of years to come. But we *are* reaching that Godhood by degrees; each pinnacle we reach we become a little more attuned to the Infinite State. And gradually, little by little, it will all be explained by the soul, which in turn becomes our best teacher.

Therefore we are reaching toward that same state of consciousness that the Pillars of Light be in today. We are gradually working into their world of reality. It may be a billion, or even billions of years before we reach it, but eventually we shall. That is our rightful heritage; that is the future; that is *your* future as the years go by. What be your consciousness ten million years from now? Or even one million years from now? Just think—a million years from now. Then think about, we will say, ten million years and then fifteen million years from now. It becomes a tremendous thought. And when we say fifty million years, or a billion years, it becomes staggering! However, you *are*; you are still in existence. Somewhere you will be whatever you shall be, whatever you have earned the right to be. More than likely you will be a Pillar of Light.

And the Pillars of Light, shall they become any higher, greater than what they are? Once we have all become attuned to the Infinite, become Pillars of Light, are we then to go on from there? Well, that is where I am stopping. The thought becomes too tremendous. I will only answer that by saying that when we become a Pillar of Light, in that state it is supreme.

Rub your hands together, sound the A-U-M, and call out your teacher's name, if you please. One . . . two . . . three . . . AUM.